JAZZ DRUMMING STEP BY STEP

Technique • Context • Ear Training

By

James Morton

"A lifetime of learning in one book."
-James Moody

Audio Tracks

To download the corresponding audio tracks for this book simply go to:

http://mortonmusic.org/jazz-drumming-audio/

And use access code: **382958**

"*Jazz Drumming Step By Step is a fantastic, very comprehensive book on jazz drumming! It will lead one to a great education and vast skills in coordination, jazz history, vocalizing, keyboard basics, creativity, phrasing, soloing, stickings, ear training, musical insight and more. I can't wait to use it with my students!*"

– Dan Britt, musician, educator, author of *Drumopedia*

Contents

INTRODUCTION

More than a century ago, when jazz was being born in New Orleans, an era of communication was also beginning. The technology of today, which offers instant access to music, entertainment, and information on any subject, was unforseen a quarter of a century ago, much less a hundred years ago. The pioneering musicians who were cooking up this new concoction were doing so without available recipes. The instruments they used were from a limilted pool of resources, some of which were left over from the Civil War. The recording process was in its primitive, experimental stage, and of course there were no books like this one to instruct on the mechanics of playing this new style of music. These early musicians, who only had each other as mentors and models, were very much on the frontier, winging it, making it up as they went. Which, in essence, is what jazz is.

Today we have the opposite situation. We have had the benefit of a century's growth of jazz, and as we learn our craft today, we follow in some pretty large footsteps as we study the lives and innovations of those who raised jazz to new levels. Thanks to the marketplace and technological advances, the quality of musical instruments and equipment have never been better, and improvements are constantly being offered. As far as instructional materials go, the amount and variety available are staggering to contemplate. Books, trade magazines, CDs, videos, software, and internet sites abound. We are in the Information Age, and if information is desired, information can be had, and easily. Is there room in such a world for another jazz book? I think there is.

In writing this book, I had three main objectives I wanted to meet. First of all, I wanted this book to have **context**, musical and historical. The history of jazz is presented in sections throughout the book, along with biographies of significant musicians of each era. Drummers may be aware of Elvin, Tony, and Buddy, but other jazz musicians know who they were too. Its hard to imagine any musician studying jazz on *any* instrument not knowing about Duke, Bird, or Miles. Understanding historical context may not seem pertinent to the playing of a style of music, but actually it is. Everything we know, everything we've heard, everything we've learned informs and colors what we play.

Secondly, I wanted this book to be **comprehensive.** The material is offered in a series of orderly steps. As you progress through the book, you can look back on what you have accomplished, and take those skills to the steps ahead.

I also wanted this book to foster **creativity.** The basis of creativity in all art is the ability to restate an idea in a different way. Since the ability to create is often a confusing and daunting challenge for the aspiring jazz musician, I viewed this objective as particularly important. So in addition to the standard comping and coordination exercises found in this and in other books, creative exercises are arranged throughout here. One needs a vocabulary and the technique to create an idea, but we also need to be free *from* stock formulas in order to further create. This brings us to the very core of what any musician should strive for: control of the instrument. If you truly control your instrument, you can play what you read, you can respond to an idea you hear someone else state, and you can express any new ideas that come to your mind. In music, technique is vitally important, and yet still subservient to creativity. In jazz, ideas are paramount.

I appreciate your interest in this book, and wish you well on your musical path.

Photo credits: Many thanks to those who graciously contributed to photos seen in this book, including William F. Ludwig, Jr., James & Linda Moody, Herb Brockstein, and Avedis Zildjian.

Symbols, Guides, & Abbreviations

Check boxes - Check off the boxes as you complete each step. You can keep tabs on your progress this way.

example:

√

☐	STEP A 4: BEAT PERCEPTION/LISTENING SKILLS

Definitions - Any word highlighted in yellow will be defined on the same page in a light green box.

example:

. . .know where the downbeat is. . .

> **Downbeat**
> The first beat of a given measure.

Research & Listening Guides - Recommended albums that are representative of the styles/eras being discussed are presented, along with other resources such as books, videos, and web sites.

Dig Deeper

"Satchmo" (Masters of American Music Series, CBS Music Video Enterprises, CBS Records Inc., 51 West 52nd St., New York, NY 10019). A trip into jazz history as clips and interviews with Tony Bennett, Dave Brubeck, Lester Bowie, Milt Hinton, and drummer Barrett Deems recount Armstrong's life. "West End Blues" and "Mack The Knife" among many music performances.

Exclamation Point - Critical points to the development of jazz drumming are presented with the following symbol:

Abbreviations:

RH	Right hand	CYM	Ride cymbal
LH	Left hand	SN	Snare drum
RF	Right foot	BD	Bass drum
LF	Left foot	HH	Hi-hat

Legend Of Notation:

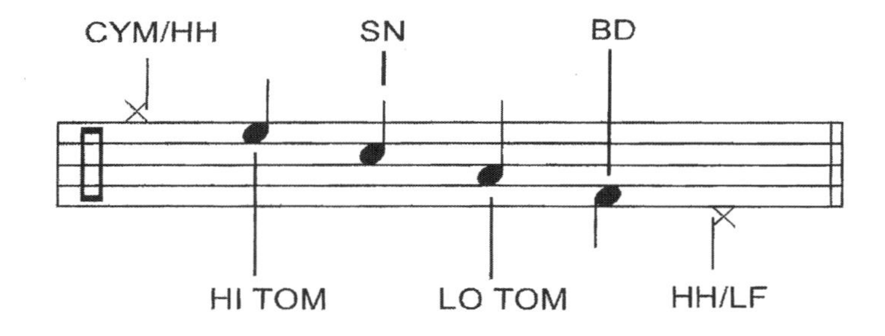

Your First Step: Getting A Keyboard

In order for you to successfully complete all the steps on your way to becoming a musical drummer, you need to purchase a keyboard. It need not be expensive (I found one at a discount store for under $10.00), and can any size. Basic keyboard information is introduced in the first section, and phrasing and singing exercises are a vital part of this book. Don't worry if you've never played a keyboard before. We are going to use this tool to become better musicians, and thus better drummers. Now go out now and get one. I'll wait. . .

Beat Perception
Meter Perception
Jazz History – The Early Years
Biography: Louis Armstrong
The Instruments Of Early Jazz
The Drummers Of Early Jazz
Keyboard Basics
Hi-Hat Technique
Reading/Coordination/Singing
Interpretive Exercises

ITS ALL IN YOUR HEAD

Most professional musicians realize that their ability to hear what is going on around them is of *equal* importance to the notes they actually play. In very basic terms, musicians need to be aware of and respond to several things at once, kind of what nowadays is called "multi-tasking." This is one of the most fundamental skills a musician must possess - so fundamental, in fact, that it is easy to skip over in pursuit of more tangible musical skills. All of us multi-task perceptually to a certain extent in our everyday life. When you walk down the street, you are aware of your immediate steps, but you are also aware of the street light up ahead, or perhaps what the store has on display in the window as you pass. But consider what a musician might have to consider, all at once:

Where am I (in the chart or song form)?
Where is the soloist going?
How is the pianist comping?
How is the balance of sound?
Am I in sync with the bass player?
When do we get paid?
Do we get to eat at this gig?
Who is that sitting over there?

Comping
Short for "accompany," to comp means to play in a supportive way, backing the soloist up with rhythmic interjections that ideally inspire the soloist and keep the music flowing. All rhythm section members must have comping skillls.

THE BEAT GOES ON

Beat
A regular and rhythmical unit of time. The consistent underlying pulsation that serves as a reference for the performance of music.

Quarter Note
The note most often associated with a beat:
♩ = 1 beat

Most popular songs, regardless of style, have an inherent pulse, or beat, upon which every other element of the music is built on. In popular music, for the most part, the beat is so strongly stated that it is apparent to anyone, even non-musicians, Even with music without a drummer, other elements, such as the phrasing of the melody, the chord changes, and the comping of other rhythm section instruments should suggest to the listener where the beat lies. The basic feel of jazz is the quarter note, and the musician who most consistently expresses the quarter note is the bass player (see page 62, "Your New Best Friend"). *The most fundamental thing a musician should be able to do is sense the pulse, or beat, of the music.*

Older Than The Mountains:
At the risk of sounding like a new age guru, it is interesting to sometimes reflect on the idea of rhythm in nature. Rhythm is the most primary component in music, and it is present in all of nature. A short list: your heartbeat, your breathing, the waves of the ocean, the rotation of the earth, the cycles of the moon, the four seasons, etc. With a little thought, you could add to this list yourself.

√

Step A 2: Beat Perception/Listening Skills

- Get together with a musician friend or teacher to help you.
- Play a jazz recording from a CD or radio at random.
- Find the pulse or beat of the song (focus on the bass player). Do this until you can find the beat.

Where's The One?

Now that the beat can be felt, the beats need to be grouped according to meter. Most popular and jazz songs are in 4/4 time, or four beats to the measure. Just as the musical elements of a performance (melody, harmony, phrasing, accenting, etc.) suggest a beat, they also suggest a combination of strong and weak beats. For most musicians, sensing the "one" (or "downbeat") of a measure may seem to come naturally. For inexperienced musicians, being able to do this may seem somewhat baffling. The following exercise should help.

√

Step A 3: Meter Perception/Listening Skills

- Get together with a musician friend or teacher to help you.
- Play a jazz recording from a CD or radio at random.
- Find the pulse or beat of the song.
- Now find the downbeat (or "one" of each measure). Careful listening to the melody, chord changes, bass line, and the phrasing of the instruments will give you clues. Confirm this with your friend or teacher. Do this until you can easily find the downbeat of each measure of a song.

Downbeat

The first beat of a given measure.

Measure

The basic unit of meter, made up of notes and rests between two bar lines. The number of beats per measure is determined by the time signature. Over the years, the terms "measure" and "bar" have come to be used interchangeably.

Meter

The term used in both poetry and music to describe the regular sequence of accented and unaccented beats.

Time Signature

The two numbers at the beginning of a piece of music that indicate (1) the meter of the piece (number of beats per measure) and (2) the note value that represents the beat.

Step A 4: Beat Perception/Listening Skills

- Do this exercise **away** from the drumset.
- Sit in a chair, back straight, relaxed and alert.
- Play track 1 of the CD.
- Listen to the beat for a few measures, then tap your RF to match the beat. Keep your heel on the floor as you tap the beat.
- After a few measures, tap your RH against your right knee, so that your RH and RF are in sync.
- Now tap your LF to match the beat. Keep your heel on the floor as you tap your LF. Your LF, RF, and RH are in sync now.
- After a few measures, tap your LH against your left knee, so that all four limbs are now in sync.
- Count aloud for at least eight measures: "1, 2, 3, 4, 1, 2, 3, 4," etc.

Step A 5: Beat Perception/Reading/Coordination

- Do this exercise **away** from the drumset.
- Sit in a chair, back straight, relaxed and alert.
- Play track 1 of the CD.
- Play the two written exercises on the next page with all four limbs tapping the written quarter notes together, in sync. Don't play the rests.
- Count the beats aloud as you play (notes and rests): "1, 2, 3, 4, 1, 2, 3, 4," etc.
- Now do the same with tracks 2 through 6 on the CD.

Track 1 - ♩= 88
Track 2 - ♩= 100
Track 3 - ♩= 120
Track 4 - ♩= 144
Track 5 - ♩= 160
Track 6 - ♩= 180

Reading Page # 1

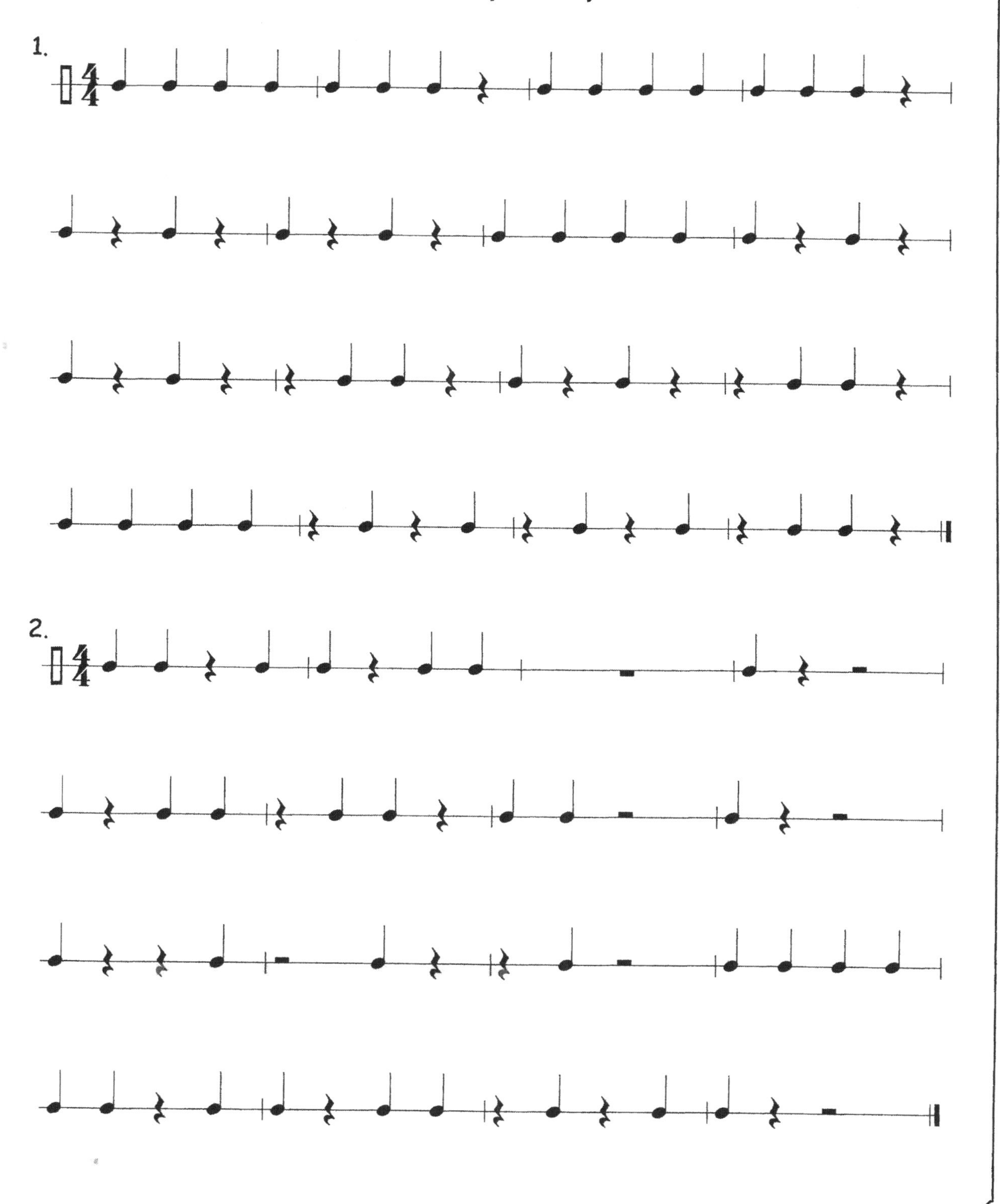

√

STEP A 6: READING/COORDINATION/SINGING

- Play track 1 of the CD.
- Play the exercises on Reading Page 1 (the previous page) with the BD (RF). Sing along with the BD, using "boom" or "bom" (don't sing the rests).
- Now play the same exercises with just the ride cymbal (RH). Sing along with the CYM,using "ting" or "ding" (don't sing the rests).
- Now play the same exercises with just the hi-hat (LF). Sing along with the HH, using "chick" (don't sing the rests).
- Now play the same exercises with just the snare drum (LH). Sing along with the SN, using "bop," "bap" or "tah" (don't sing the rests).
- Now do the same with tracks 2 through 6 on the CD.

√

STEP A 7: READING/COORDINATION/SINGING

- Play track 1 of the CD.
- RH/CYM: Play light quarter notes throughout.
- As your RH plays quarter notes on the ride cymbal, play the written exercises on page 11 with the BD. Sing along with the BD part, using "boom" or "bam" (don't sing the rests).
- Now repeat the exercise, playing the written part with your LH/SN (while maintaining quarter notes on the cymbal). Sing along with the SN part, using "bop," "bap" or "tah" (don't sing the rests).
- Now repeat the exercise, playing the written part with your LF/HH (while maintaining quarter notes on the cymbal). Sing along with the HH part, using "chick" (don't sing the rests).
- Now do the same with tracks 2 through 6 on the CD.

The Mighty Quarter Note

"I *love* quarter notes. I do more with quarter notes than I do anything else. That's just the way I feel."

Grady Tate
Modern Drummer, June, 2001

THE IMPORTANCE OF VOCALIZING

In 1979, the great violinist Isaac Stern visited China, to perform and give master classes.* A young violinist was struggling through a musical passage. She was hitting all the notes in the right places, but something was missing. Stern asked the girl to sing the passage, which she did. Then he told her to play it *like she had just sang it*. An amazing thing happened. The girl's performance improved significantly. What had happened? What she could play only mechanically moments before, she was now playing musically, because her voice gave her the correct phrasing, and a mental template to play against.

Research has shown that we learn more thoroughly when more than one of our senses are engaged. When musicians are able to vocalize what they need to play, they seem to more aesthetically grasp the shape of each note. Since the voice really is the oldest instrument (not the drums, as some think), and because we usually learn to speak before we play another instrument, we can use that skill to our advantage. Most people can phrase musically with their voice before they can master the same skill on an instrument that requires much practice.

Drum instructors have been saying for many years that if you can count it, you can play it. An addendum to that would be that if you can sing it, you can play it better. So sing away!

Q. What is this man doing in a drum book?

A. He has something important to share with you.

Isaac Stern described his style of playing as like the "natural rise and fall of the human voice . . . You sing in your head, and you play what you hear."

* Isaac Stern's trip to China is wondrously chronicled in the documentary, "From Mao to Mozart: Isaac Stern in China." Produced by Docurama (docurama.com), and available on DVD and VHS. ISBN 0-7670-3222-5

JAZZ HISTORY - THE BEGINNING

When Louis Armstrong was asked "What is jazz?" he is said to have replied, "If you have to ask, you'll never get to know." The fact that defining jazz has always been an elusive and subjective endeavor is evidence of jazz' flexibility and ability to assimilate, and yet there are historical and stylistic developments that can be chronicled.

Although jazz is appreciated and played throughout the world, it is a uniquely American development and a twentieth century phenomenon. Every style of music is in some degree influenced by its predecessors and contemporaries, and the origins of jazz are rooted in black folk music (which has its roots in West African music, evolving eventually into the blues), European music (which contributed styles, forms, and theoretical concepts), and black influenced popular music of the late nineteenth century (the banjo music of the minstrel shows, marches as played by black marching bands, hymns, and ragtime, a popular piano style of the day).

New Orleans. New Orleans, Louisiana is generally credited as the birthplace of jazz, and the earliest documented jazz style came from that city around the turn of the twentieth century. It wasn't until 1917 that a band called The Original Dixieland Jazz Band made a recording, creating a national sensation. Two other New Orleans bands followed soon after: The New Orleans Rhythm Kings, and the Creole Jazz Band, led by King Oliver, an influential cornetist.

The most influential jazz musician to come out of New Orleans was Louis Armstrong, who was King Oliver's second cornetist before striking out on his own. Armstrong was truly the first jazz virtuoso, extending improvisation with his solos, creating whole new melodies based on the chord progressions of the songs. His singing approach was the same, and he set the standard for all future vocalists with his scat singing. Indeed, his innovative style might be viewed as a forerunner of swing. New Orleans jazz was characterized by counterpoint between the lead trumpeter, who would state the melody with whatever embellishments he felt at the moment, and the clarinetist, who would simultaneously improvise a counter-melody. The trombonist would improvise a bass line, and the rhythm section would provide strong metrical support.

Chicago and New York City. Jazz began another era with the migration of many musicians to Chicago. A definitive "Chicago style" emerged, with emphasis on improvisational solos, tighter rhythms, and more sophisticated arrangements. It was in Chicago that Louis Armstrong began attracting attention. By 1924, Armstrong had moved to New York, where he worked as a member of the Fletcher Henderson Orchestra, a forerunner of the big band swing scene that would become the national rage in the '30s and '40s. Eventually, many other musicians settled in New York, which also became a major jazz city.

Scat singing
Using the voice as an instrument, without using words. Louis Armstrong and Ella Fitzgerald were masters of this.

Counterpoint
Music which contains two or more melodic lines.

Louis Armstrong Biography

One would be hard pressed to invent a more interesting and inspiring musician to usher in this new form of music than Louis Armstrong. His story is truly legendary, and his personality, playing, and singing still resonate today.

Armstrong was born on August 4, 1901 in New Orleans, and grew up poor in a tough neighborhood called the "Battlefield." In order to help support the family, the young boy began working cleaning graves, working on a junk wagon, selling coal to prostitutes, and singing on street corners for pennies (showing an early talent for music and sense of showmanship). Soon he was teaching himself to play the comet. His life then took an unexpected tum.

On New Year's Eve, 1913, 11 year old Louis was busted for shooting a pistol in the air, and was sent to the Colored Waif's Home for Boys, a juvenile detention center. While his confinement was no doubt a sad situation, it was there that he received his first and only formal music education, playing in the band.

Upon release from the detention home, Armstrong began playing in clubs, parades, and funerals, and soon caught the attention of the local professionals. Joe "King" Oliver, a fine cornetist, took an interest in Armstrong and began mentoring him. When Oliver moved to Chicago, Armstrong took his place in Kid Ory's band, a popular New Orleans group. Armstrong further honed his skills by playing on riverboats that steamed up and down the Mississippi River. In 1922 Oliver invited Armstrong to come to Chicago to become his second cornetist. Thus, people beyond the vicinity of New Orleans were soon to be aware of his astounding talent.

Dig Deeper

"Satchmo" (Masters of American Music Series, CBS Music Video Enterprises, CBS Records Inc., 51 West 52nd St., New York, NY 10019). A trip into jazz history as clips and interviews with Tony Bennett, Dave Brubeck, Lester Bowie, Milt Hinton, and drummer Barrett Deems recount Armstrong's life.

In 1924, Armstrong moved to New York City to play with one of the most popular bands in the country, the Fletcher Henderson Orchestra. The next year he returned to Chicago and recorded his first songs as a band leader, of the Hot Five. From then on he was a star, not only as a jazz artist, but also as an entertainer, singer, and movie star. In 1947, he formed a group called the All Stars, continuing to tour around the world, eaming accolades and acclaim as he introduced the music he helped create to millions of people. Louis Armstrong died on July 6, 1971, and left such a strong musical foundation for jazz to grow on, that literally every other jazz musician that came after him owed him a huge debt of gratitude. As Dizzy Gillespie succinctly put it, "Without him, no me."

A Series Of Firsts

1. The first great jazz musician.
2. His 1925 recording of "Heebie Jeebies" introduced scat singing.
3. Introduced "cats" and "chops" into the jazz lexicon.
4. His 1929 recording of "Ain't Misbehavin'" was the first pop song interpreted in a jazz style.
5. Most importantly, Armstrong brought to us the idea of the extended improvisational solo.

THE INSTRUMENTS OF EARLY JAZZ

Black musicians in early twentieth century New Orleans played in parade bands, honky-tonk blues bands, and dance bands, so the instruments that were used in the first jazz bands reflected that background. The **cornet** (a shorter, fatter version of the trumpet), **clarinet**, **trombone** and **drums** obviously came from parade bands, and early New Orleans jazz prominently featured those instruments. **String bass**, **piano**, and **violin** were mainstays of the dance bands of the area. Banjo and tuba actually came a little later, in dixieland bands.

Jazz, in a sense, was music that eventually moved indoors, and it was the invention of the foot pedal (W. F. Ludwig held a patent on it in 1910) that brought the drummer control over the snare and bass drum at the same time. Without that invention, it is doubtful that the drumset as we know it today would have evolved. Early drumsets were scarcely more than those two drums (the hi-hat did not exist at the time). Bass drums were quite large, and eventually other items, such as wood blocks, Chinese toms, temple blocks and cymbals were attached to them. These smaller percussion instruments were called "trappings." The early drumset was called a **"trap set**." In fact the woodblock was used frequently in early recordings, as the recording devices then could not accomodate the forceful sound of the bass drum and snare. Because of this, the drummer was always in the back of the band when recording.

Here's how the Leedy catalog described their Professional Outfit: "The Professional Outfit is composed entirely of the highest grade articles. No better selection could be assembled. The drummers holding down the best jobs in the country have no better tools than these... positively the last word in drummers equipment." The Professional Outfit went for ninety dollars!

THE DRUMMERS OF EARLY JAZZ

Notable drummers during this time included Tony Sparbora, also known as Tony Spargo (The Original Dixieland Jazz Band) and Paul Barbarin (Creole Jazz Band), but Zutty Singleton and Warren "Baby" Dodds were the most influential. Singleton, a self taught drummer born in New Orleans in 1898, played with the Tuxedo Jazz Band, the Maple Leaf Band, and later with Louis Armstrong's Hot Five. Singleton's drumming featured press rolls on the backbeat, which can be construed as the a predecessor to the jazz cymbal pattern.

Dodds, also born in New Orleans in 1898, performed and recorded with several musicians of the day, including Jelly Roll Morton. Baby Dodds' brother Johnny was also known as a fine musician, playing clarinet in King Oliver's Creole Jazz Band. A fellow clarinetist at the time, Gavin Bushell, remarked, "The Dodds' brothers . . . felt very highly about what they were doing, as though they were doing something nobody else could do. I'd say they did regard themselves as artists."

Dodds is credited with pioneering the use of fills , and also for converting the snare press roll into the jazz ride cymbal pattern, perhaps the most singular evolutionary step in the development of modern drumming.

Although timekeeping patterns were played primarily on the snare in a rudimental fashion, woodblocks, cowbells, cymbals, tom-toms, and several other percussion effects augmented the now developing drumset. Drummers during this era gradually made a subtle transformation from a strict, duple, rudimental march approach to a freer, more swinging feel.

Baby Dodds

Early drummer on an early drumset. Note the clarinets on the floor.

Zutty Singleton

His playing featured press rolls on the backbeat.

KEYBOARD BASICS

(Note: If you are already familiar with the notes of the keyboard, skip to page 22).

Imagine that you had never seen a keyboard before. What would be the first thing that you would notice? Probably that there are black and white keys. Now what would be the second thing you would notice? Right. The black groups are arranged in groups of twos and threes. Being aware of this is your first step toward being keyboard literate.

The Musical Alphabet

The musical alphabet consists of seven letters: A, B, C, D, E, F, & G. These notes are found on the white keys. To the immediate left of any group or two black keys is the note C. To the immediate left of any group of three black keys is the note F:

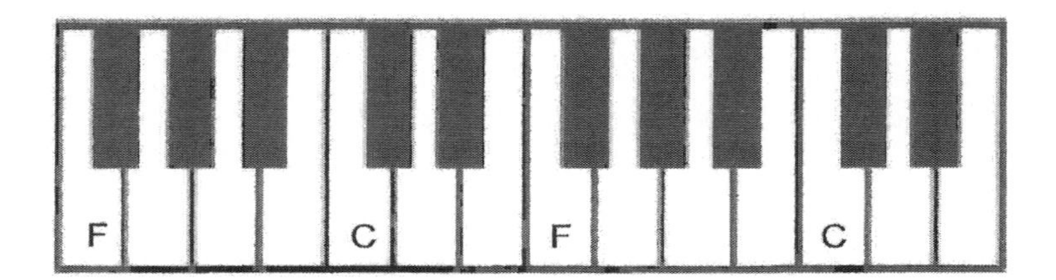

Like a lot of things in music, math, and life, if you know one thing, you can find out other things by relative reasoning. We can now fill in the other white keys:

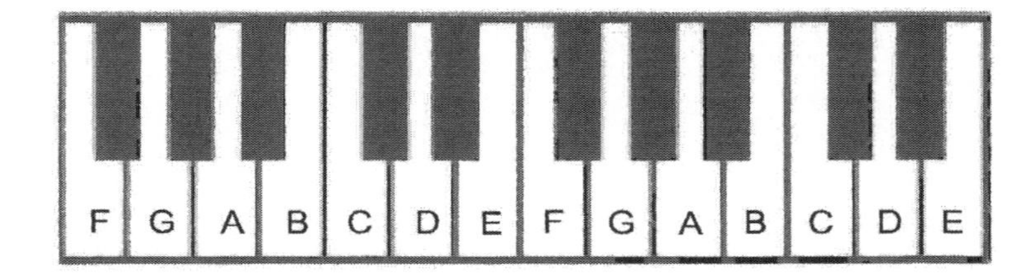

The notes on the white keys repeat themselves: A, B, C, D, E, F, G, A, B, C, D, E, F, G, etc.

Middle C

On any standard piano, the **c** closest to the middle of the piano is called "middle C." Middle C is also usually very close to the piano's brand name or logo. On other keyboards (most of which are shorter in length than that of a piano) middle C is often indicated by an arrow or mark somewhere on the body of the keyboard.

Find middle C on your keyboard, then familiarize yourself with the names of the other white keys. For practice, have someone point to a white key on a keyboard. See how quickly you can identify the note. In time, this skill will become automatic.

Fill in the names of the keyboard white notes.

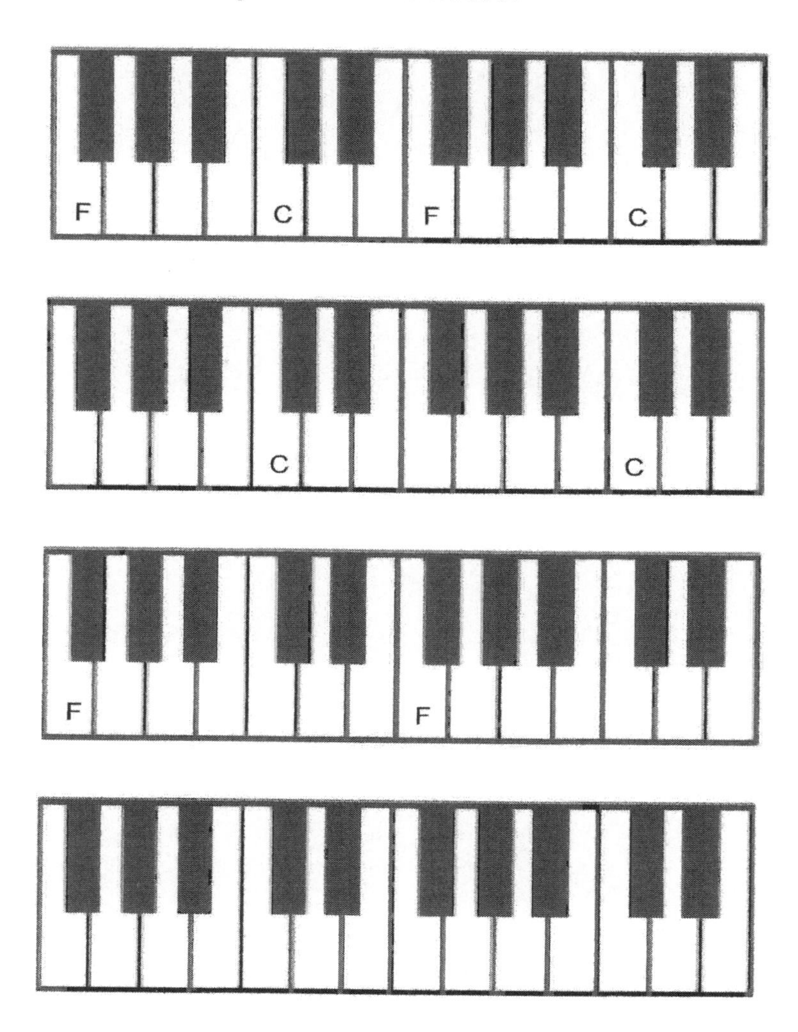

Sharps And Flats

As we noticed earlier, the black notes are in groups of twos and threes. These notes are called either **sharps** or **flats.**

The nearest black key going up (to the right) is called a **sharp**. The sign for the sharp is this:

♯

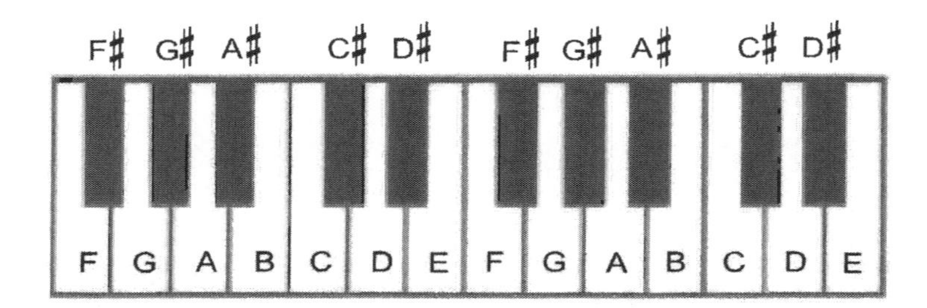

The nearest black key going down (to the left) is called a **flat.** The sign for the flat is this:

♭

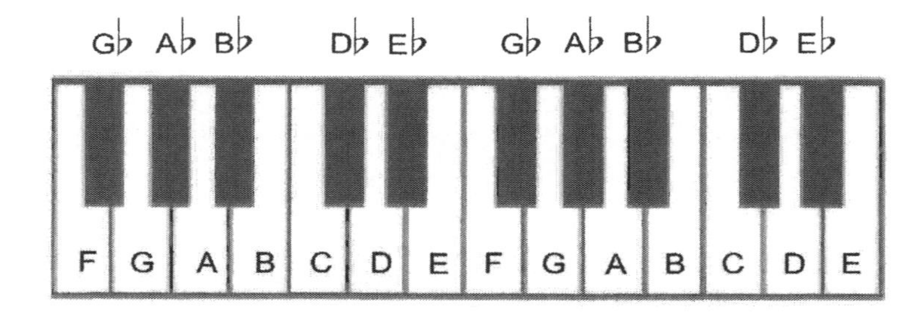

You might have noticed that there can be notes on the keyboard that have two different names (F♯ and G♭, C♯ and D♭, etc.). Notes that sound the same but have two different names are said to be "enharmonic" (from the Greek, meaning literally "together sound").

If you are new to the keyboard, I want you to hang in there. There is only one more page to go, and you'll need the very little information that is presented here to do the keyboard exercises that correspond to the drum exercises.

Identify the black notes here as sharps. The first one is done for you.

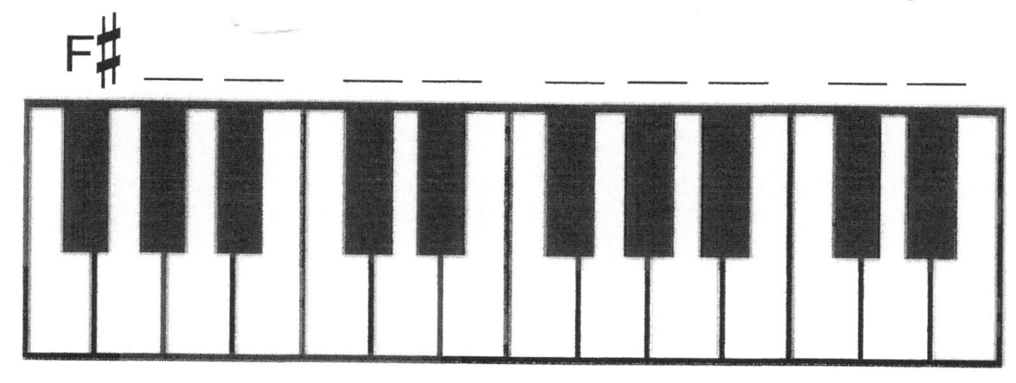

Identify the black notes here as flats. The first one is done for you.

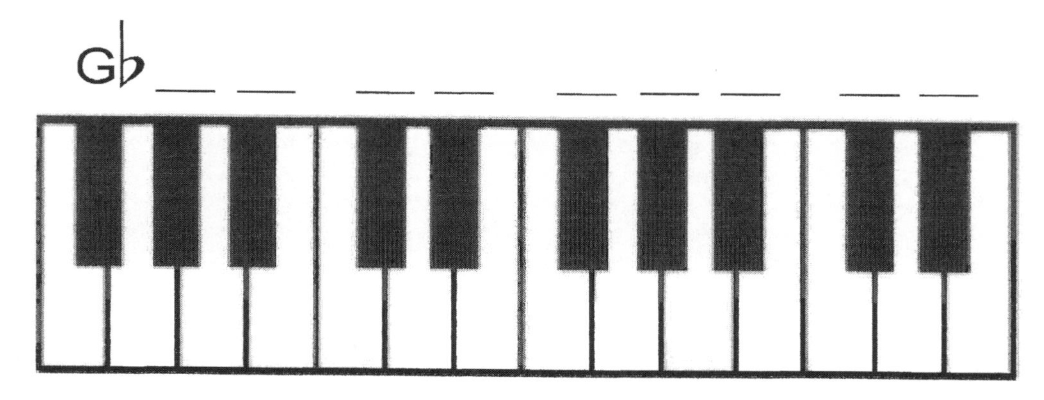

STEP A 16: READING/KEYBOARD SINGING EXERCISE

- Find the E♭ above middle c.
- Play track one of the CD.
- Play the exercises on Reading Page 1 on page 11 using the E♭. Use any finger of your right hand.
- Sing along as you play the E♭, using "tah." Match the pitch the best you can.
- Repeat this exercise against track 2 through 6 of the CD.

E♭

Middle C

YOUR LEFT FOOT

Rock and roll (what early rock music was called) came into being in the early '50s, and since then its dominant characteristic has been a strong backbeat. Early rock and roll used the 12 bar blues almost exclusively, and like country music, remains harmonically simple, almost by neccessity, as a vehicle for the lyrics. Rock music gets its energy from its emotional, direct expression, and a strong backbeat provides its drive and power. Whether its Martha and the Vandella's "Dancing In the Street" (1964) or Bruce Springsteen's "Born In the USA" (1984), or whatever is on the charts today, the drummer's left hand has been hitting the snare on "2" and "4" from the beginning.

Three Popular Music Styles Defined, Succinctly (and not too seriously):

Country music: Three Chords and the truth.
Rock music: Dancing on your troubles.
Jazz: Music that comes before and after the bass solo!

In jazz, although the backbeat is sometimes strongly stated, more often the "2" and "4" is played with more subtlety, with the drummer using his left foot to close the hi-hat on those beats. There is therefore more of a sense of equalibrium between the beats in jazz than in rock.

Using the left foot to play the hi-hat on "2" and "4" while playing other rhythms with the other limbs is part of the stylistic and traditional heritage of jazz and *must* be mastered. The subtle "chick" sound of the cymbals closing adds both a bouyancy to the swing feeling and a sense of having a landmark in feeling the time.

"The hi-hat just adds an added impulse to the time - to the beat. That's why time is so important because if you have the time feeling - the swinging feeling - you can become as free as you want as long as that basic element is there."

Shelly Manne
Down Beat, June, 1964

Backbeat

The second and fourth beat of a 4/4 measure.

12 Bar Blues

One of the most influential of styles, the blues has influenced virtually every other music style in America. The blues evolved into different forms, but the most enduring has been the twelve bar blues, a twelve measure cycle that repeats itself:

I IV

I V I

HEEL-TOE HI-HAT TECHNIQUE

Although there are various ways of playing the hi-hat with the left foot, I have found that using the heel-toe method in *practice* (even if other techniques are used elsewhere) to be an effective way to "lock in" the quarter note feel of jazz, and to facilitate the coordination of all the limbs.

- Do this exercise **away** from the drumset.
- Sit in a chair, back straight, relaxed and alert.
- Play track 1 of the CD.
- Rock your left foot in time to the bass line of the CD, with the heel down on beats 1 & 3, and the toes down on beats 2 & 4:

"one"

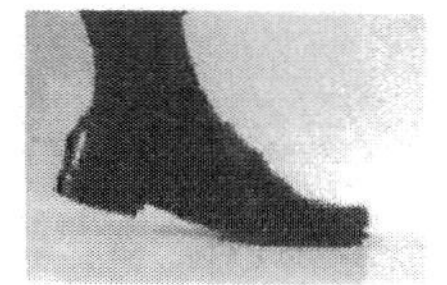
"two"

"three"

"four"

- Add quarter notes with your right foot, keeping your heel on the ground, and tapping all the beats with the toes. Note the obvious: your feet are employing a different technique for each foot. Make sure the tapping points are perfectly in sync with each other and in time with the CD,
- Repeat this exercise against tracks 2 through 6 of the CD.

Think Outside Of The Box:

One skill that jazz musicians should have is the ability to express the same idea in a different way each time it is played. You might have noticed that we are getting a lot of mileage out of Reading Page One (page 11). Well, we're just getting started! A creative musician can take the simplest page of music and do interesting things with it indefinitely. Being able to do this is evidence of creativity and the ability to internalize (really feel) what you are playing, whether you are on your instrument or not. The following exercises may not seem standard fare for your basic drum book, but they will lead to your having a stronger sense of phrasing and control in your playing.

Step A 19: Reading/Coordination/Phrasing/Singing

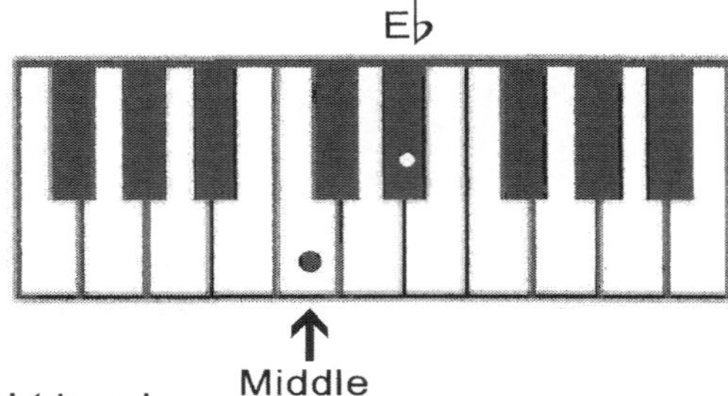

- Find the E♭ above middle C.
- Play track 1 of the CD.
- Play the exercises on Reading Page One on page 11, using the E♭. Use any finger of your right hand.
- As you play the keyboard with your right hand, rock your left foot in time with the beat, heel down on 1 & 3, and toe down on 2 & 4.
- Sing along as you play the E♭, using "tah." Match the pitch the best you can.
- Repeat this exercise against tracks 2 through 6 on the CD.

> Extra Challenge: Play the exercise while your left hand snaps its fingers on 2 & 4, matching your left foot tapping its toes on 2 & 4.

Step A 20: Technique/Coordination/Reading/Singing

- Do this exercise on the drumset.
- Play track 1 of the CD.
- Rock your LF/HH in time: heel down on beats 1 & 3, toes down on beats 2 & 4. Let the HH cymbals close crisply on the backbeat, making a "chick" sound.
- With your LF/HH keeping time on 2 & 4, play the exercises on page 11, using your RH/CYM. Sing along with the cymbal, using "ting" or "ding." Don't sing the rests.
- With your LF/HH keeping time on 2 & 4, play the same exercises on the snare, using your left hand. Sing along with the snare, using "bop," "bap," or "tah." Don't sing the rests.
- With your LF/HH keeping time on 2 & 4, play the same exercises on the bass drum, using your right foot. Sing along with the BD, using "boom." Don't sing the rests.
- Repeat this exercise against tracks 2 through 6 on the CD.

> Extra Challenge: Play these exercises against your LF/HH playing 2 & 4 with different combinations of the other limbs playing in unison:
>
> RH & RF
> RH & LH
> RF & LH
> RH & RF & LH

√

☐ STEP A 21: INTERPRETIVE EXERCISE

- Play track 1 of the CD. Apply the following exercise against Reading Page One (page 11).
- Play RF/BD quarter notes, LF/HH on 2 & 4.
- Hands play alternating quarter notes (R L R L etc.). Move to the high tom on the written quarter notes (notes on beats 1 & 3 will be played with the RH, notes on beats 2 & 4 will be played with the LH). All rests will be played on the snare. Sing the tom part as you play it, using "bop" or "bom" (don't sing the rests).
- Repeat this exercise against tracks 2 through 6 on the CD.

√

☐ STEP A 22: INTERPRETIVE EXERCISE

- Play track 1 of the CD. Apply the following exercise against Reading Page One (page 11).
- Play RF/BD quarter notes, LF/HH on 2 & 4.
- Hands play alternating quarter notes (R L R L etc.). Move to the high tom and low tom an all written quarter notes (written notes on 1 & 3 will be played on the low tom with the RH, written notes on 2 & 4 will be played on the high tom with the LH). Sing the tom parts as you play them, using "bop" or "bom" (don't sing the rests). Try to match the pitch difference between the toms as you sing.
- Repeat this exercise against tracks 2 through 6 on the CD.

√

☐ STEP A 23: INTERPRETIVE EXERCISE

- Play track 1 of the CD. Apply the following exercise against Reading Page One (page 11).
- Play RF/BD quarter notes, LF/HH on 2 & 4.
- RH stays *positioned* on the high tom, and plays all written quarter notes. Sing the tom part as you play it, using "bop" or "bom" (don't sing the rests). The LH stays *positioned* on the snare drum and plays all "missing" quarter notes (the rests).
- Repeat this exercise against tracks 2 through 6 on the CD.

Extra Challenge: Play the above exercise with the hands reversed: LH on high tom and RH on snare.

√

Step A 24: Interpretive Exercise

- Play track 1 of the CD. Apply the following exercises against Reading Page One (page 11).
- LF/HH on 2 & 4.
- RH/CYM and RF/BD play written notes together, in unison. As you play the CYM and BD together, sing the written part, imitating either the CYM or BD sound.
- The LH stays positioned on the snare drum and plays all "missing" quarter notes (the rests).
- Repeat this exercise against tracks 2 through 6 on the CD.

Extra Challenge: Play the above exercise with the hands reversed: LH on cymbal and RH on snare.

√

Step A 25: Technique/Coordination/Reading/Singing

- Play track 1 of the CD. Apply the following exercises against Reading Page One (page 11).
- LF/HH on 2 & 4.
- RH/CYM and LH/SN play written notes together, in unison. As you play the CYM and SN together, sing the written part, imitating either the CYM or SN sound.
- RF/BD plays all "missing" quarter notes (the rests).
- Repeat this exercise against tracks 2 through 6 on the CD.

What Stan Kenton Said About Jazz:

"A session in jazz is comparable to an open forum where theories and opinions are discussed openly and freely. Without inhibition or the fear of being reprimanded, a soloist rises and speaks without the aid of notes or previous preparation. Speeches with words of various inflections and insinuations are replaced with a flow of melodic, rhythmic music. One soloist will speak for himself on a chosen topic and then retire to hear the feelings of another on the same subject. On occasions, they will speak of happy things, then those of a serious nature, sometimes somber and even tragic. All phases of life's emotions are felt and experienced in jazz. Some of the music is complex and reaches far below the surface while other forms dwell lightly. There are speakers in improvised jazz who are eloquent in their ability. Musical words flow freely. Others tend to speak in short sentences with a simple vocabulary. However, if sincerity prevails, everyone is felt, understood and appreciated."

Swinging Eighth Notes
The Big Bands
Drummers Of The Big Bands
Ride Cymbal Rhythm
Independence
Comping Patterns
Sticking Fluency
The Properties Of Sound
The Shape Of Each Note
Ear Training/Phrasing
Comping/Creativity

Swinging Eighth Notes

As we learned in Section A, early jazz was the blending of various forms of music, and owes much of its loose rhythmic feel to the blues and ragtime part of the blend. Indeed, it was the relaxing of the traditional pitch and rhythmical strictures that gave jazz its characteristic sound and feel. The biggest rhythmic change in jazz came with the eventual playing of eighth notes unevenly. The upbeats (the "ands") were, in a sense, moved closer to the next beat. Just how they were played varied, depending on the style, historical period, tempo, and the musicians playing.

Eventually, eighth notes became to be played most often with an underlying triplet feel:

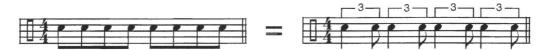

Most rhythmic figures in jazz are written with various combinations of quarter notes and eighth notes, and are played with a swing interpretation. The eighth notes are interpreted with an underlying triplet feel. This is called "jazz" or "swing" interpretation (or feel).

This method of notation is standard on all instruments, and is used as a "musical shorthand" to indicate swinging rhythms. It is also easier to sightread, once you get used to it. Here are some sample rhythms, written with quarter and eighth notes, and then literally:

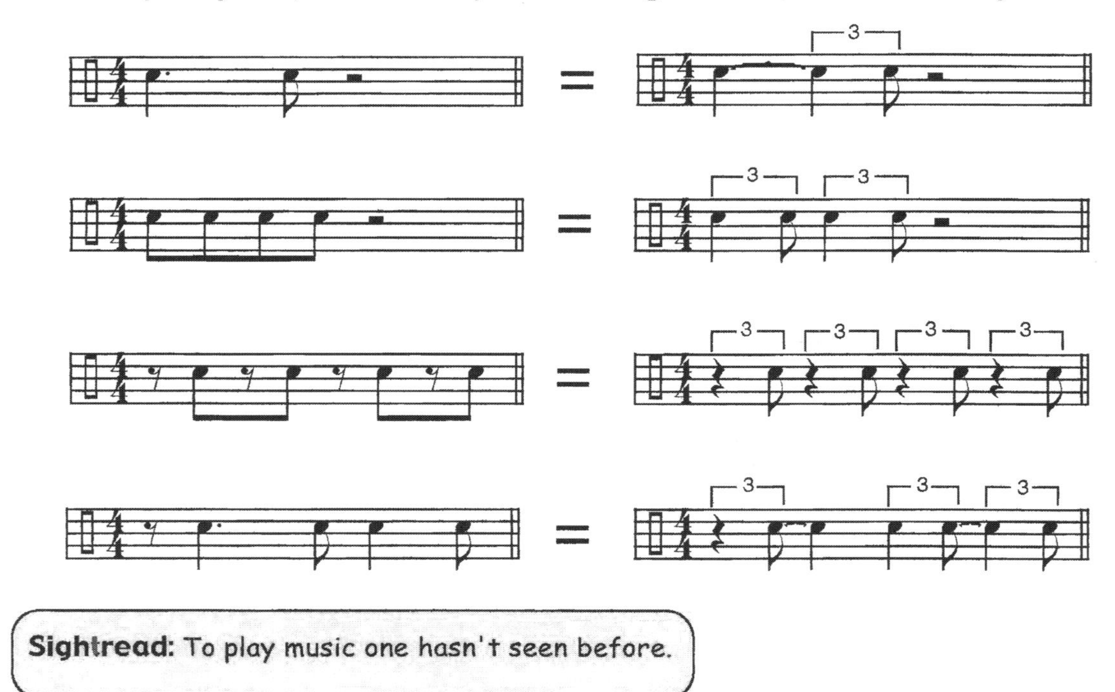

Sightread: To play music one hasn't seen before.

√

STEP B 2: SWINGING EIGHTH NOTES/READING/SINGING

- Play Track 1 of the CD. Apply the following exercise against the following two pages (Reading Pages 2 & 3).
- RF/BD: Light quarter notes, LF/HH on 2 & 4.
- Play the written exercises on the snare using this sticking:
  RH plays all notes on the beat.
  LH plays all the "ands."
- Sing the written part as you play it, using any combination of syllables you are comfortable with (bop, do, be, dee, bah, dah, etc.).
- Repeat this exercise against tracks 2 through 6 of the CD.

√

STEP B 3: SWINGING EIGHTH NOTES/READING/SINGING

- Play Track 1 of the CD. Apply the following exercise against the following two pages (Reading Pages 2 & 3).
- RF/BD: Light quarter notes, LF/HH on 2 & 4.
- Play the written exercises with both hands in unison:
  RH/CYM
  LH/SN
- Sing the written part as you play it, using any combination of syllables you are comfortable with (bop, do, be, dee, bah, dah, etc.).
- Repeat this exercise against tracks 2 through 6 of the CD.

√

STEP B 4: SWINGING EIGHTH NOTES/READING/SINGING

- Find the E♭ above middle c.
- Play Track 1 of the CD.
- Play the exercises on Reading Pages 2 & 3, using the E♭. Use any finger of your RH.
- As you play the keyboard with your RH, rock your LF in time with the beat, heel down on 1 & 3, and toe down on 2 & 4.

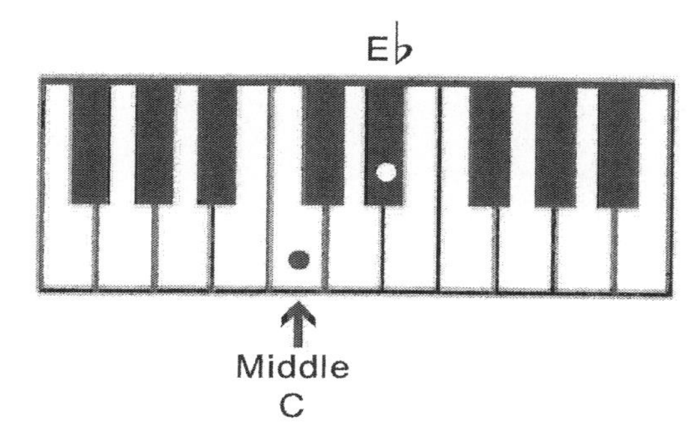

- Sing along as you play the E♭, using "tah." Match the pitch the best you can.
- Repeat this exercise against tracks 2 through 6 of the CD.

Reading Page # 2

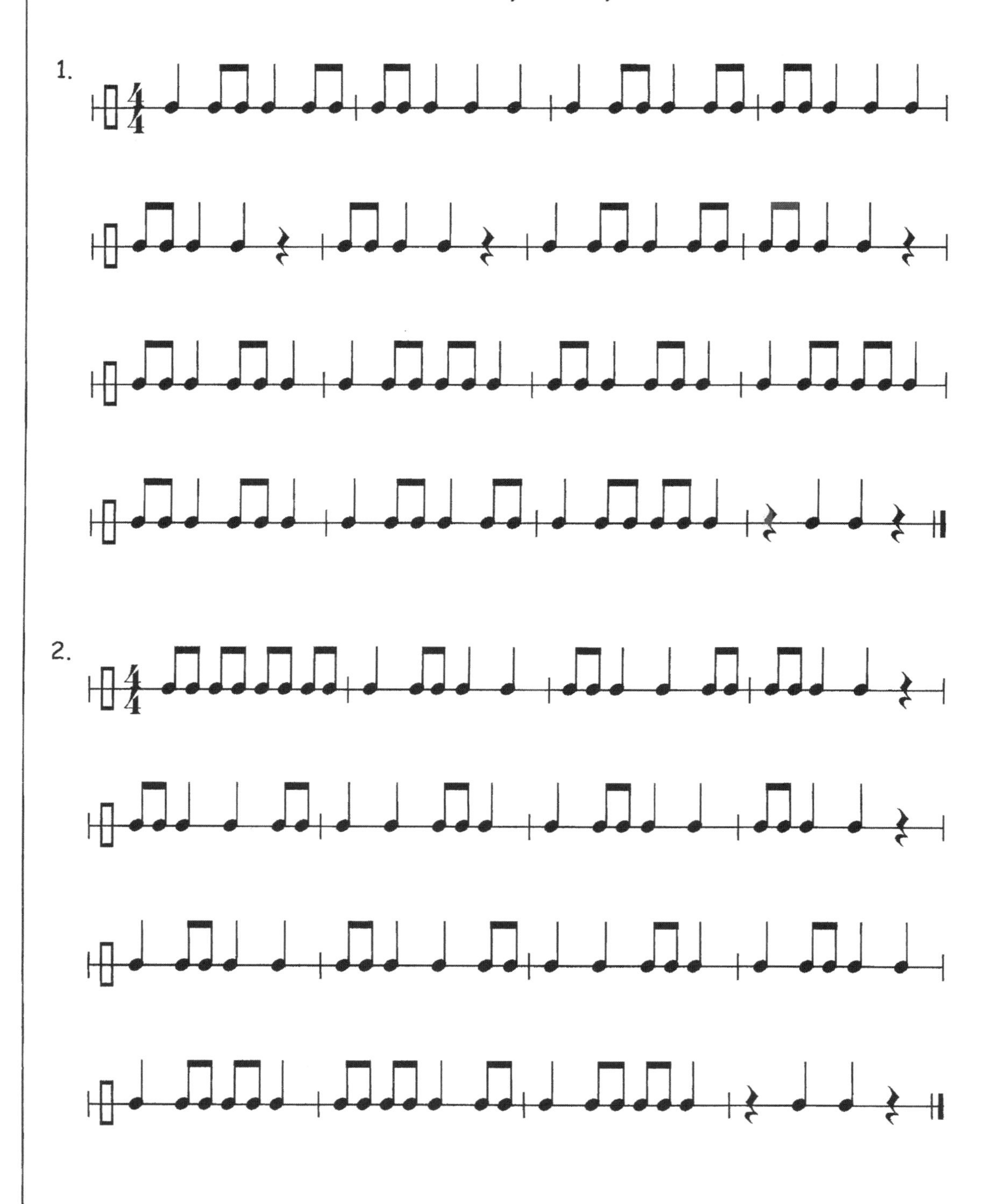

Reading Page # 3

STEP B 5: FILLING IN THE BLANKS/COORDINATION

This exercise to be played against Reading Pages 2 & 3 (pp. 30-31).

- RF/BD: Light quarter notes, LF/HH on 2 & 4.
- Hands play swinging eighth notes, with alternating sticking (R L R L R L R L, ETC.) throughout.
- Play the written notes on the high tom, with all the "missing" eighth notes on the snare.

For example, the first line of Reading Page 2 looks like this:

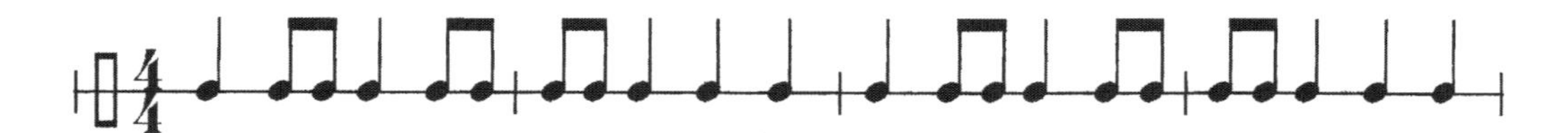

And would be played like this:

- Sing the written part (high tom) as you play it, using any combination of syllables you are comfortable with.
- Play this exercise against tracks 1 through 6 of the CD.

STEP B 6: FILLING IN THE BLANKS/COORDINATION

This exercise to be played against Reading Pages 2 & 3 (pp. 30-31).

- RF/BD: Light quarter notes, LF/HH on 2 & 4.
- Hands play swinging eighth notes, with alternating sticking (R L R L R L R L, ETC.) throughout.
- Play the written notes on the snare, with all the "missing" eighth notes on the high tom.

For example, the first line of Reading Page 2 looks like this:

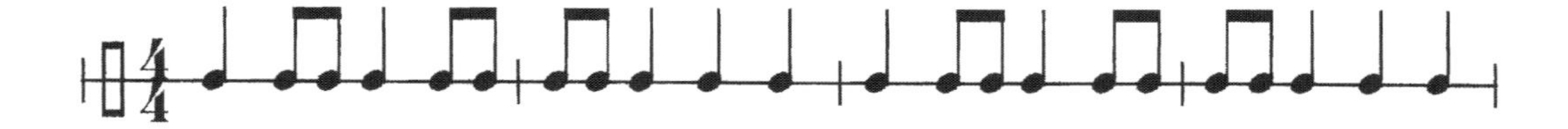

And would be played like this:

- Sing the written part (the snare) as you play it, using any combination of syllables you are comfortable with.
- Play this exercise against tracks 1 through 6 of the CD.

√

STEP B 7: FILLING IN THE BLANKS/COORDINATION

This exercise to be played against Reading Pages 2 & 3 (pp. 30-31).

- RF/BD: Light quarter notes, LF/HH on 2 & 4.
- Hands play swinging eighth notes, with alternating sticking (R L R L R L R L, ETC.) throughout.
- Play the written notes on two toms, with all the notes on the beat played with the RH on the floor tom. All the written notes on the upbeats (the and's) will be played with the LH on the high tom. All "missing" eighth notes to be played on the snare with either hand.

  For example, the first line of Reading Page 2 looks like this:

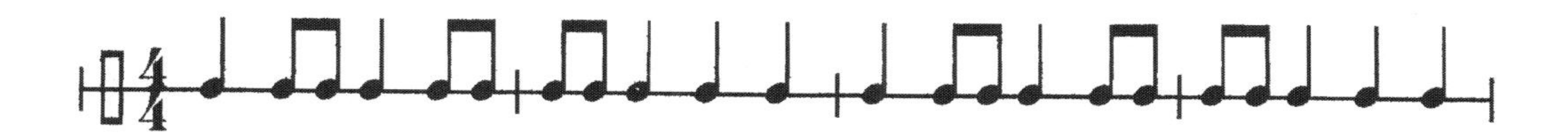

  And would be played like this:

- Sing the written part (the two toms) as you play it, using any combination of syllables you are comfortable with. As you sing, try to match the pitches of the two toms.
- Play this exercise against tracks 1 through 6 of the CD.

THE BIG BANDS

Big band swing came into national prominence around 1935, and in terms of public appeal, it was the rock'n'roll of its day, with literally hundreds of bands playing ballrooms throughout the country, In terms of lasting influence and importance, a few bands stand out. Two bands that had a lasting impact: the ensembles of Duke Ellington and Count Basie.

The Duke. Edward Kennedy "Duke" Ellington was born in Washington, D.C. in 1899, and began playing professionally at the age of seventeen. In 1923, he moved to New York, formed a ten piece band, and was soon a mainstay at the famed Cotton Club. A prolific writer, Ellington used his band as a vehicle for his own artistic expression, and what are now famous standards soon emerged: "Mood Indigo," "Sophisticated Lady," and of course "Satin Doll." Ellington's trademark song, however, was "Take The 'A' Train," written by his arranger Billy Strayhorn. Evidence of his lasting influence is seen by the fact that his music is still performed nightly in countless clubs, and even a revue of his music was a Broadway smash a few years ago. Ellington's band, at the time, was probably the most daring and eclectic, with innovative arrangements and harmonies, and to perform with his band was a high honor among musicians. Louis Bellson, who joined Ellington's band in 1951, said, "There was something different every night. Duke always gave us a great deal of freedom. I learned about tempos and blending from Benny [Goodman] and Harry [James] and Basie, and about endurance from Tommy [Dorsey]. But from Duke I learned the importance of sound. Playing with his band was the highlight of my career." Jazz critic Ralph Gleason wrote that Ellington was the "single greatest talent to be produced in the history of jazz."

Duke Ellington

Ensemble
A group of musicians who perform together.

Standards
Compositions that continously get played through the years.

Louis Bellson
"There was something different every night."

Sam Woodyard
Played with the Duke
1953-1973

The Count. Throughout the development of Chicago and New York as jazz centers, musicians in Kansas City were developing their own brand of swing, and in 1936, Count Basie's band epitomized this new style, a blend of big band swing and the blues. William "Count" Basie was born in Red Bank, New Jersey, in 1904. While stranded on a tour in Kansas City, Basie joined Benny Moten's band. When Moten died, Basie formed his own band. Basie's band was distinct from the other bands of the day by its ultra-tight rhythm section (composed of Jo Jones, whose pulsating ride cymbal changed the course of drumming, bassist Walter Page, guitarist Freddie Green, and Basie, with his trademark economical touch), its smooth ensemble blend, and its outstanding soloists, among them the great saxophonist Lester Young. Basie's bandstand featured several great drummers at different tenures, among them Jo Jones, Sonny Payne, and Butch Miles.

Count Basie

Butch, you got the gig:

When Butch Miles auditioned for Basie's band, he ended up playing with Basie for several weeks without knowing he was "officially" in. After carefully dropping hints to Basie to let him know his status, Basie, who was economical in conversation as he was on the piano, said to Butch, "Well, you're still here, aren't you?"

Besides showcasing great soloists and drummers, Basie's band also featured at different times three outstanding vocalists: Jimmy Rushing, Joe Williams, and the legendary Billie Holiday. The Basie signature song was "One O' Clock Jump," a riff-based instrumental.

Some Notable Big Bands:

Charlie Barnett
Count Basie
Benny Berigan
Jimmy Dorsey
Tommy Dorsey
Benny Goodman
Duke Ellington
Fletcher Henderson
Woody Herman
Harry James
Jimmy Lunceford
Glenn Miller
Artie Shaw
Chick Webb

Barrett Deems, Gene & Buddy

Some Notable Big Band Drummers:

Louis Bellson
Sid Catlett
Cozy Cole
Sonny Greer
Jo Jones
Rufus Jones
Gene Krupa
Mel Lewis
Sonny Payne
Buddy Rich
Dave Tough
Chick Webb
Shadow Wilson
Sam Woodyard

Riff: A short, catchy phrase, repeated several times.

DRUMMERS OF THE BIG BANDS

Gene Krupa
The first drum star - check out the angle of the snare!

Gene Krupa. One of the most famous and influential drummers in musical history also made the Chicago to New York transit, after spending his formative years in the Windy City, developing his craft in the shadow of the great black drummers of the time. Gene Krupa was born in Chicago in 1909. After considering and rejecting the priesthood as a vocation, he began to play drums around the Chicago area, working with different groups. Krupa was a quick study, and was greatly influenced by two transplanted New Orleans drummers, Zutty Singleton and Baby Dodds. Krupa once stated, "I picked up from Zutty Singleton and Baby Dodds the difference between starting a roll or sequence of beats with the left or right hand, and how the tone and inflection changed entirely when you shifted hands. . . most white drummers of the day thought drums were something you beat the hell out of. . . few of them realized that the drums had a broad range of tonal variations so they could be played to fit the harmonic pattern as well as a rhythmical one." Krupa moved to New York in 1929, worked with several bands, and joined the Benny Goodman band in 1935. Soon the Goodman band became the hottest band in the land (Goodman was called the "King Of Swing"), and the charismatic Krupa garnered his share of the spotlight. Krupa was regularly featured as a soloist on "Sing, Sing, Sing," and this did much to bring the drummer to a new height of credibility and acceptance. In 1938, Krupa formed his own band, and more drum orientated standards emerged, among them "Drum Boogie" and "Wire Brush Stomp."

Not another drum joke:

Q. What do you call a guy who hangs out with musicians?
A. The drummer!

The jokes haven't stopped (there are jokes about every instrument), but it was Gene Krupa, as Louis Bellson said, who brought the drummer out of the orchestra pit onto the stage, bringing a new respect for the drumset as an instrument.

Let's Get Small

Besides leading his own big band, Benny Goodman pioneered the small group combo as a creative outlet. With Gene Krupa on Drums and Teddy Wilson on piano, the Goodman trio first appeared to jazz lovers on record. Although reluctant at first to appear in public with his trio, Goodman eventually did, and showed the public that the world would not end if black and white musicians played together. Later, the discovery of vibraphonist Lionel Hampton made the trio a swinging quartet.

Dave Tough. A drumming contemporary of Krupa who was also nurtured amid the transplanted black musicians in the '20s Chicago scene was Dave Tough. Tough was born in 1908, and like Krupa, made the Chicago to New York migration, and became very well known for his swinging, sensitive approach with such bands as Tommy Dorsey, Artie Shaw, Benny Goodman, and later with Woody Herman, with whose band reached the apex of his career, Unfortunately, Tough's life and career mirrored that of the great Chicago cornetist Bix Biederbeck. Both were intelligent, literate, and talented, and yet both were victims of alcoholism and poor health. Tough died prematurely in 1949, from a fall resulting from an epileptic seizure. Baby Dodds, Tough's mentor and prime influence, said, "Tough was like a clock. Stick him under a band and he'd make everybody play."

Dave Tough

Dropping Bombs: Hitting intermittent accents with the bass drum, as opposed to keeping time with quarter notes.

Significant other drummers. As the big band era flourished in the late '30s, other drummers made lasting contributions to jazz: Sonny Greer (who distinguished himself throughout the early Ellington years), Cozy Cole, Chick Webb (whose very swinging band launched the career of Ella Fitzgerald), Jo Jones (whose work with Count Basie, featuring a swinging ride cymbal, pioneering use of the hi-hat, and the creative use of "dropping bombs" put a definitive stamp on drumming at the time), Sidney Catlett, and of course, Buddy Rich.

Some BIG Big Band Drummers

The debonair Sonny Greer, the significant Jo Jones, and the exciting Buddy Rich.

Buddy Rich. Bernard "Buddy" Rich was born in Brooklyn in 1917, the son of a husband and wife vaudeville team. At the age of eighteen months he was already appearing with his parents, and by age four was touring as "Traps the Drum Wonder." After appearing at the Hickory House with Joe Marsala, Rich played in succession with Bunny Berigan, Benny Carter, Artie Shaw, Tommy Dorsey, and Harry James. After intermittent periods of fronting his own band, Rich made the move permanent in 1968. Possessing a phenomenal technique that has yet to be matched, Rich played with an innate musical perception that made him a drummer's drummer. Rich was also a convincing singer, and his bass drum technique was undoubtedly related to his tap dancing ability. Rich died in 1987, and several memorial tributes featuring his band playing with current top drummers were recorded and released.

Buddy And Basie

Buddy was a big fan of Count Basie, and a friend of Jo Jones, Basie's fine drummer. One night in September, 1944, with World War II in full force, Jones and Lester Young, Basie's star saxophonist, were served with their draft notices, and were gone the next morning. Basie was in a fix. Buddy was brought on for the two week engagement set at the Plantation Club in Los Angeles. Basie later remarked that whenever Buddy was sitting in, the rest of the band would actually show up early for the gig. On the last night of the engagement, Basie presented Buddy with a blank check, which Buddy tore up. Basie later gave Buddy a gold watch with the inscription: "To Buddy From The Count. L.A. Thanks."

Buddy in the '60s. The first trumpeter is obviously thinking way ahead, ducking to avoid all future projectiles.

Buddy Rich Stories

Talk to enough jazz musicians, and sooner or later you'll hear some Buddy Rich stories - almost everyone has one to tell. Buddy was definitely a colorful character. Here's one of many:

Gunnar Biggs, a bassist friend of mine who spent some time in Buddy's band on the road, confirmed that being in Buddy's band was no picnic. "You couldn't get away," he said. "We were playing Las Vegas, and one afternoon I was out by the pool, getting some sun, trying to forget everything for a while. Well, I've got my eyes closed, I'm totally relaxed. Buddy sneaks up on me and whispers in my ear, 'If you make a mistake tonight, I'm going to kill you!'" What a wakeup call!

There is a treasure trove of available albums documentaries, and books on the big band/swing era. Here are a few to get you started:

Albums

Benny Goodman - Live At Carnegie Hall (Columbia G2K 40244). A historical period piece: the "King of Swing" and his band and friends shake up Carnegie Hall on January 16, 1938. Recorded with a single overhead mike, the sound is not pristine, but the joint is jumping and Gene Krupa is swinging all over the place.

Ellington At Newport (Columbia CK 40587). Another historical landmark: The Duke makes his comeback at Newport on July 7, 1956. Drummer Sam Woodyard pushes the band.

Mercy Mercy - The Buddy Rich Big Band (Blue Note 54331). The absolutely phenomenal Buddy pushing his band to the outer limits.

Big Swing Face - The Buddy Rich Big Band (Pacific Jazz CDP 7243 8 37989 2 6). Object lesson in how to swing a band. Standouts include "Norwegian Wood," "Big Swing Face," and the legendary "Love For Sale."

Atomic Basie (Blue Note 23635). Many Basie fans name this as their favorite album. The whole album is great, but "Li'l Darlin'" alone is worth it for a lesson on how to swing S-L-O-W.

Basie At The Sands (Reprise WPCR - 1874). Basie warming up the crowd before Frank Sinatra. Any Basie album with Sonny Payne on it is recommended (a very exciting drummer)

Consummation (Blue Note 38226). This Thad Jones/Mel Lewis album is a great taste of '70s big band. Jones played flugelhorn and drummer Mel Lewis, though never flashy, always played with consummate taste. A great lesson in big band drumming.

Videos

on the road with duke ellington (Docurama NVG-9502). Variety called this "a superb profile on an elusive subject." This documentary was filmed six years before Duke's passing, and is an intimate look at one of the giants of jazz. We see Ellington in concert, backstage, and in hotel rooms. We learn that he had the same breakfast every morning (steak, potatoes, and hot water) as he wouldn't know when the next meal might be. "Satin Doll," "Take the 'A' Train," and an appearance by Louis Armstrong are highlights.

Clasic Jazz Drummers: Swing And Beyond (Hudson Music ISBN 0-634-04656-X). A treasure trove of video clips highlighting significant jazz drummers. Big Sid Catlett with Louis Armstrong, Gene and Buddy, Panama Francis, Gus Johnson, Philly Jo Jones, and others. A historic bonus: the only known video of Baby Dodds. Highly Recommended.

Books

Drummin' Men - The Heartbeat Of Jazz, by Burt Korall (Oxford University Press ISBN 0-19-515762-1). An incisive look at the drummers who drove the swing band era. Chick Webb, Gene Krupa, the underrated Ray McKinley, Jo Jones, Sid Catlett, Dave Tough, Buddy Rich, and others are looked at through the author's and orther musicians' eyes.

Good Morning Blues (Da Capo Press ISBN 0-306-81107-3). William Basie sits down with writer Albert Murray, and the result is this autobiography of one of the giants of jazz, and the reading is as smooth and easy as the Basie band was. Full of anecdotes about himself and his contemporaries: Frank Sinatra, Sammy Davis, Jr., Quincy Jones, Billie Holiday, Tony Bennett, and others. A look at the 20th century as well as a history of jazz from the inside.

JAZZ RIDE CYMBAL RHYTHM

The standard ride pattern that most jazz drummers use matches the quarter note pulse. Two notes are added, right before the 3rd and 1st beats. These two notes are sometimes called "skip notes."

The jazz ride pattern is usually written like this:

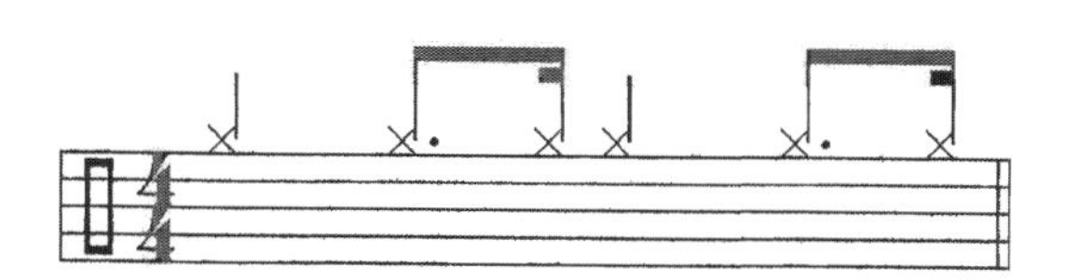

It is generally played like this:

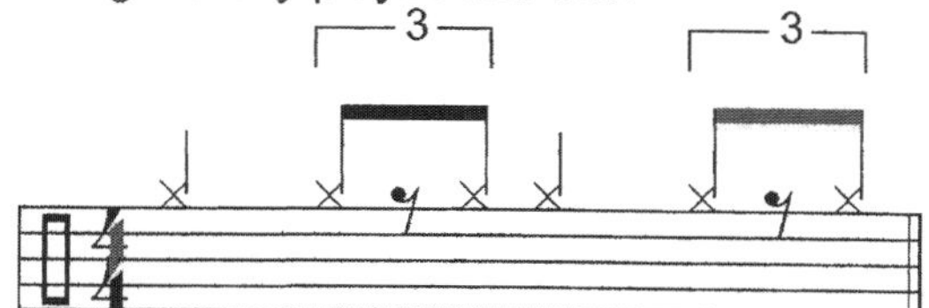

STEP B 7: RIDE CYMBAL RHYTHM EXERCISE

- Practice the jazz ride rhythm below slowly, counting triplets (count all triplets - play the counts that are in bold type). Repeat several times, counting steadily. This exercise will help you gain the proper proportion and feel for the jazz ride rhythm.

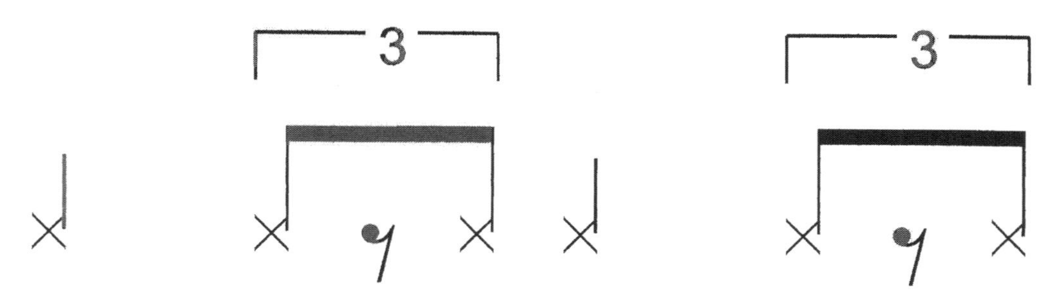

One Trip Let **Two** Trip **Let** **Three** Trip Let **Four** Trip **Let**

- Now practice the jazz ride rhythm against tracks 1 through 6 of the CD. Rock your LF/HH in time, closing the HH on beats 2 & 4. Keep **very light** quarter notes with the BD.

- Make sure your limbs are in sync with each other, and that your playing is relaxed and consistent. Play the ride cymbal with a light touch.

When musicians talk about their favorite drummers, they invariably mention the way those drummers kept time on the ride cymbal. Great jazz drummers had signature sounds in their timekeeping, and could actually be recognized by their ride cymbals (Tony Williams, Elvin Jones, Jimmy Cobb, Buddy Rich, etc.). Get started on *your* sound by focusing on the smoothness and accuracy of your ride pattern.

INDEPENDENCE

The drumming community has long owed a debt of gratitude to Jim Chapin, who in 1948 wrote the first book of its kind to deal in jazz independence studies. His book "Advanced Techniques for the Modern Drummer," is still being used today, and several other books have since been written with the same goal in mind: to help develop the drummer's coordinational skills in the jazz style.

Independence or Interdependence?
(it depends)

The word "independence" has been used since the Chapin book to describe basically ostinato skills: being able to play various rhythms with the LH/SN and RF/BD against the jazz ride cymbal pattern. These skills have to be sharpened by any serious drum student, and the same kind of studies are included in this book as well.

Other writers have recently suggested that the word "independence," as defined in the above paragraph, is somewhat of a misnomer, as truly independent limbs would be something to be avoided. Those writers have put forth the term "interdependence" as the suggested substitute. Their reasoning is quite valid, and time will tell which word will prevail.

No matter which term is used, we as drummers, no matter what style of music, are in the ostinato and polyrhythm business. Incidently, any experienced pianist will have long paid his/her dues in those same techniques. Any piano piece utilizes polyrhythms, and boogie-woogie is a wonderfully exhuberant use of ostinato.

As long as we are all on the same page regarding what we are trying to accomplish, life will go on.

Ostinato

A short phrase that is persistently repeated, often as a rhythmical accompaniment to the melody. A drummer's use of ostinato could be: (1) soloing over bass drum quarter notes, (2) playing hi-hat eighth notes while varying the snare and bass drum patterns, and (3) improvising the snare and bass drum against the jazz ride pattern. From the Italian, meaning *obstinate* or *persistent*.

Polyrhythm

The simultaneous use of contrasting rhythms. "Poly" is a common prefix from the Greek, meaning *more than one*.

√

STEP B 9: QUARTER NOTE INDEPENDENCE: SNARE

We are now going to embark on a rather lengthy study of independence skills. We are going to make use of Reading Page One (page 11) yet again.

- On the next page (page 44), the two exercises from Reading Page One are to be played on the snare with the LH, against the jazz ride rhythm (RH/CYM) and hi-hat on 2 & 4 (LF).
- Even though it is not notated, keep **very light** quarter notes on the bass drum.
- As you play the two exercises, sing the snare part, using "bop."
- Play these exercises against tracks 1 through 6 of the CD.

√

STEP B 10: QUARTER NOTE INDEPENDENCE: BASS DRUM

- On page 45, the two exercises from Reading Page One are to be played on the bass drum against the jazz ride rhythm (RH/CYM) and hi-hat on 2 & 4 (LF).
- As you play the two exercises, sing the bass drum part, using "boom."
- Play these exercises against tracks 1 through 6 of the CD.

Much of what a jazz drummer does relates to what can be called "filling in the blanks." The next two steps are geared to help you develop that skill.

√

STEP B 11: READING AND INTERPRETATION SKILLS

- Repeat Step B 9, but instead of reading page 44, do the step while reading Reading Page One (page 11). Since only the basic rhythm is written (the SN part), you will have to place the ride cymbal, and hi-hat where they belong, without the benefit of a note by note transcription.

√

STEP B 12: READING AND INTERPRETATION SKILLS

- Repeat Step B 10, but instead of reading page 45, do the step while reading Reading Page One (page 11). Since only the basic rhythm is written (the BD part), you will have to place the ride cymbal, and hi-hat where they belong, without the benefit of a note by note transcription.

Quarter Note Independence: Snare

Quarter Note Independence: Bass Drum

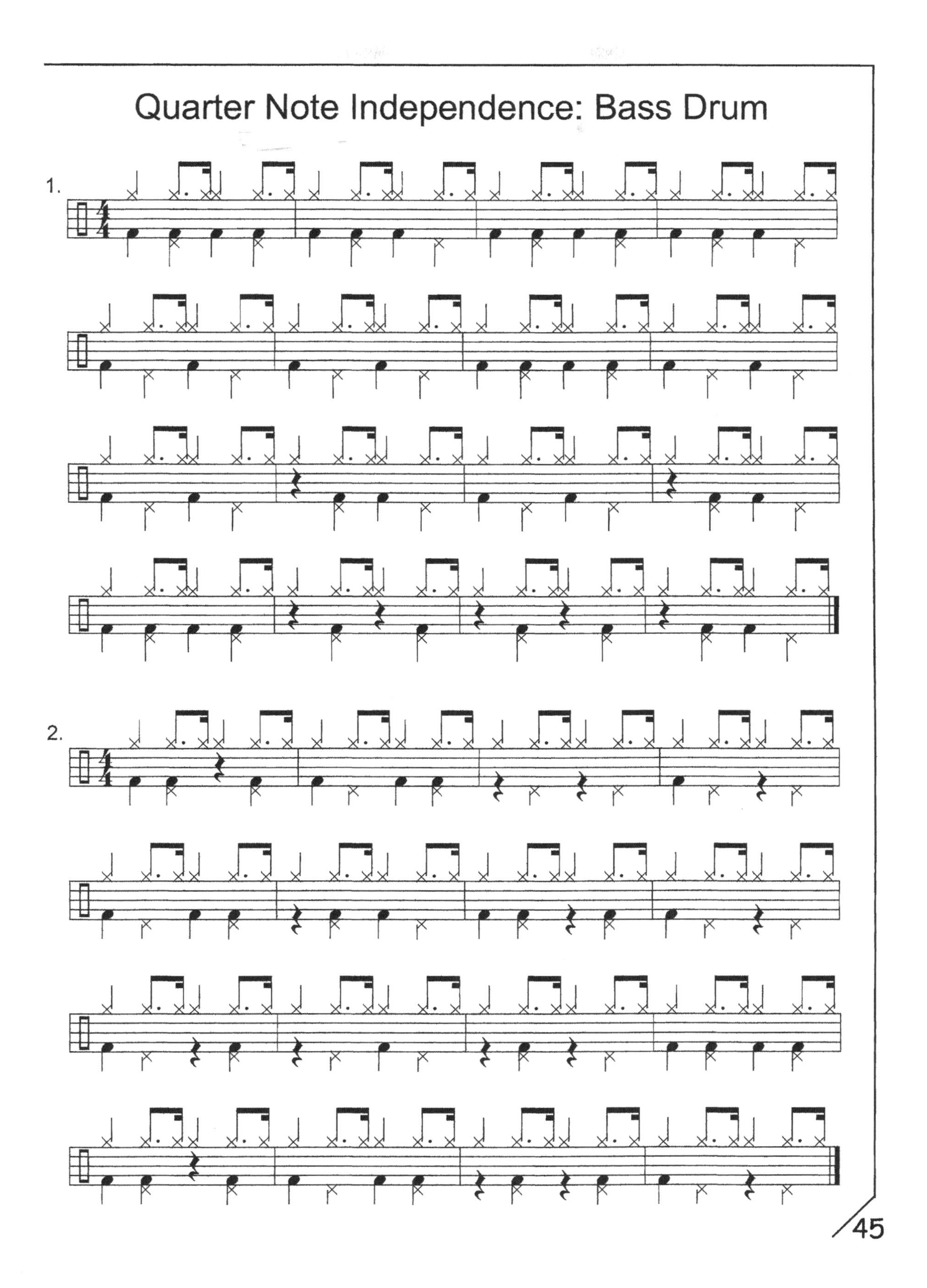

Eighth Note Independence

We are now going to apply these concepts to independence to swinging eighth notes. Most rhythms in jazz and swing are comprised of combinations of quarter and eighth notes. There are six parts to this section:

Keyboard Playing/Phrasing
Eighth Note Independence: Snare
Two measure comp patterns: Snare
Eighth Note Independence: Bass Drum
Eighth Note Independence: Snare and Bass Drum
Two measure comp patterns: Snare and Bass Drum

Follow the instructions carefully for best results.

Step B 13: Keyboard Playing/Phrasing

Follow these directions for pages 48 - 54.

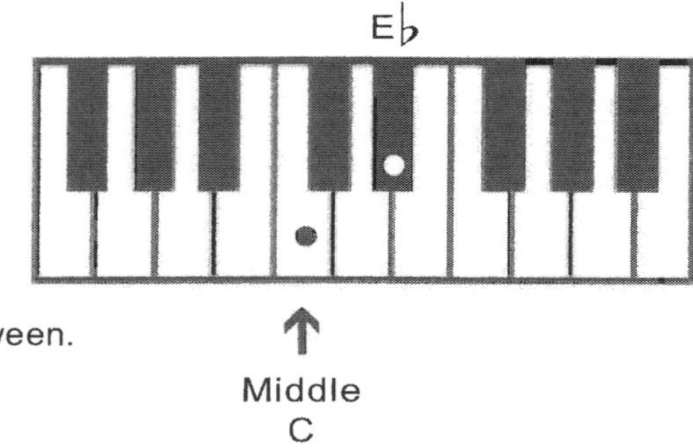

- Find the E♭ above middle c.
- Play Track 1 of the CD.
- Play the **snare rhythms** with your RH, using the E♭. Use any finger of your RH. Play each exercise with a **measure rest** in between. Repeat this sequence for each exercise. For example, exercise 1 looks like this:

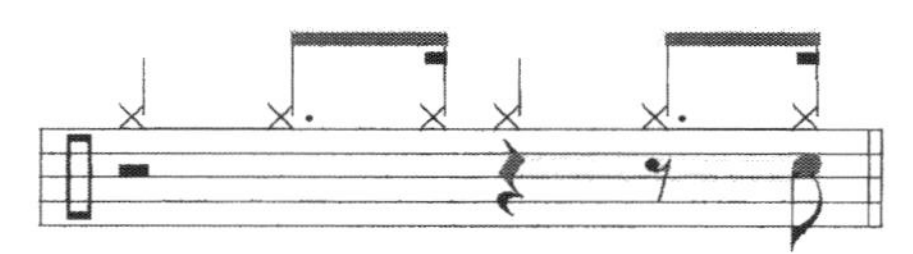

Here's how you will play it on the keyboard:

- Sing along as you play the E♭, using "tah." Match the pitch the best you can.
- Repeat this exercise against tracks 2 through 6 of the CD.

Playing these exercises with the alternating measure rest is crucial to understanding and feeling the proper phrasing. So play these exercises as directed.

√

STEP B 14: EIGHTH NOTE INDEPENDENCE: SNARE

Follow these directions for pages 48 - 54.

- The exercises on the following eight pages are to be played on the snare with the LH, against the jazz ride rhythm (RH/CYM) and hi-hat on 2 & 4 (LF).
- Even though it is not notated, keep **very light** quarter notes on the bass drum.
- As you play the two exercises, sing the snare part, using "bop," "bah," "tah," or "dah." Play each exercise with a **measure of "time"** in between. Repeat this sequence for each exercise. For example, exercise 1 looks like this:

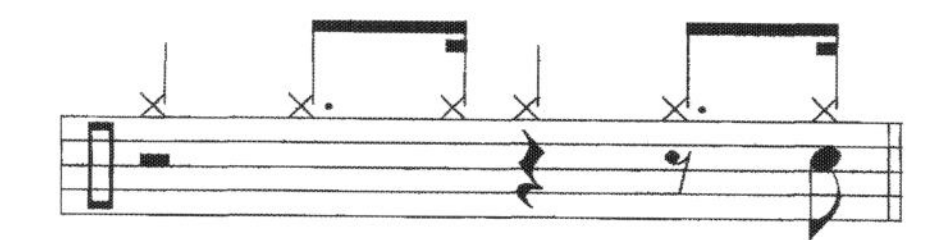

Here's how you will play it on the drumset:

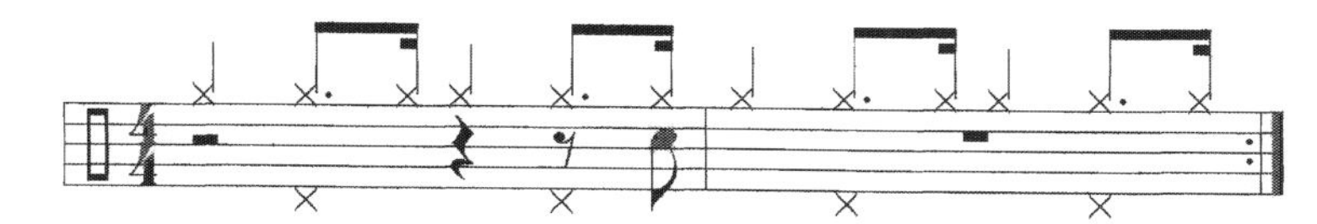

- Play these exercises against tracks 1 through 6 of the CD.

Can One Note Swing?

"A band can really swing when it swings easy. When it can play along like cutting butter. Even a single note can swing."

Count Basie
Ken Burns Jazz, Volume 6

"Swing is a matter of coordination. So when Count Basie says that he can make one note swing, what he means is that the whole preparation and everything in the rhythm and the feeling of the note is coordinated. Louis Armstrong is the master of that, but the Count, just the way he sat at the piano, you could tell before he came in he was going to swing. The way he lifted his hand before he hit the note, he was already swingin'. So bing! When he would hit it. . . you would know we were in for a treat tonight."

Wynton Marsalis
Ken Burns Jazz, Volume 6

Step B 13: Keyboard Playing/Phrasing

Step B 14: Eighth Note Independence: Snare

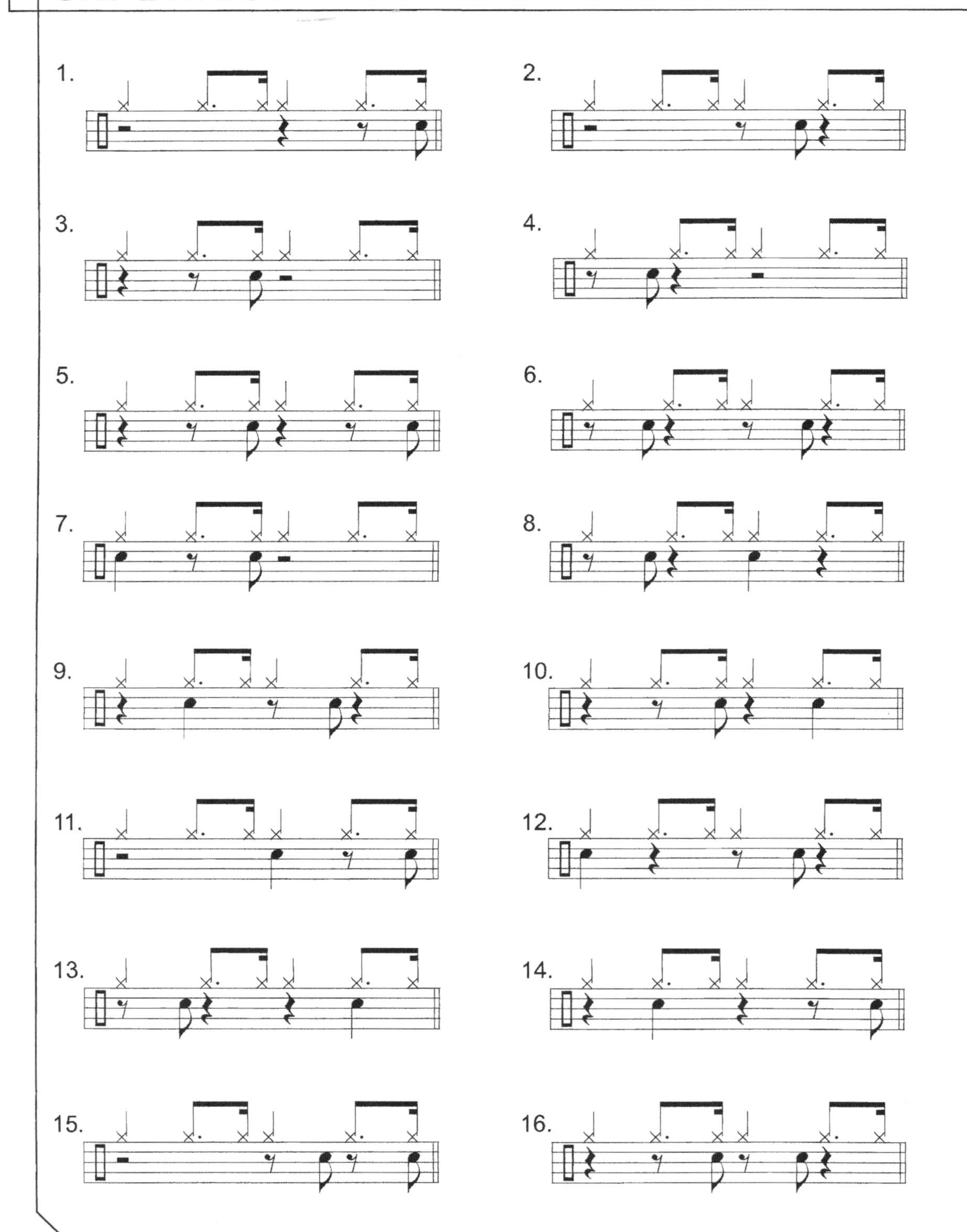

	STEP B 13: KEYBOARD PLAYING/PHRASING
	STEP B 14: EIGHTH NOTE INDEPENDENCE: SNARE

17.

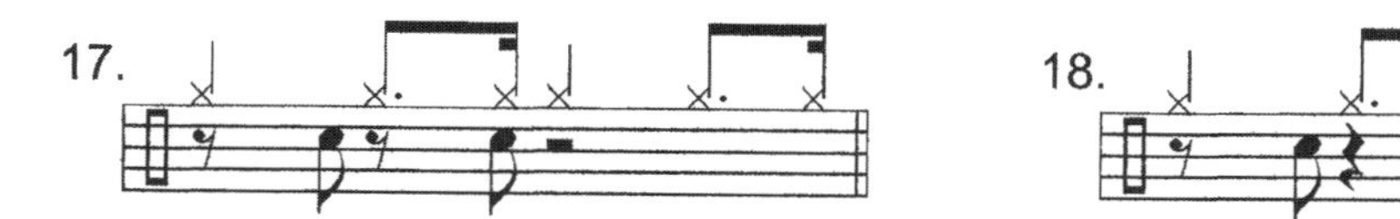

18.

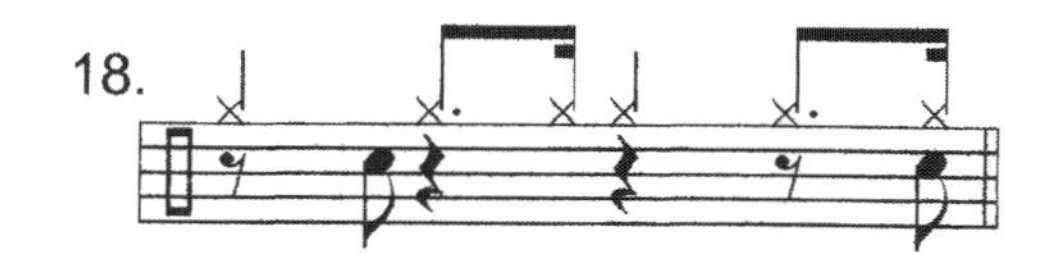

19.

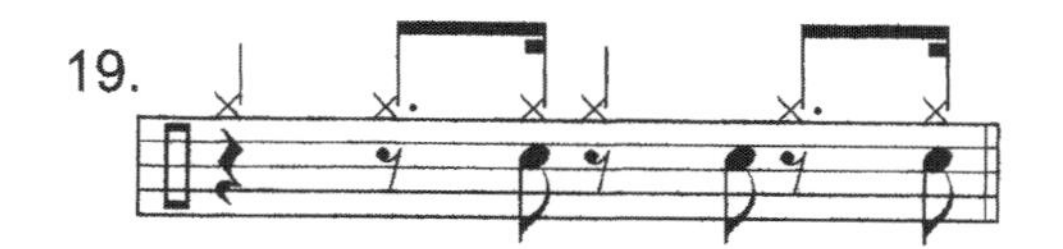

20.

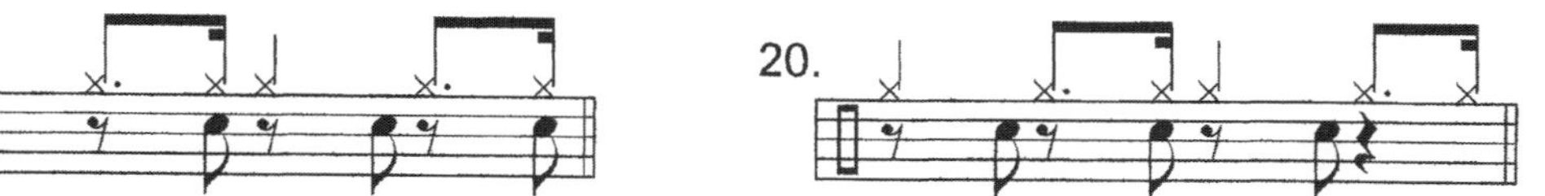

21.

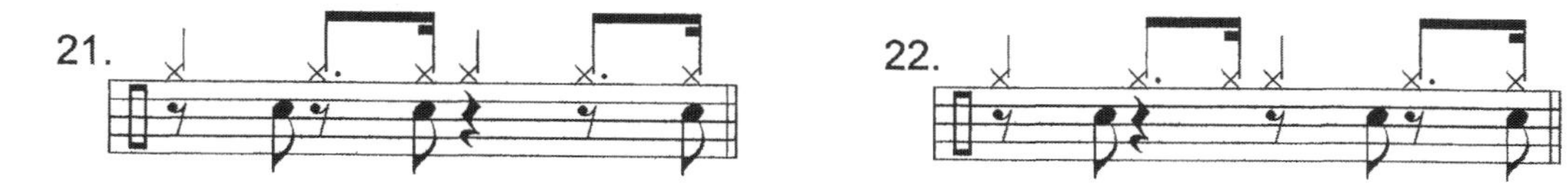

22.

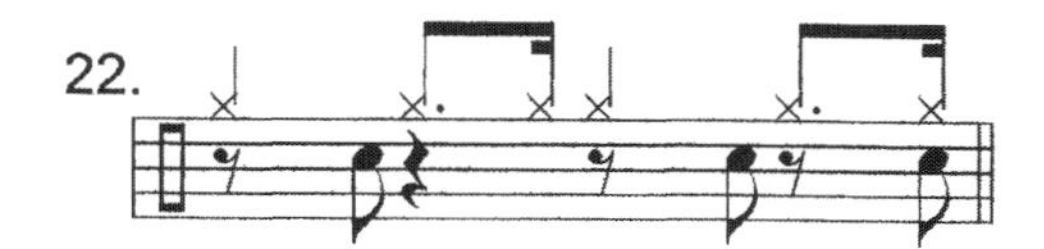

23.

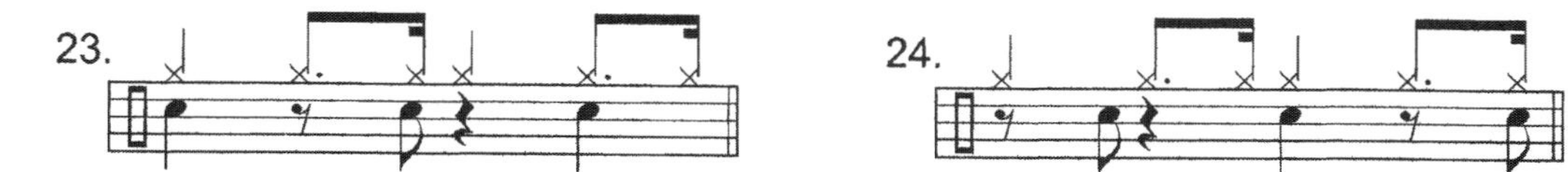

24.

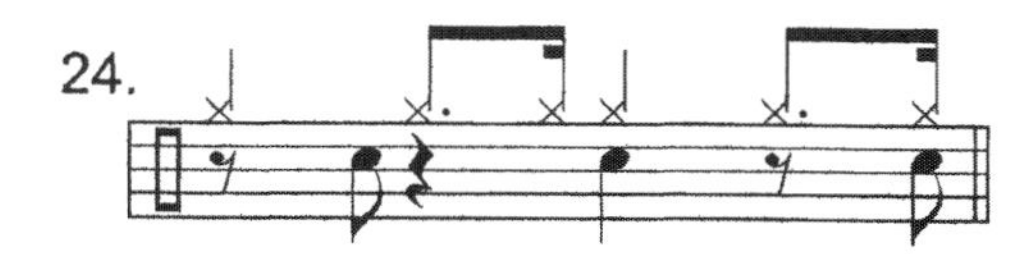

25.

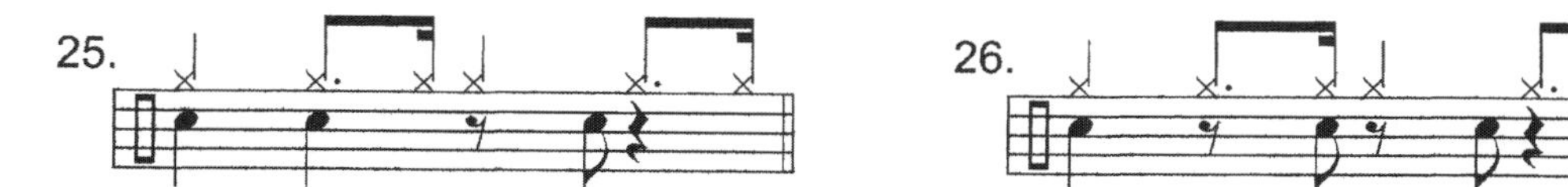

26.

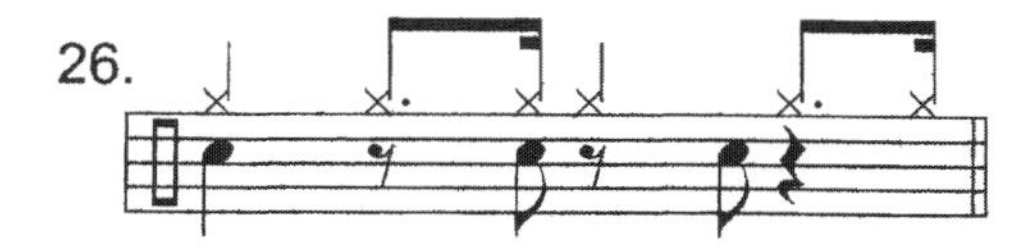

27.

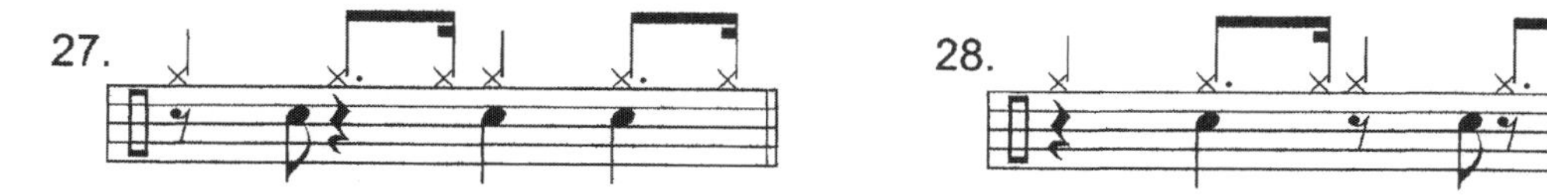

28.

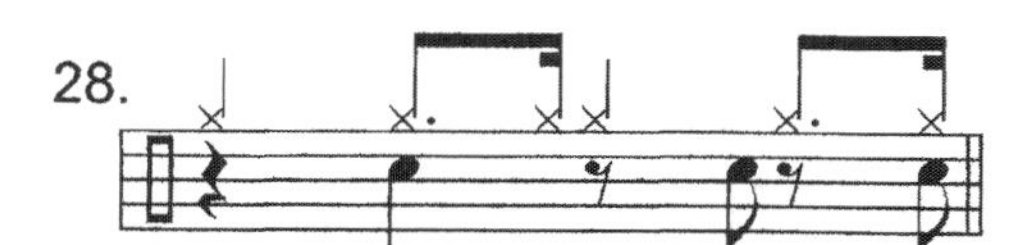

29.

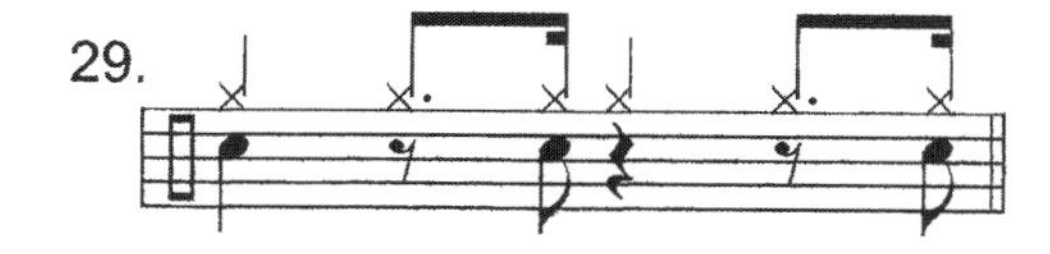

30.

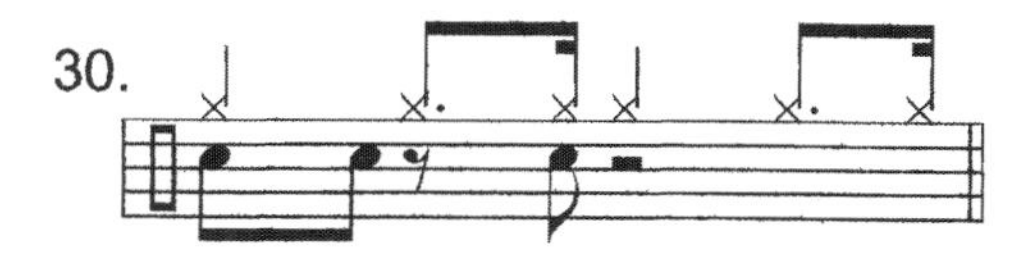

31.

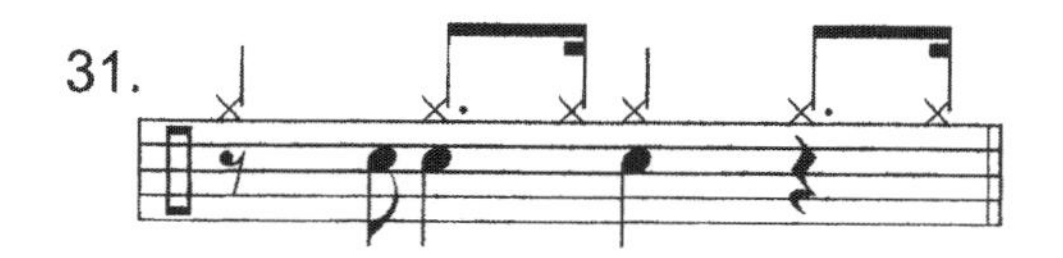

32.

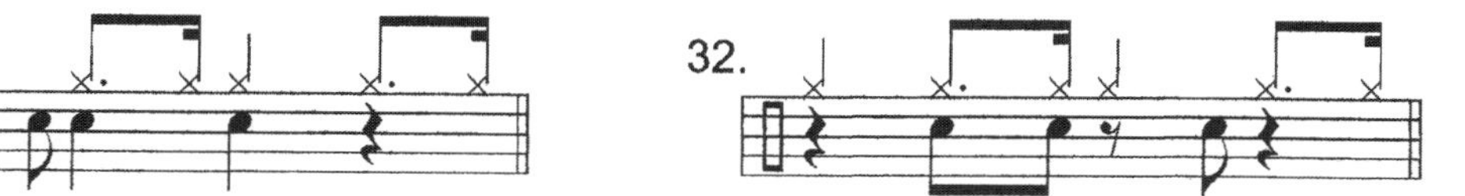

Step B 13: Keyboard Playing/Phrasing

Step B 14: Eighth Note Independence: Snare

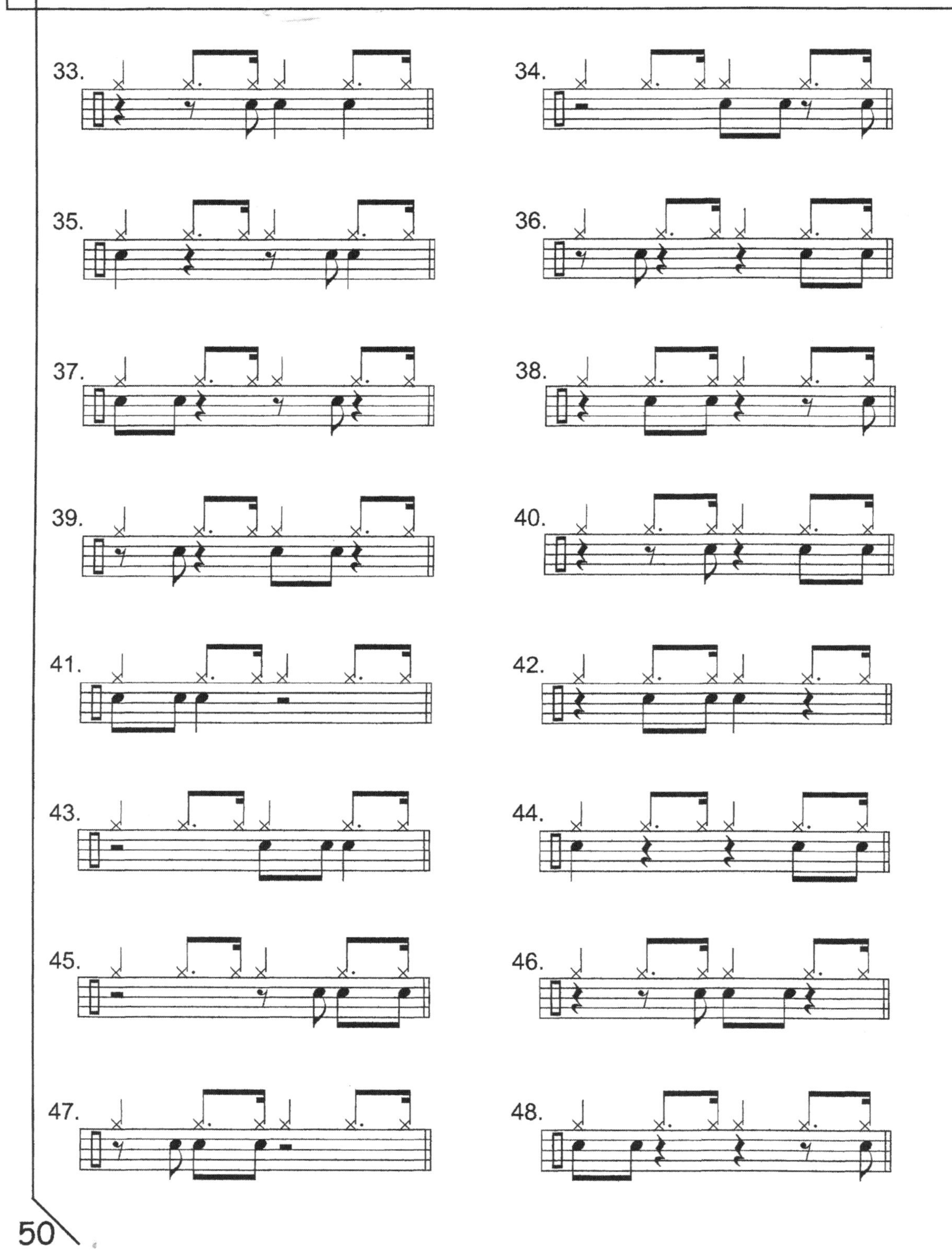

√

	STEP B 13: KEYBOARD PLAYING/PHRASING
	STEP B 14: EIGHTH NOTE INDEPENDENCE: SNARE

49. 

50. 

51. 

52. 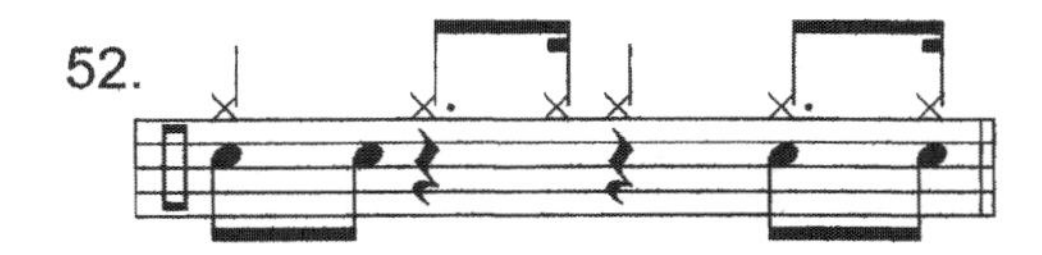

53. 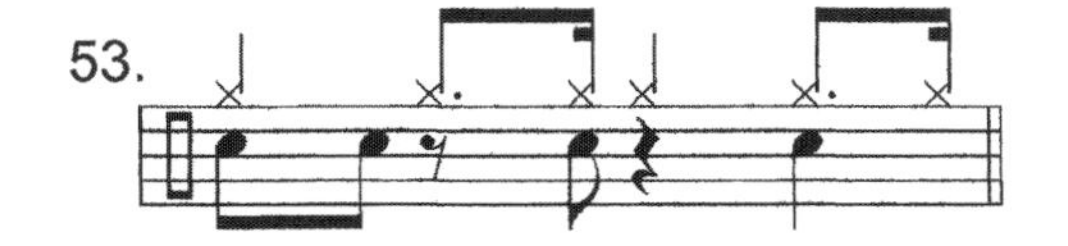

54. 

55. 

56. 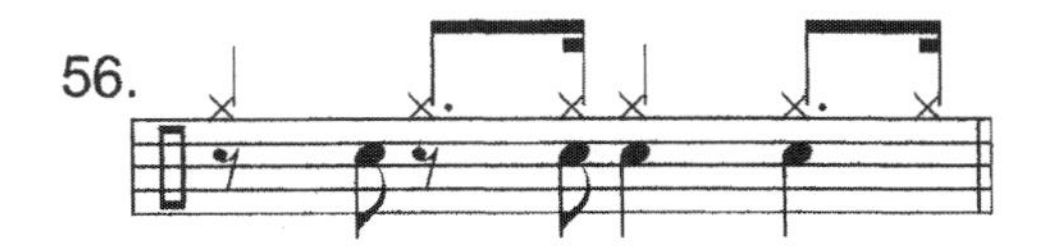

57. 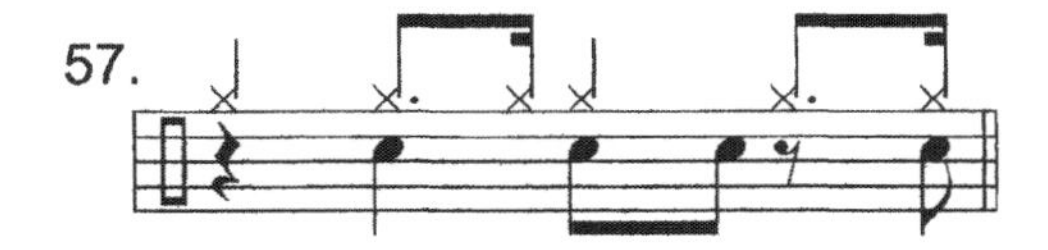

58. 

59. 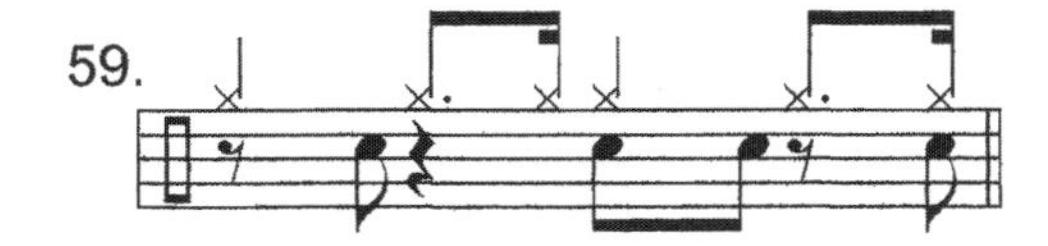

60. 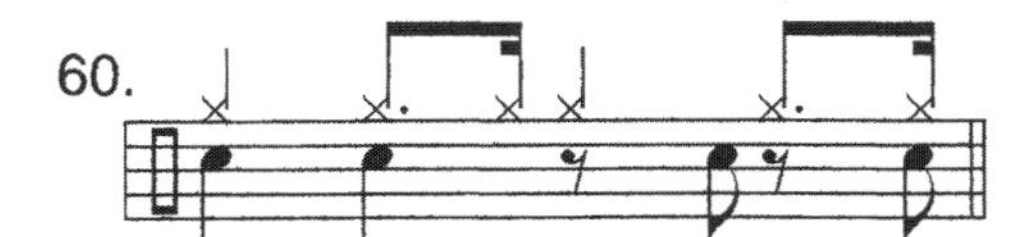

61. 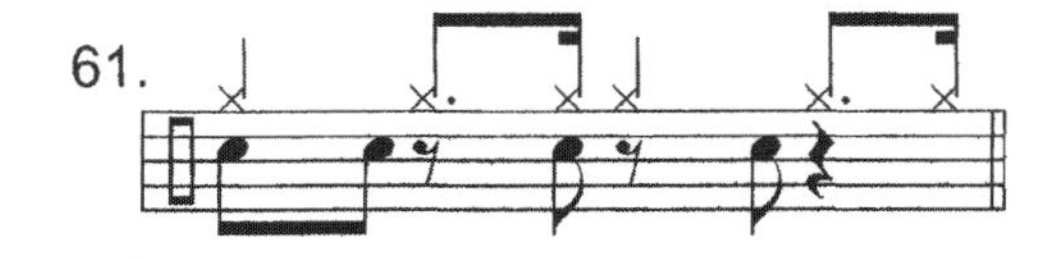

62. 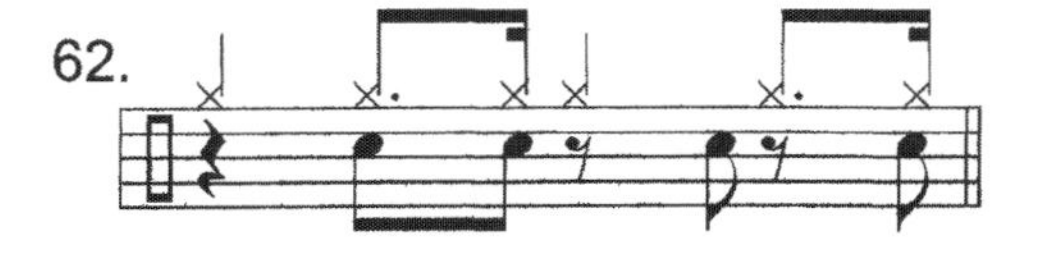

63. 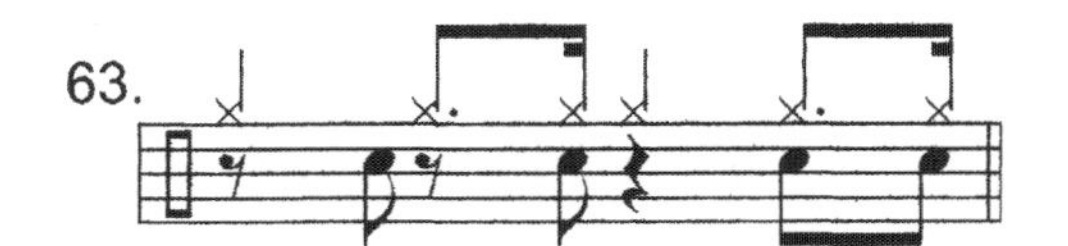

64. 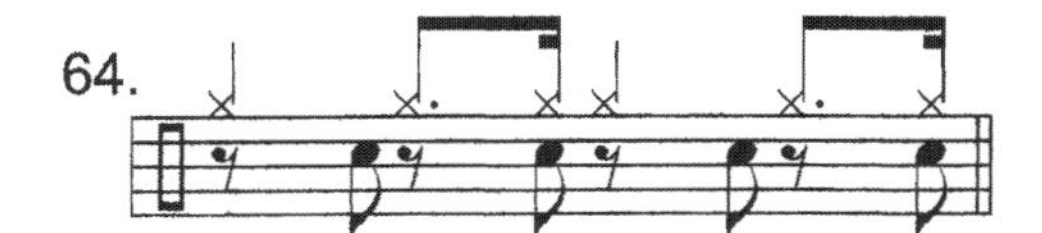

Step B 13: Keyboard Playing/Phrasing

Step B 14: Eighth Note Independence: Snare

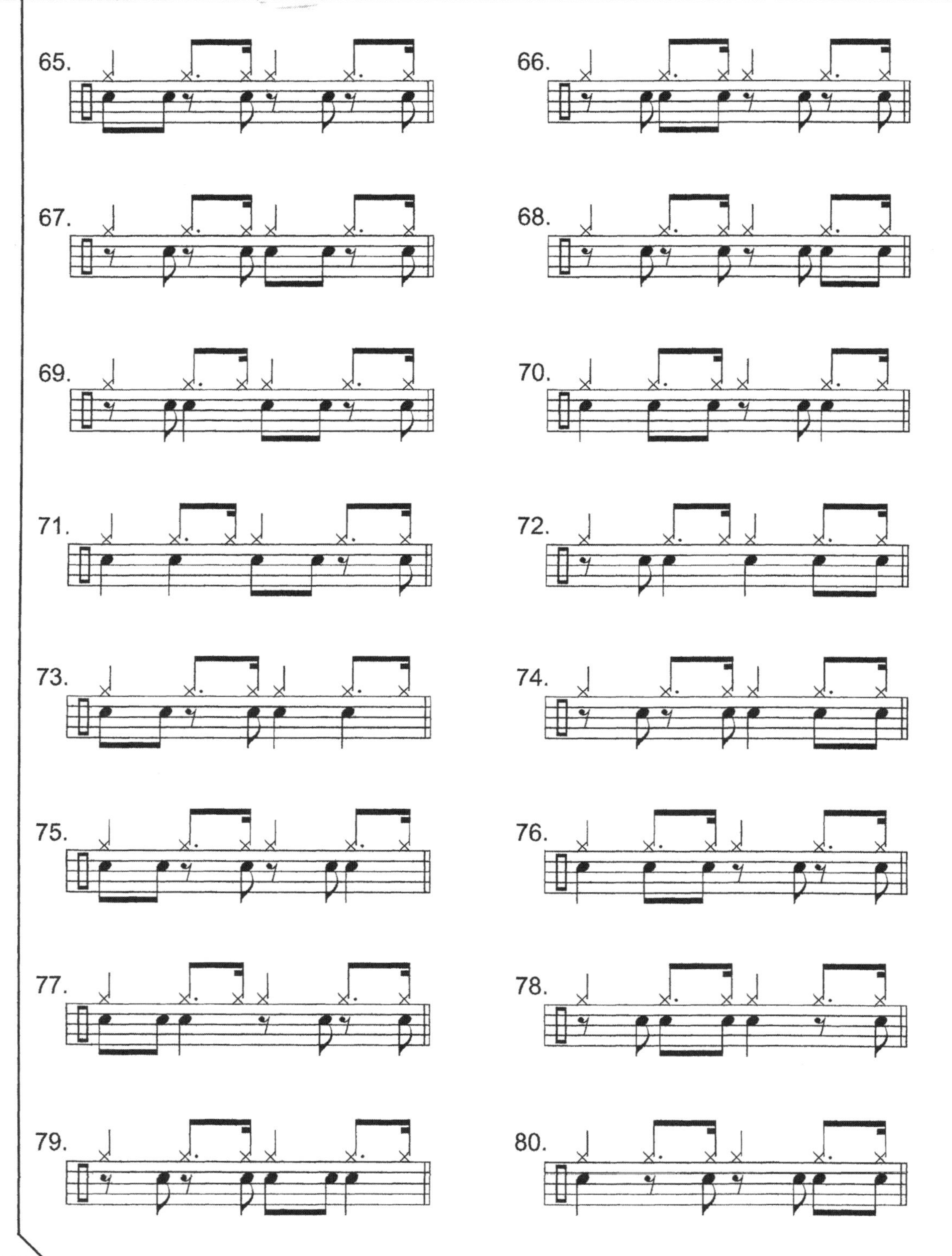

Step B 13: Keyboard Playing/Phrasing

Step B 14: Eighth Note Independence: Snare

81.

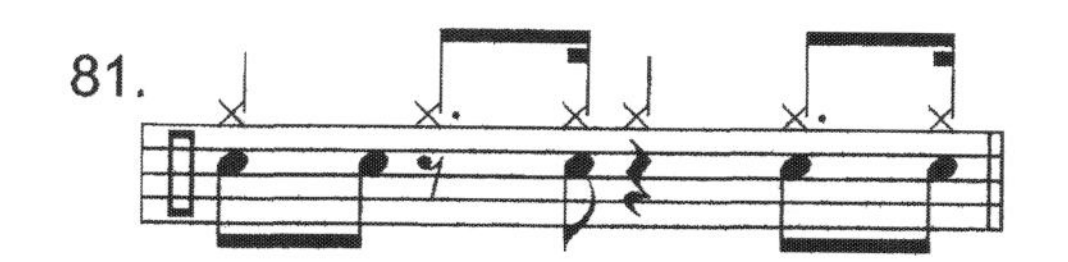

82.

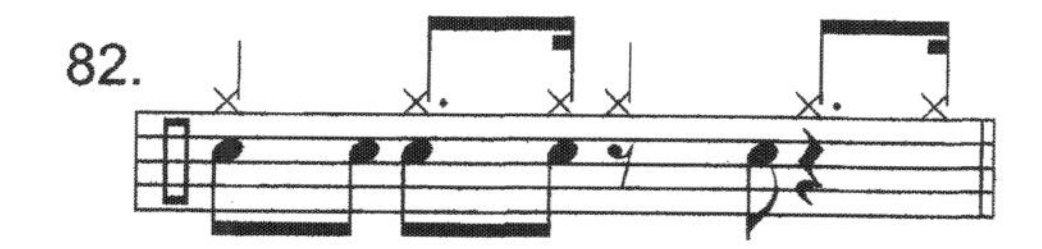

83.

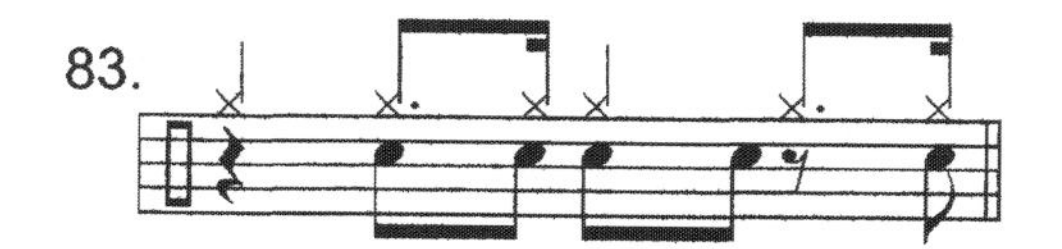

84.

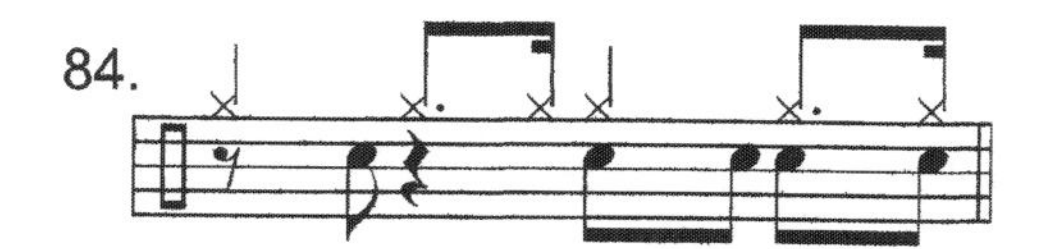

85.

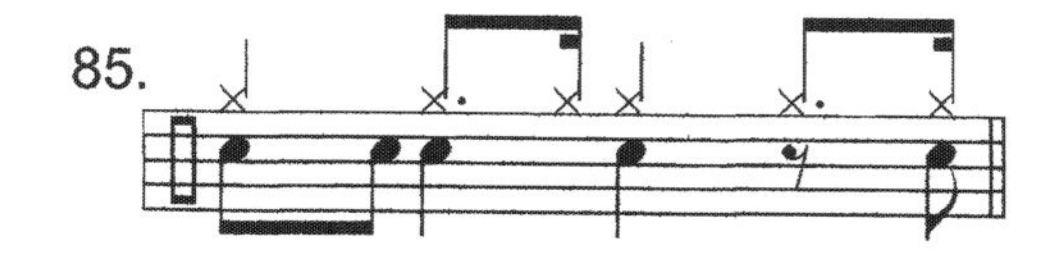

86.

87.

88.

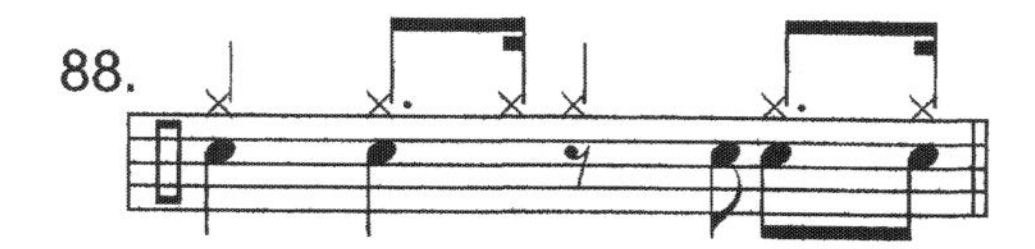

89.

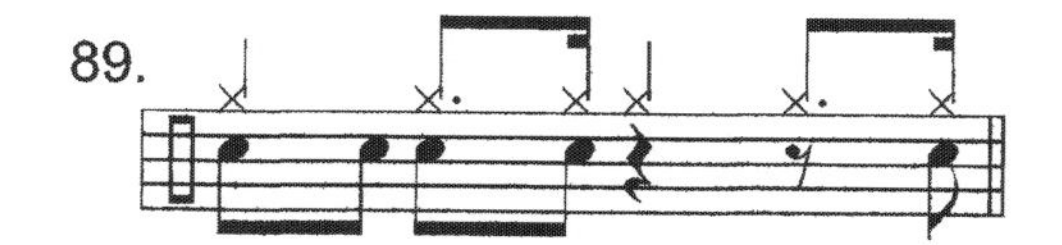

90.

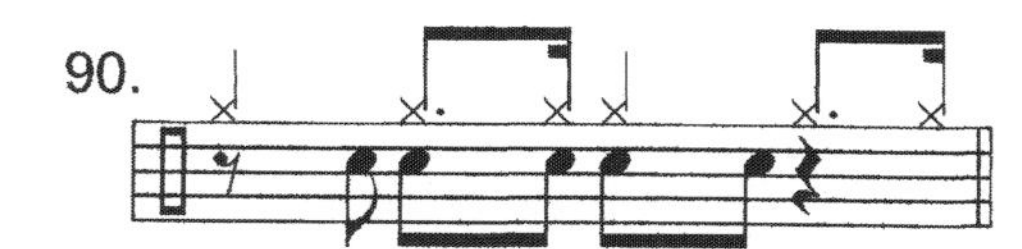

91.

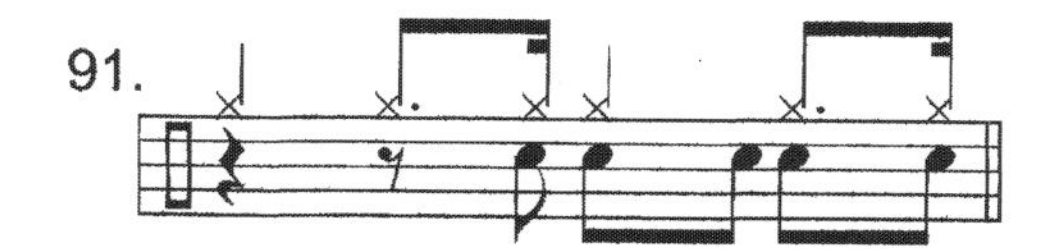

92.

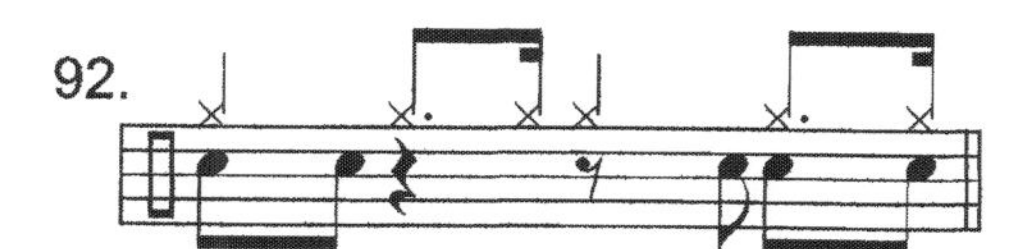

93.

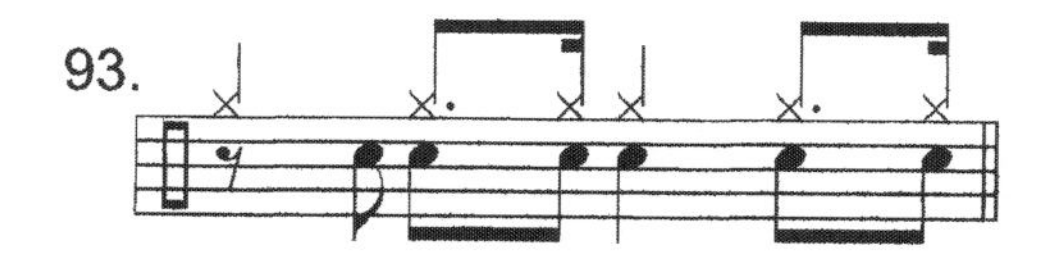

94.

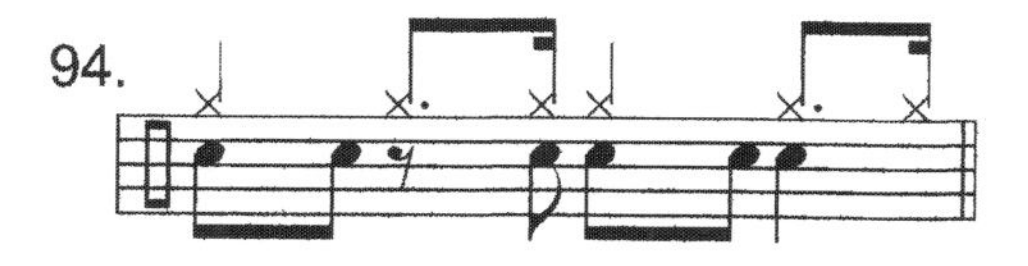

95.

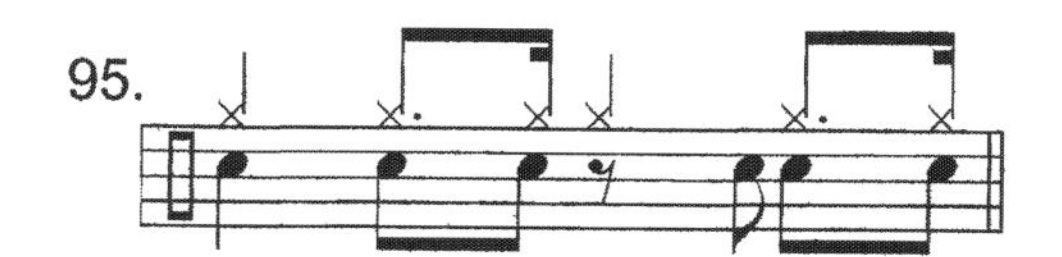

96.

Step B 13: Keyboard Playing/Phrasing

Step B 14: Eighth Note Independence: Snare

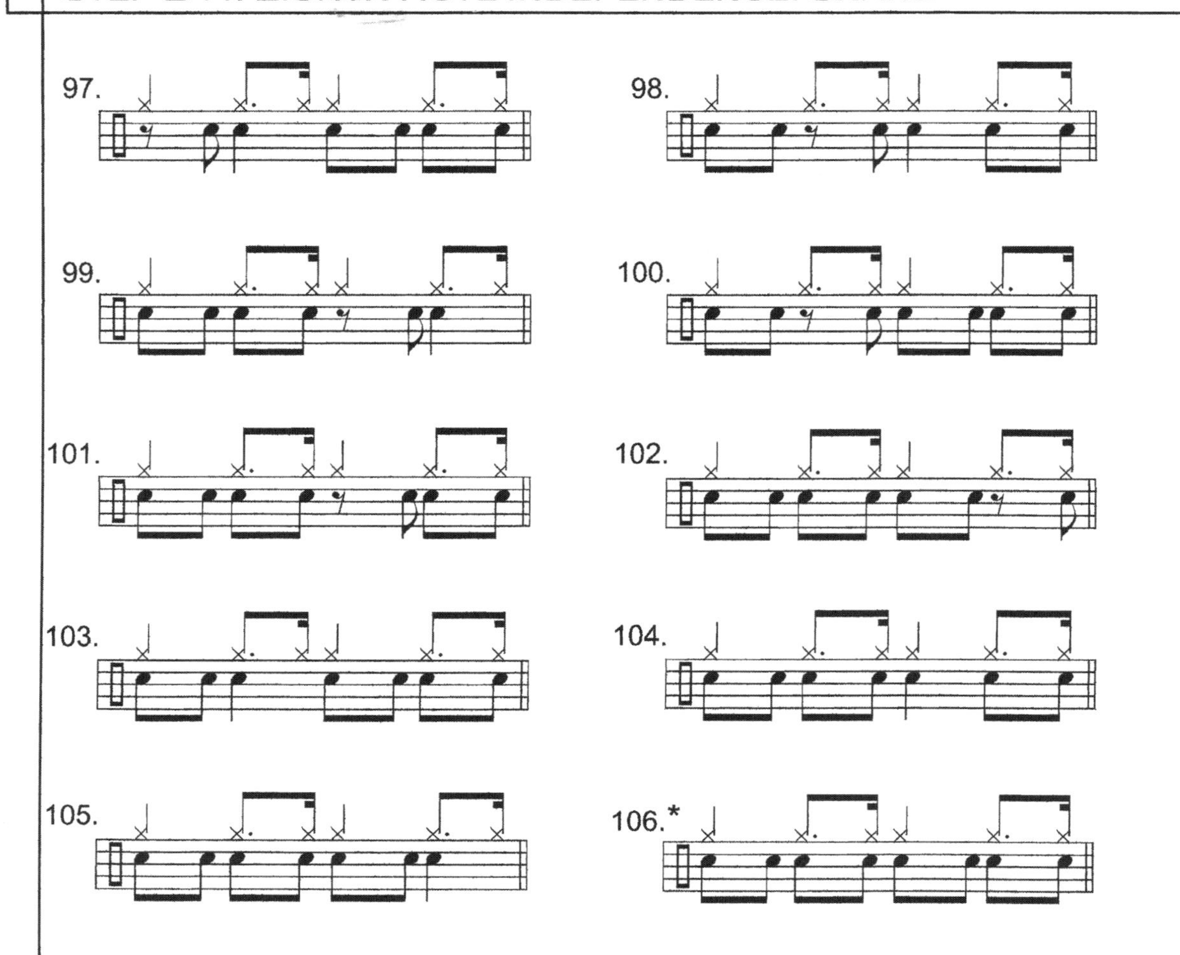

* Exercise 106 (where your left hand is playing all swinging eighth notes), is a very useful pattern, for three reasons:

1. The previous 105 exercises are all derived from this pattern.
2. It is a great exercise for the left hand.
3. It is an effective shuffle that can be used in playing situations.

√

Step B 15: Read: "Feathering, Pepper, & Filling In The Blanks

Pass the pepper, please. Musicians often talk of what a drummer does in descriptive terms. The light playing of quarter notes on the bass drum is often referred to as "feathering." The intermittent notes a drummer plays on the snare while keeping time, or comping, is sometimes called "pepper," actually an apt term, in that they (the notes) seem to add spice to timekeeping. Just as spice makes food more palatable, the "pepper" a drummer adds to timekeeping makes music more interesting. And just as an experienced chef knows just how much spice to add to his culinary creation, an intuitive drummer knows just how much "pepper" to add to the musical mix.

Filling in the blanks, continued. As discussed on page 43, all competent jazz musicians have a particular perceptual skill of "filling in the blanks" - sensing a note, phrase, chord, or rhythm that would fit in an appropriate spot in the performance. To know what is "appropriate" of course is the heart of the matter, and usually is learned through the school of experience. It is in the interaction among musicians that one learns what fits and what doesn't.

"Filling in the blanks" applies in the area of reading as well. A pianist reading a lead sheet chart must fashion an appropriate accompaniment to the written melody, think about how the chords are voiced (sometimes in response to the choices other players have made), and play in the desired style.

Here is your chance to practice filling in the blanks. On the pages to follow are 48 two measure comping patterns, with just the snare figure only. With the training you have gone through up to this point, you will now have to fashion the ride cymbal pattern and the BD and HH around the snare figure. You will also read these two measure patterns on your keyboard.

Feathering

The light playing of the BD, usually to give low end rhythmical support to a band.

Pepper

The light touches a jazz drummer plays on the snare while timekeeping.

Lead sheet

A chart with only the melody notated and chords indicated.

Thoughts On Swinging

"Swing is a slippery concept to define. Think of it as the tension created between the basic beat of the music and the actual notes and emphases played by the musicians. That tension creates the forward propulsion known as swing. Call it a natural jazz rhythm, or a relaxed state of mind, swing just grabs you when you hear it. Trust Me."

Simon Adams

"The main thing a drummer still needs to do is play time that *swings*. Spang-spang-a-lang is the hardest thing in the world to do. The time has to be alive, not just be good time. A metronome has good time."

Shelly Manne
Modern Drummer, October, 1981.

STEP B 16: TWO MEASURE PATTERNS/ KEYBOARD PLAYING

Follow these directions for pages 57 - 61.

- Find the E♭ above middle c.
- Play the **two measure snare rhythms** with your RH, using the E♭. Use any finger of your RH. Follow each exercise with a two measure rest. For example, exercise 1 looks like this:

Here's how you will play it on the keyboard:

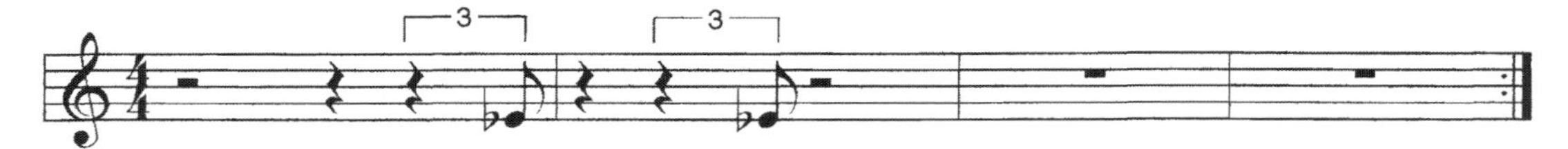

- Sing along as you play the E♭, using "tah." Match the pitch the best you can.
- **Play each exercise twice**, before moving to the next one. Thus, the playing of each exercise will be in sync with the 8 bar phrases of the CD tracks.
- Play these exercises against tracks 1 through 6 of the CD.

STEP B 17: TWO MEASURE COMP PATTERNS: SNARE

- The exercises on the following five pages are to be played on the snare with the LH, against the jazz ride rhythm (RH/CYM) and hi-hat on 2 & 4 (LF).
- Even though it is not notated, keep **very light** quarter notes on the bass drum.
- As you play the exercises, sing the snare part, using "bop," "bah," "tah," or "dah." Follow each two measure exercise with two measures of "time" (ride cymbal and hi-hat). For example, exercise 1 looks like this:

Here's how you will play it on the drumset:

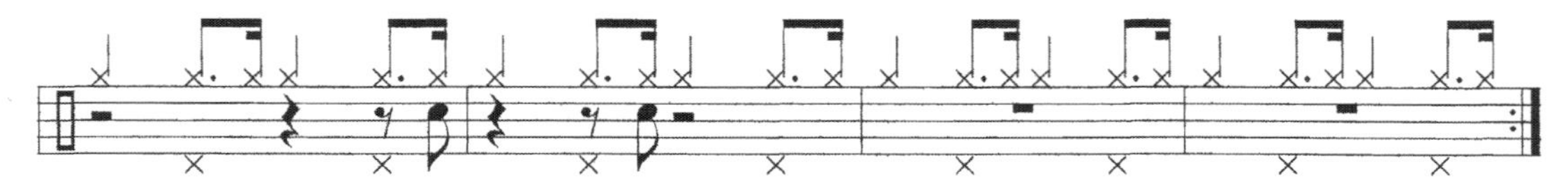

- **Play each exercise twice**, before moving to the next one. Thus, the playing of each exercise will be in sync with the 8 bar phrases of the CD tracks.
- Play these exercises against tracks 1 through 6 of the CD.

√

	STEP B 16: TWO MEASURE PATTERNS/ KEYBOARD PLAYING
	STEP B 17: TWO MEASURE COMP PATTERNS: SNARE

√

Step B 16: Two Measure Patterns/ Keyboard Playing

Step B 17: Two Measure Comp Patterns: Snare

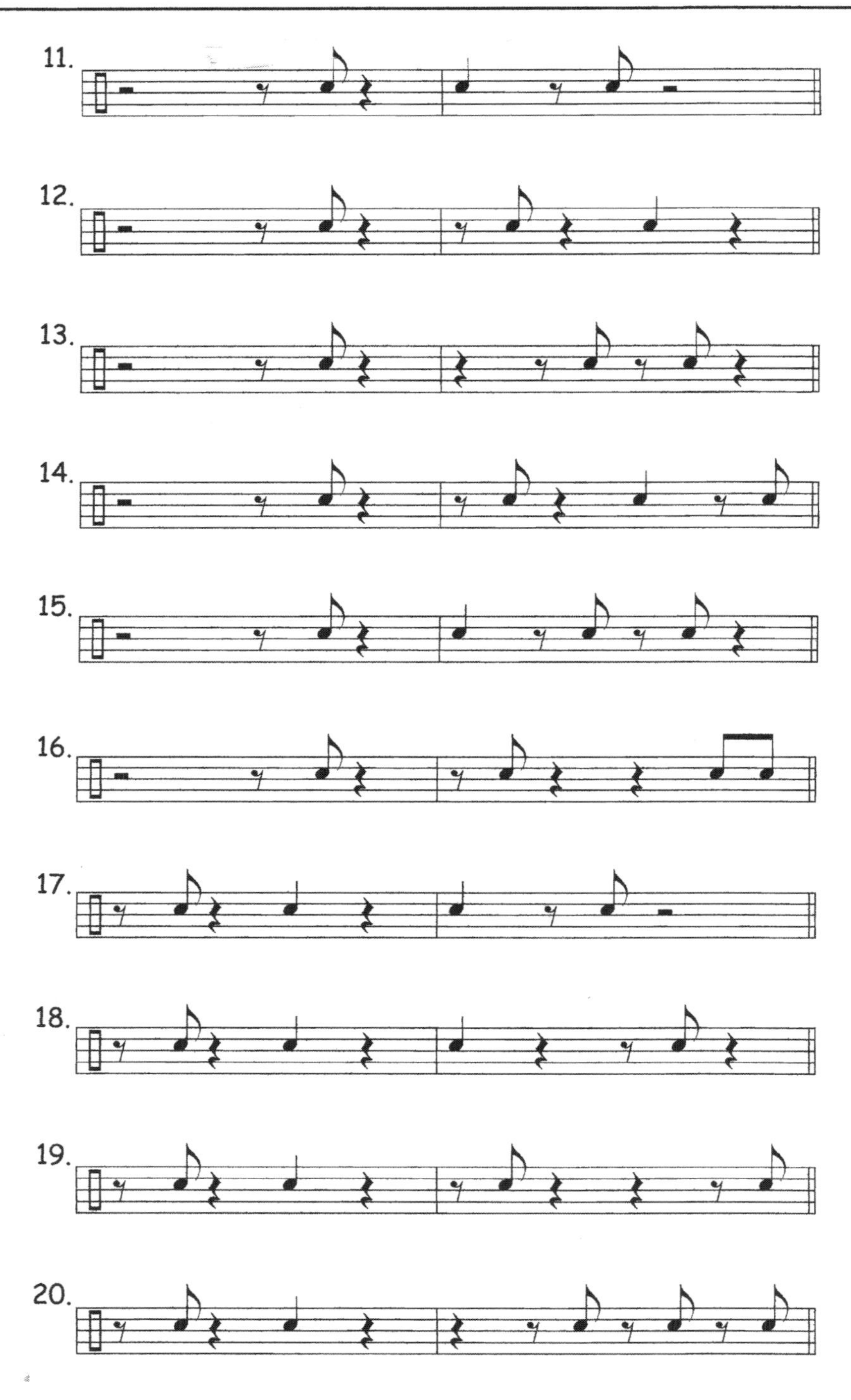

	STEP B 16: TWO MEASURE PATTERNS/ KEYBOARD PLAYING
	STEP B 17: TWO MEASURE COMP PATTERNS: SNARE

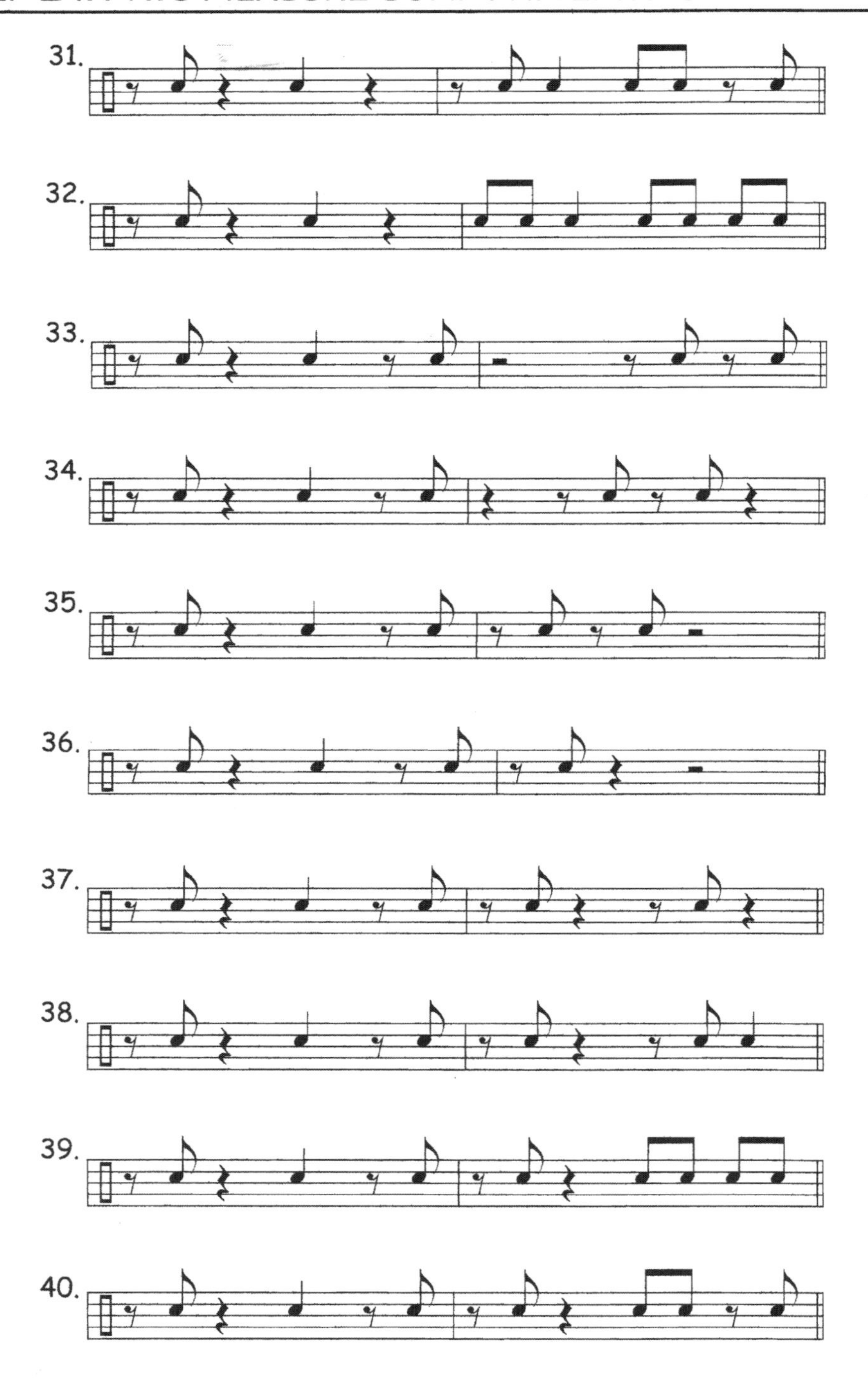
31.
32.
33.
34.
35.
36.
37.
38.
39.
40.

	Step B 16: Two Measure Patterns/ Keyboard Playing
	Step B 17: Two Measure Comp Patterns: Snare

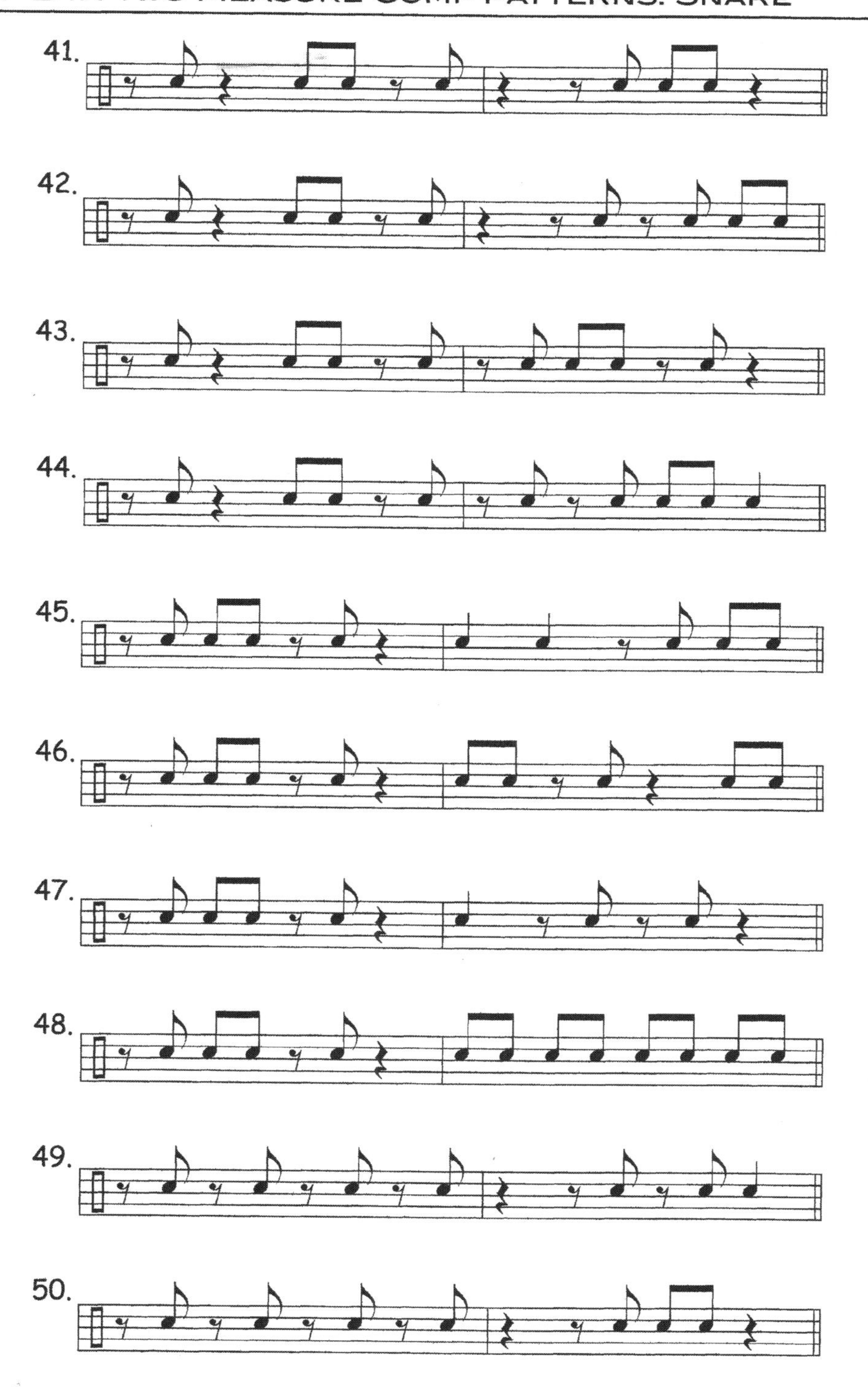

STEP B 18: READ "TAMBOU KA DANSÉ (DRUMMING IS DANCING)"

TAMBOU KA DANSÉ (DRUMMING IS DANCING)

A while back I was going through a box of rags to do some chores when I came across an old tee shirt I had bought on my honeymoon. My wife and I were on the island of Martinique (where the merengue dance originated) more than 25 years ago, when we came upon this shirt. The picture on the front featured a drummer and dancer interacting. I asked the shopowner what the inscription (tambou ka dansé) meant. He answered that it roughly meant "to drum is to dance" or "drumming is dancing." The idea of equating drumming and dancing is intriguing, and upon reflection, makes sense. Dancing is moving in time, and so is drumming. In fact, every exercise in this book is a little dance of its own. Part of the secret of playing these exercises musically is to learn the "dance" your feet are doing for each pattern. Your playing will sound smoother and more fluid.

STEP B 19: READ "MEET YOUR NEW BEST FRIEND"

MEET YOUR NEW BEST FRIEND

Perhaps no other musician in a jazz band is more in tune with the pulse of the music than the bass player. The traditional acoustic instrument is known by various names: **string bass**, **upright bass**, or **double bass**. In most situations the bassist plays quarter notes, outlining the chord progression with his choice of notes, thereby "walking" band, both rhythmically and harmonically. Therefore, a good bassist has a strong sense of time as well as an awareness of the chord progressions and form.

Because of the bassist's dual role includes timekeeping, it is vital that you two "lock in" with each other. Listen with rabbit ears. Listen, listen, listen. A good bass player can make a gig a lot of fun, and not feel like work at all.

Some well known bass players: Jimmy Blanton (Duke Ellington), Walter Page (Count Basie), Oscar Pettiford, Ray Brown (pictured), Charles Mingus, Gene Wright (Dave Brubeck Quartet), Paul Chambers (Miles Davis), Percy Heath, Charlie Haden, Dave Holland, Scott LaFaro, and Ron Carter.

Walking Bass: A style of bass playing where the bassist plays quarter notes (marking the pulse), using notes that clearly outline the chord progression.

STEP B 20: EIGHTH NOTE INDEPENDENCE: BASS DRUM

Follow these directions for pages 64 - 68.

- The exercises on the following five pages are to be played on the BD with the RF, against the jazz ride rhythm (RH/CYM) and hi-hat on 2 & 4 (LF).*

- As you play the exercises, sing the BD part, using "boom" or "bom."
  Play each exercise with a **measure of "time"** in between. Repeat this sequence for each exercise. For example, exercise 1 looks like this:

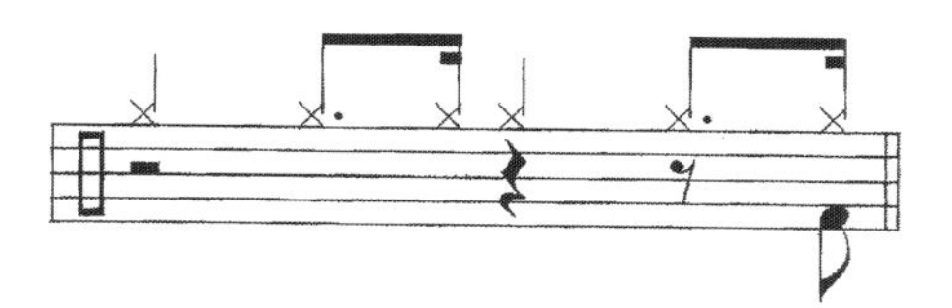

Here's how you will play it on the drumset:

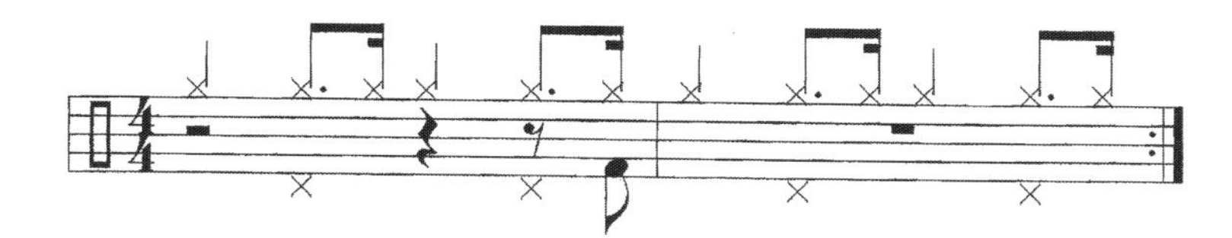

- Play these exercises against tracks 1 through 6 of the CD.

Step B 20: Eighth Note Independence: Bass Drum

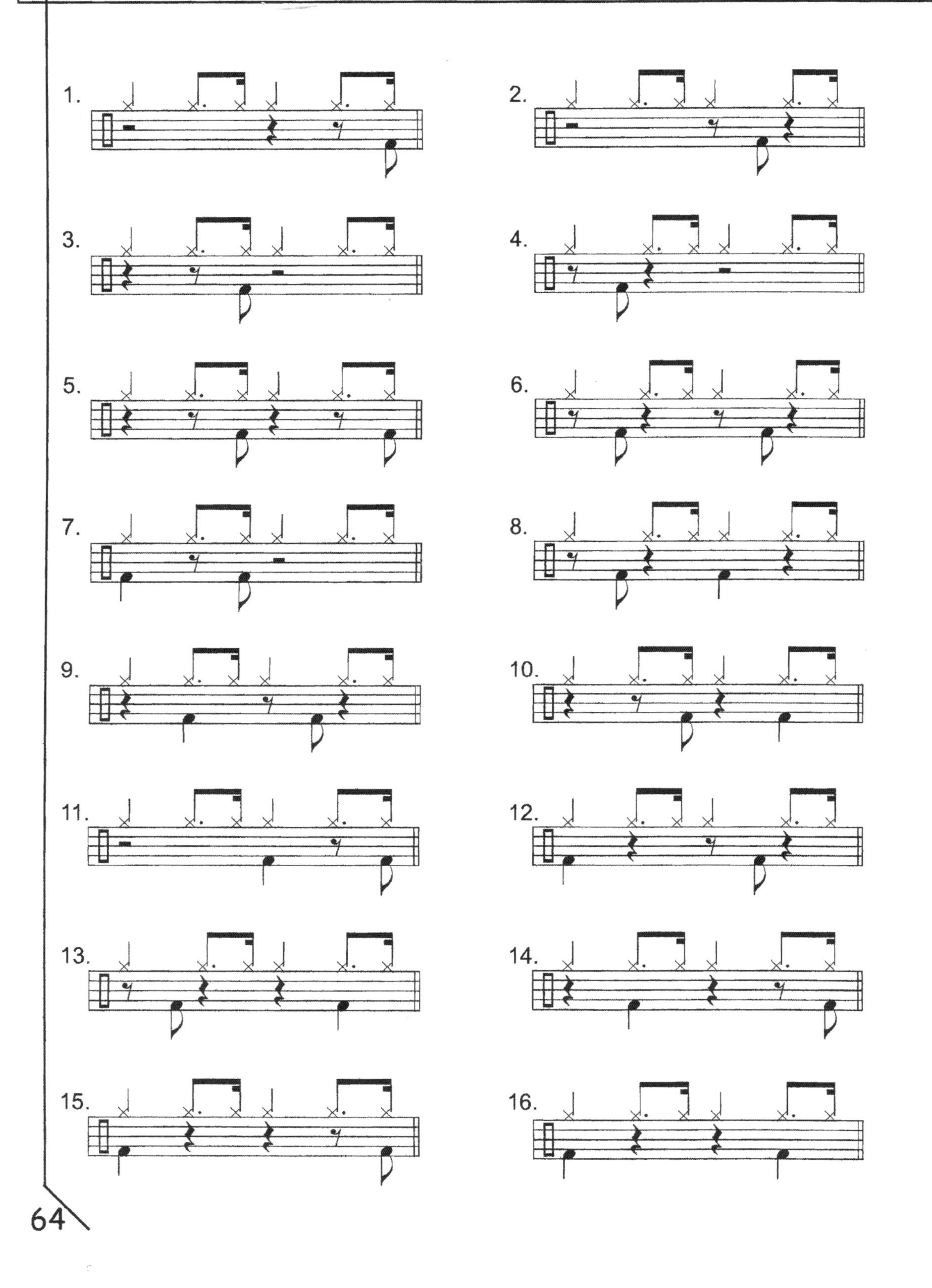

Step B 20: Eighth Note Independence: Bass Drum

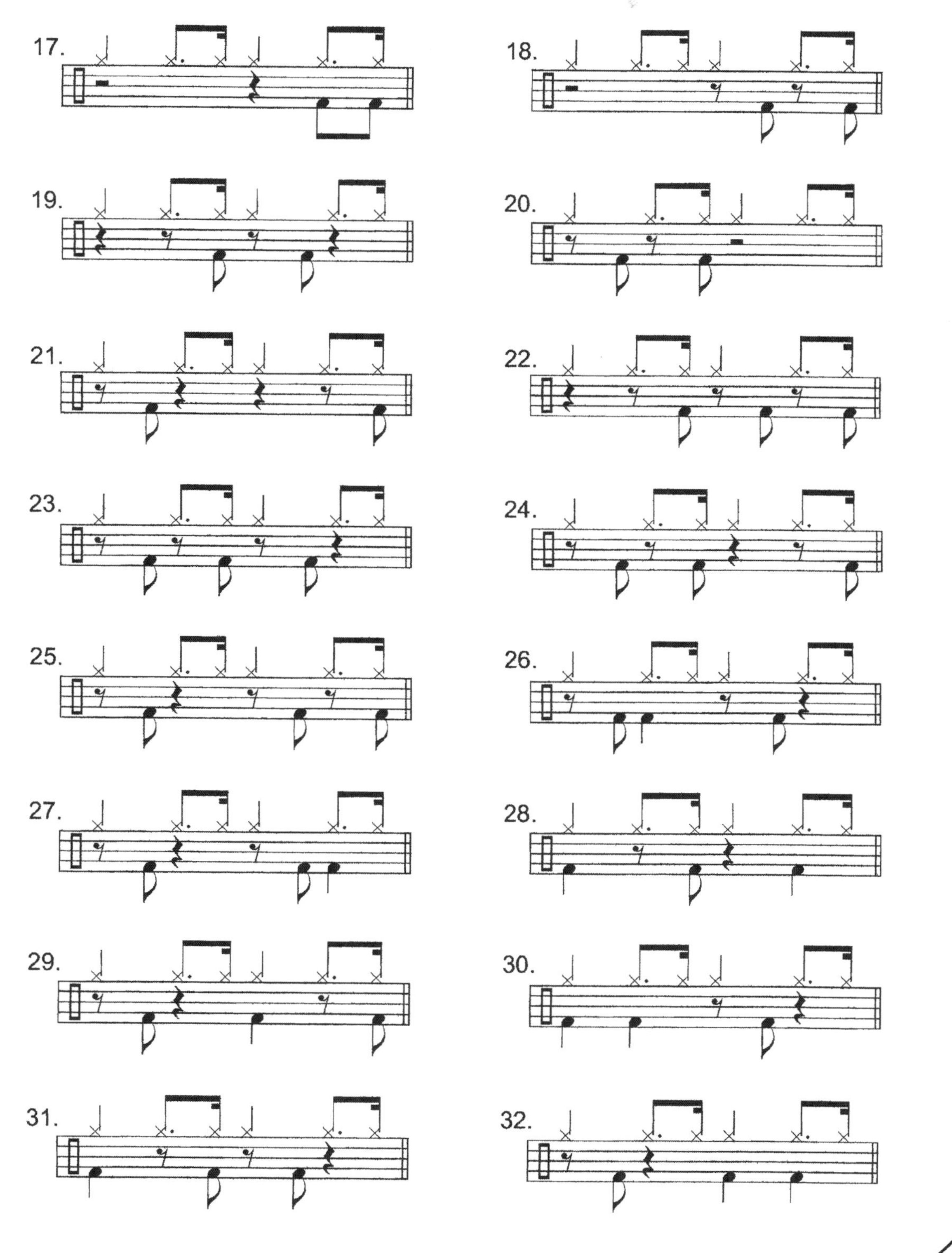

Step B 20: Eighth Note Independence: Bass Drum

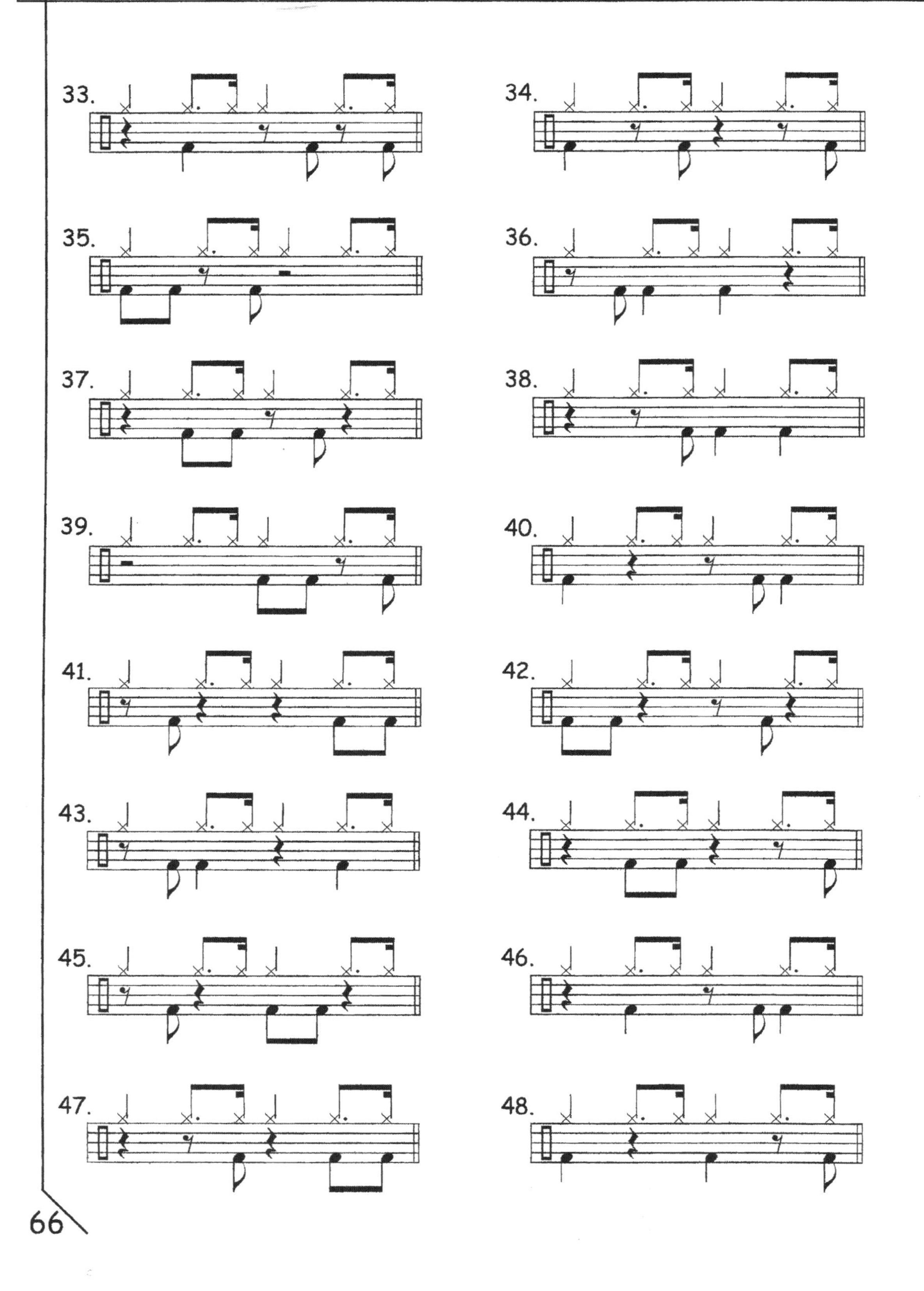

Step B 20: Eighth Note Independence: Bass Drum

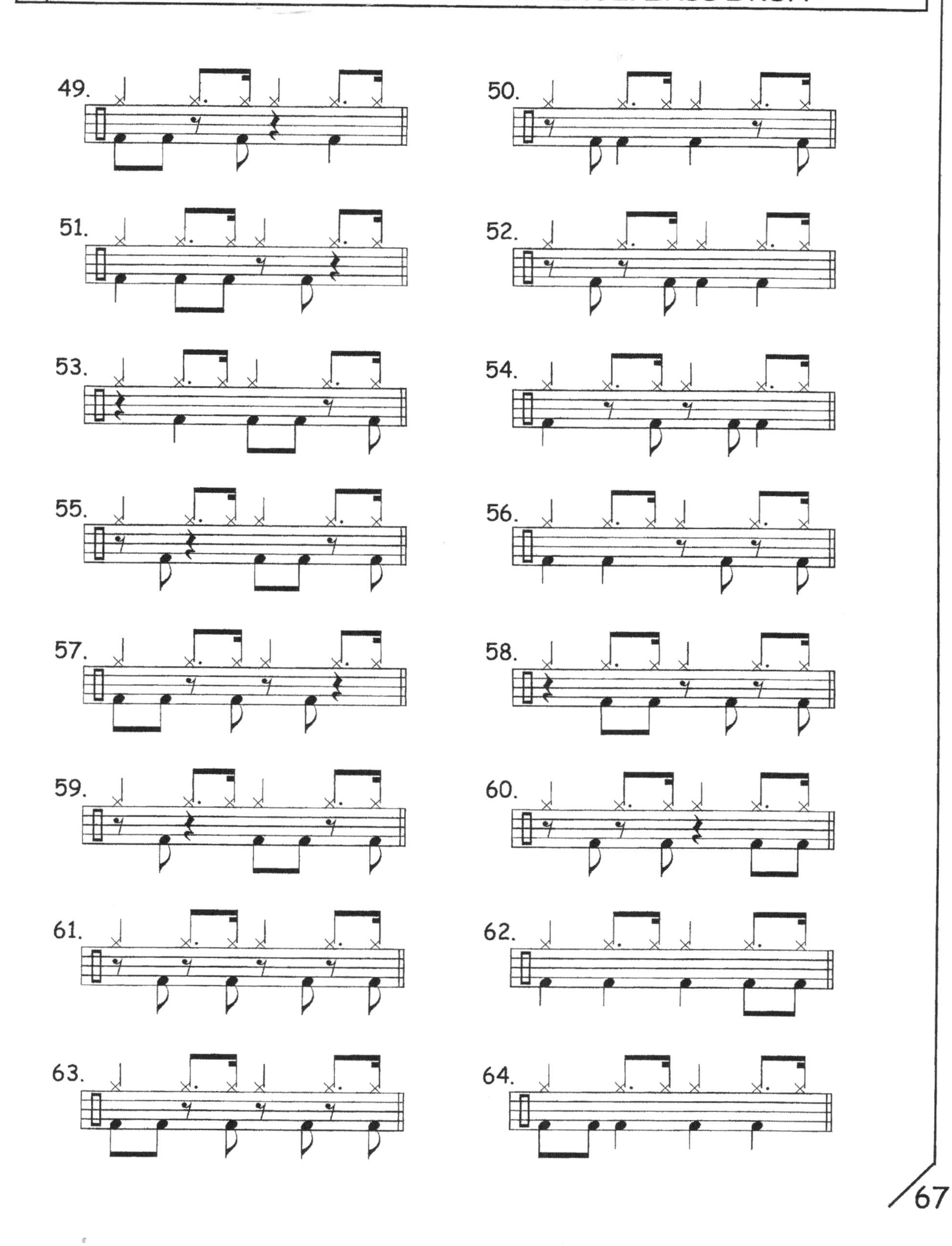

Step B 20: Eighth Note Independence: Bass Drum

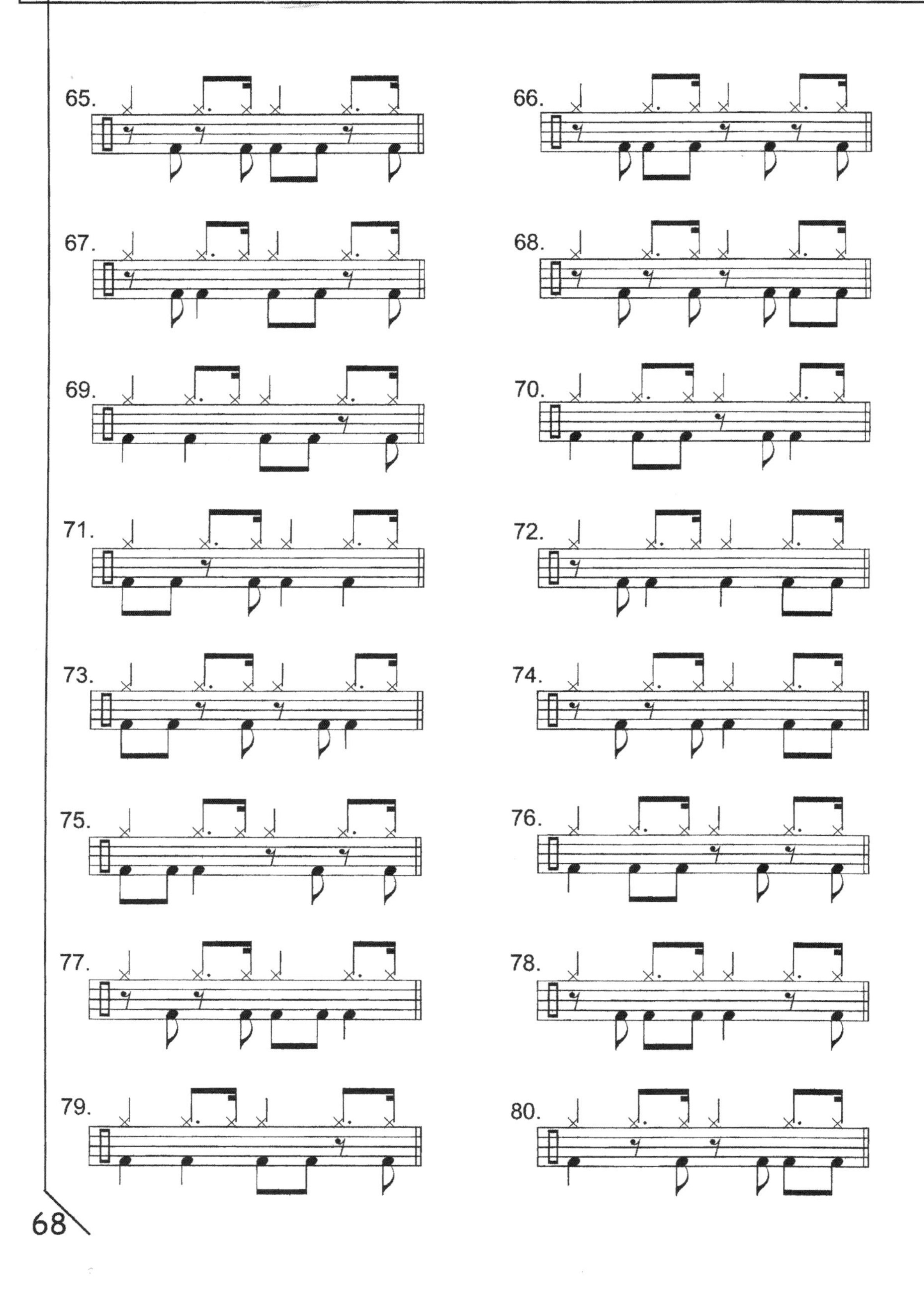

√

Step B 20: Keyboard Playing/Phrasing/Melody Awareness

- Follow these directions for pages 70 - 85.

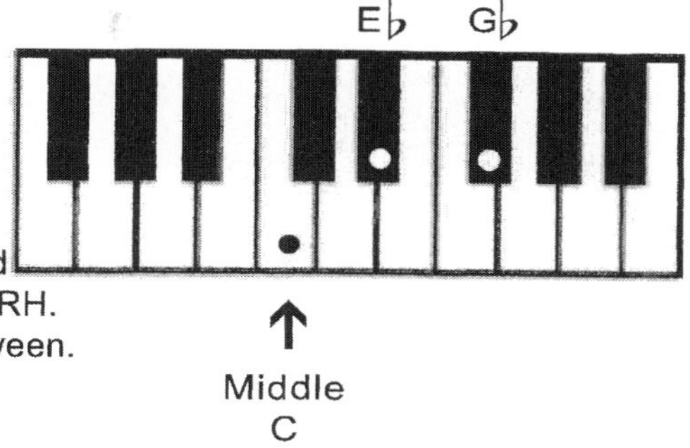

- Find the E♭ and G♭ above middle c.

- Play the **snare and bass drum rhythms** with your RH, using the G♭ for the SN part, and the E♭ for the BD. Use any two fingers of your RH. Play each exercise with a **measure rest** in between. Repeat this sequence for each exercise. For example, exercise 1 looks like this:

Here's how you will play it on the keyboard:

- Sing along as you play the G♭ and E♭, using "dah." Match the pitch the best you can.

- Play these exercises against tracks 1 through 6 of the CD.

√

Step B 21: Eighth Note Independence: Snare & Bass Drum

- Follow these directions for pages 70 - 85.

- The exercises on the following pages are to be played on the SN/LH and BD/RF, against the jazz ride rhythm (RH/CYM) and HH on 2 & 4 (LF).

- As you play each exercise, sing the SN and BD part, using "tah" or "dah" for the SN, 'boom" or "bom" for the BD. Play each exercise with a **measure of "time"** in between. Repeat this sequence for each exercise. For example, exercise 1 looks like this:

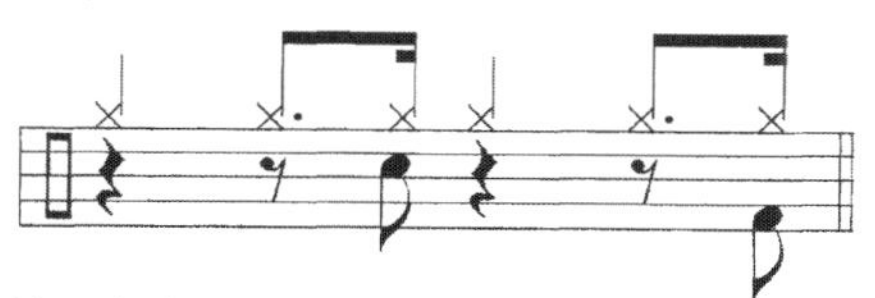

Here's how you will play it on the drumset:

- Play these exercises against tracks 1 through 6 of the CD.

Step B 20: Keyboard Playing/Phrasing/Melody Awareness

Step B 21: Eighth Note Independence: Snare & Bass Drum

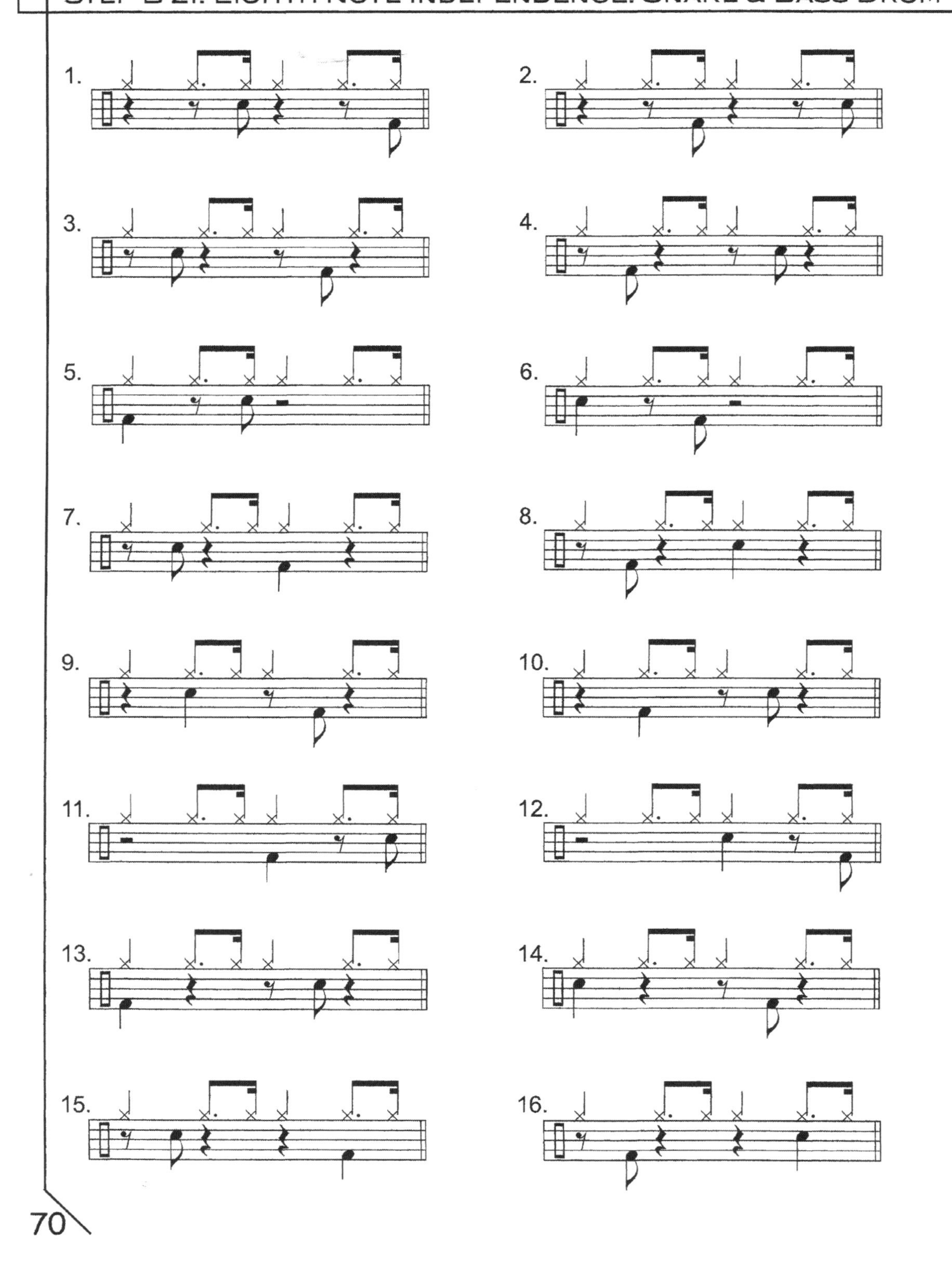

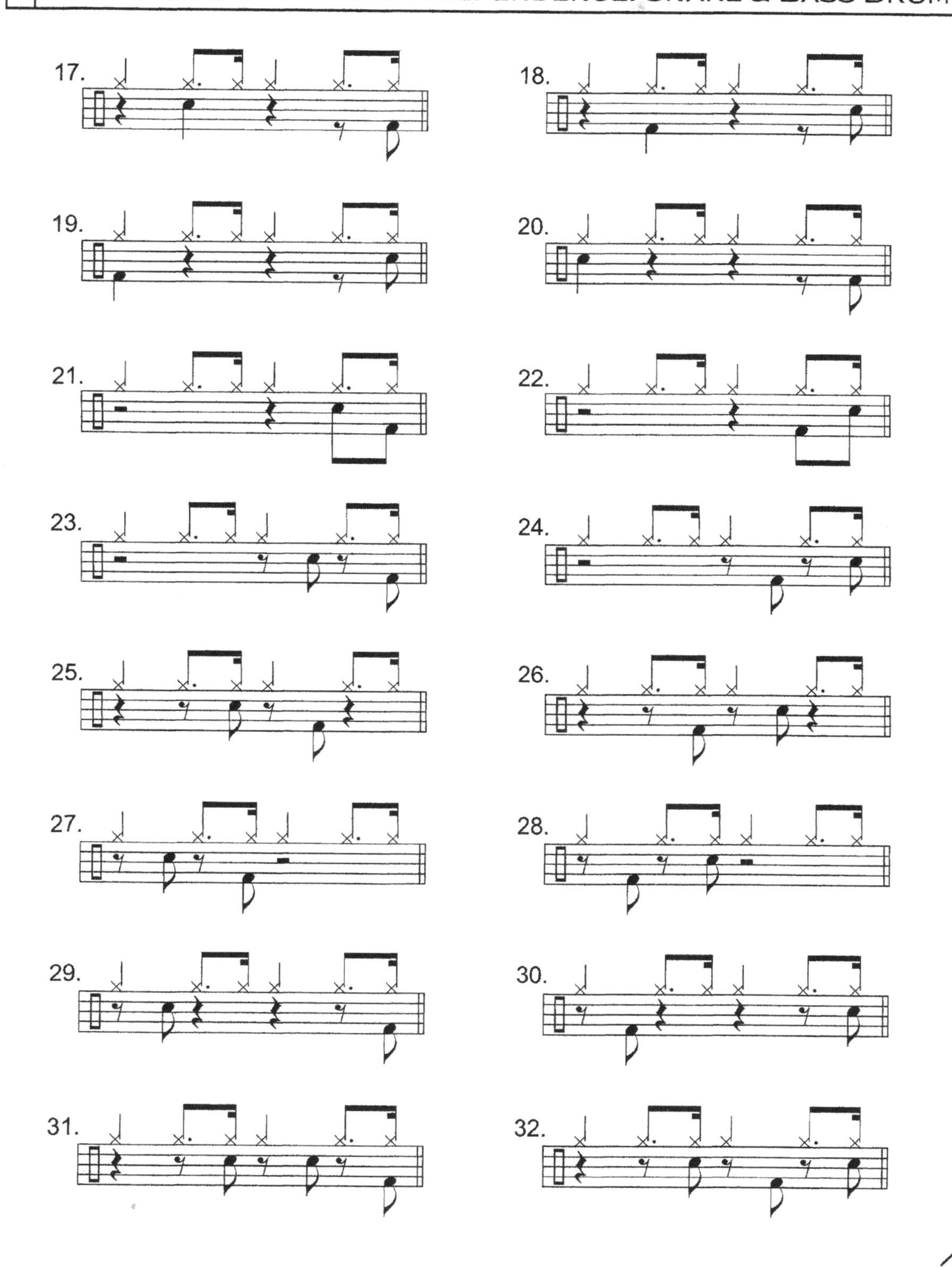
17.
18.
19.
20.
21.
22.
23.
24.
25.
26.
27.
28.
29.
30.
31.
32.

Step B 20: Keyboard Playing/Phrasing/Melody Awareness

Step B 21: Eighth Note Independence: Snare & Bass Drum

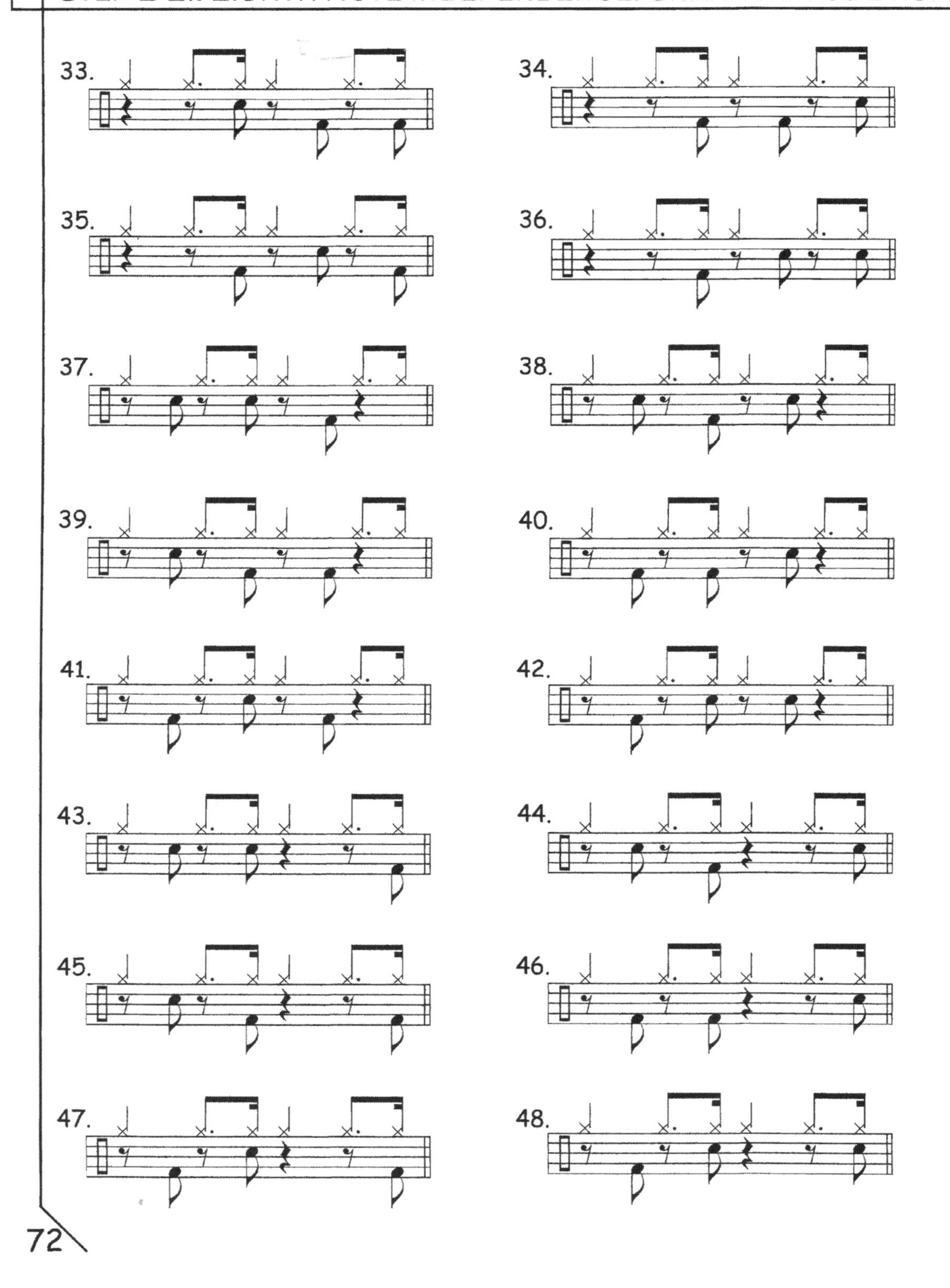

√

	STEP B 20: KEYBOARD PLAYING/PHRASING/MELODY AWARENESS
	STEP B 21: EIGHTH NOTE INDEPENDENCE: SNARE & BASS DRUM

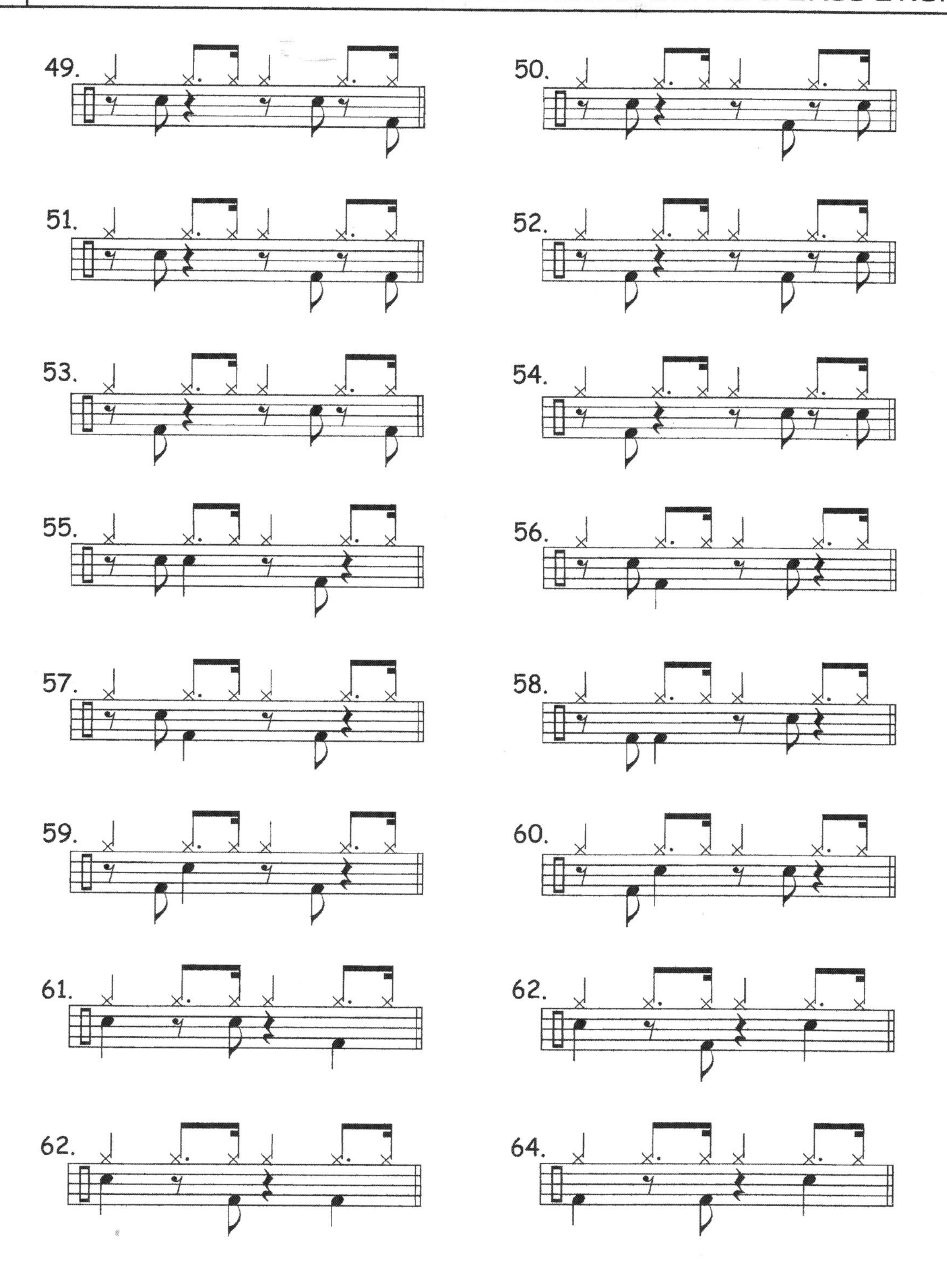

Step B 20: Keyboard Playing/Phrasing/Melody Awareness

Step B 21: Eighth Note Independence: Snare & Bass Drum

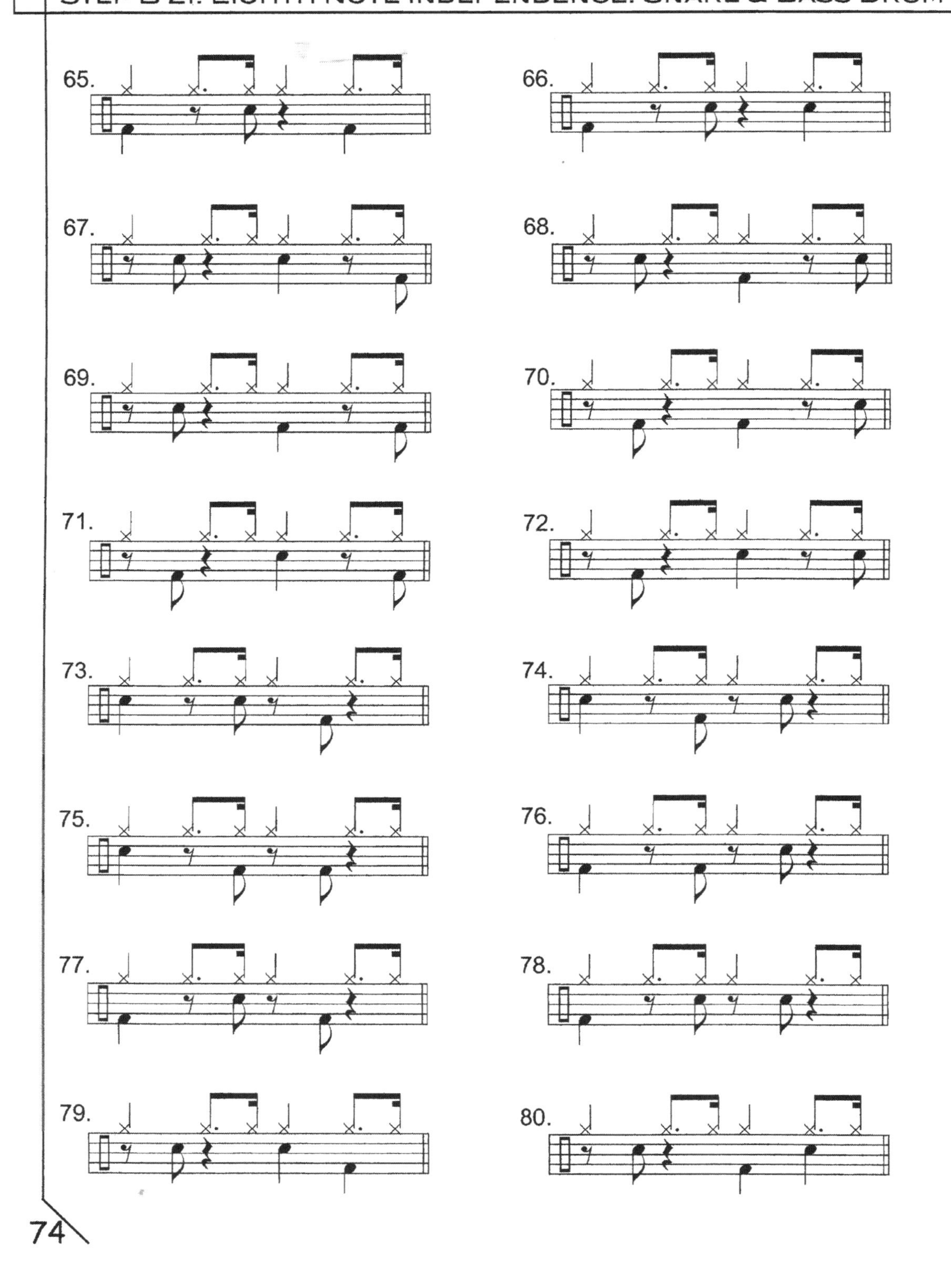

	STEP B 20: KEYBOARD PLAYING/PHRASING/MELODY AWARENESS
	STEP B 21: EIGHTH NOTE INDEPENDENCE: SNARE & BASS DRUM

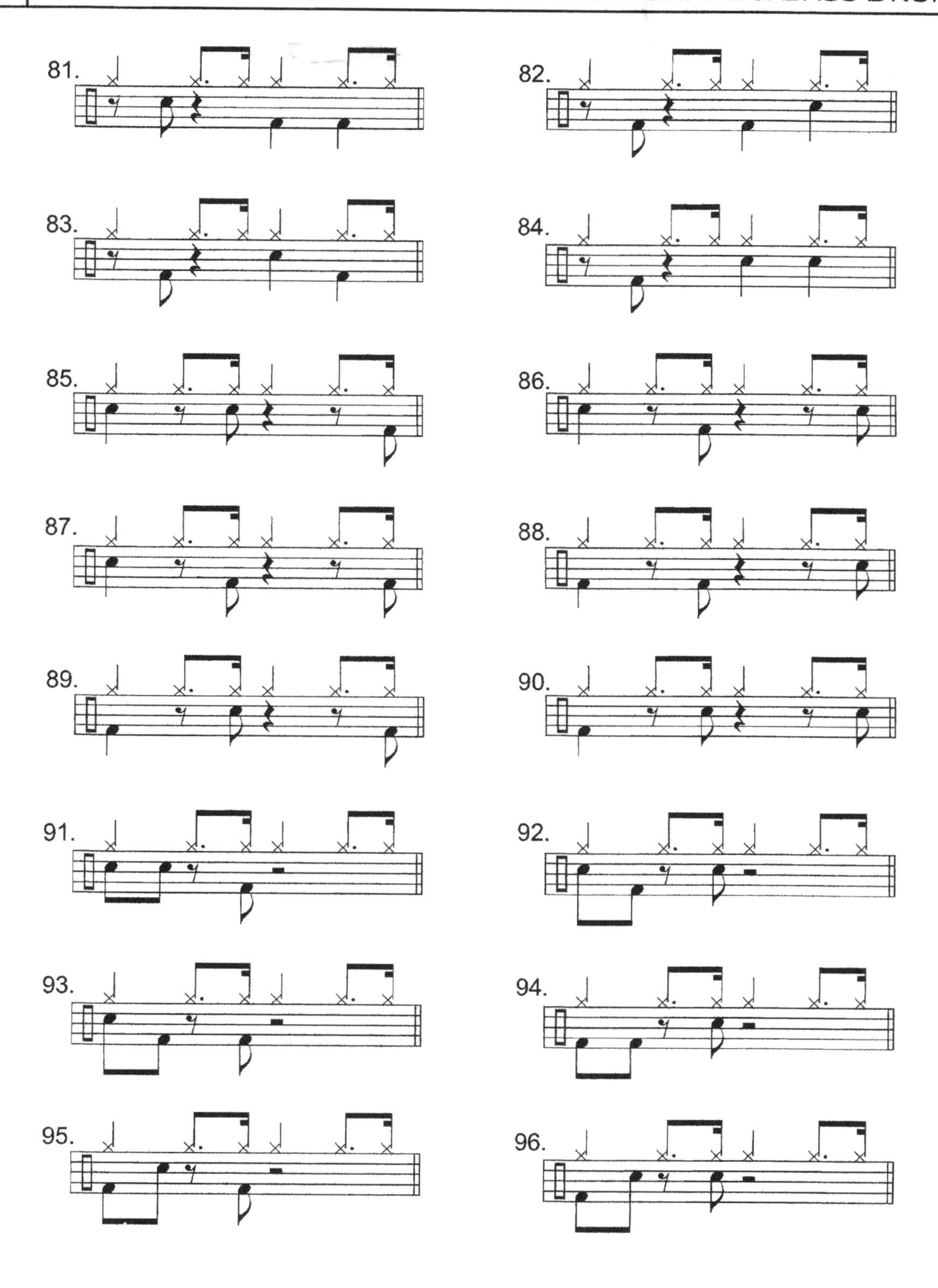

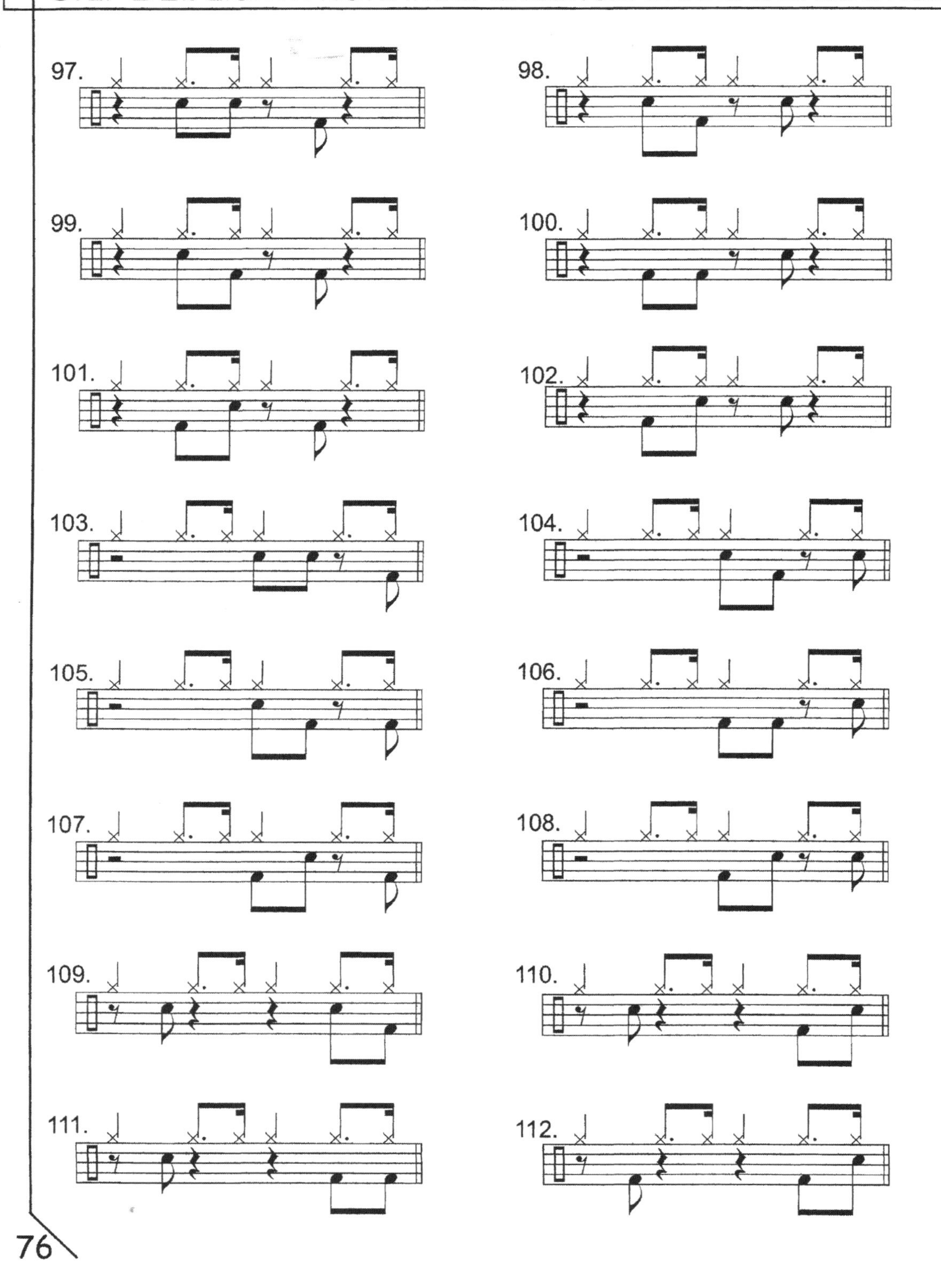
97.
98.
99.
100.
101.
102.
103.
104.
105.
106.
107.
108.
109.
110.
111.
112.

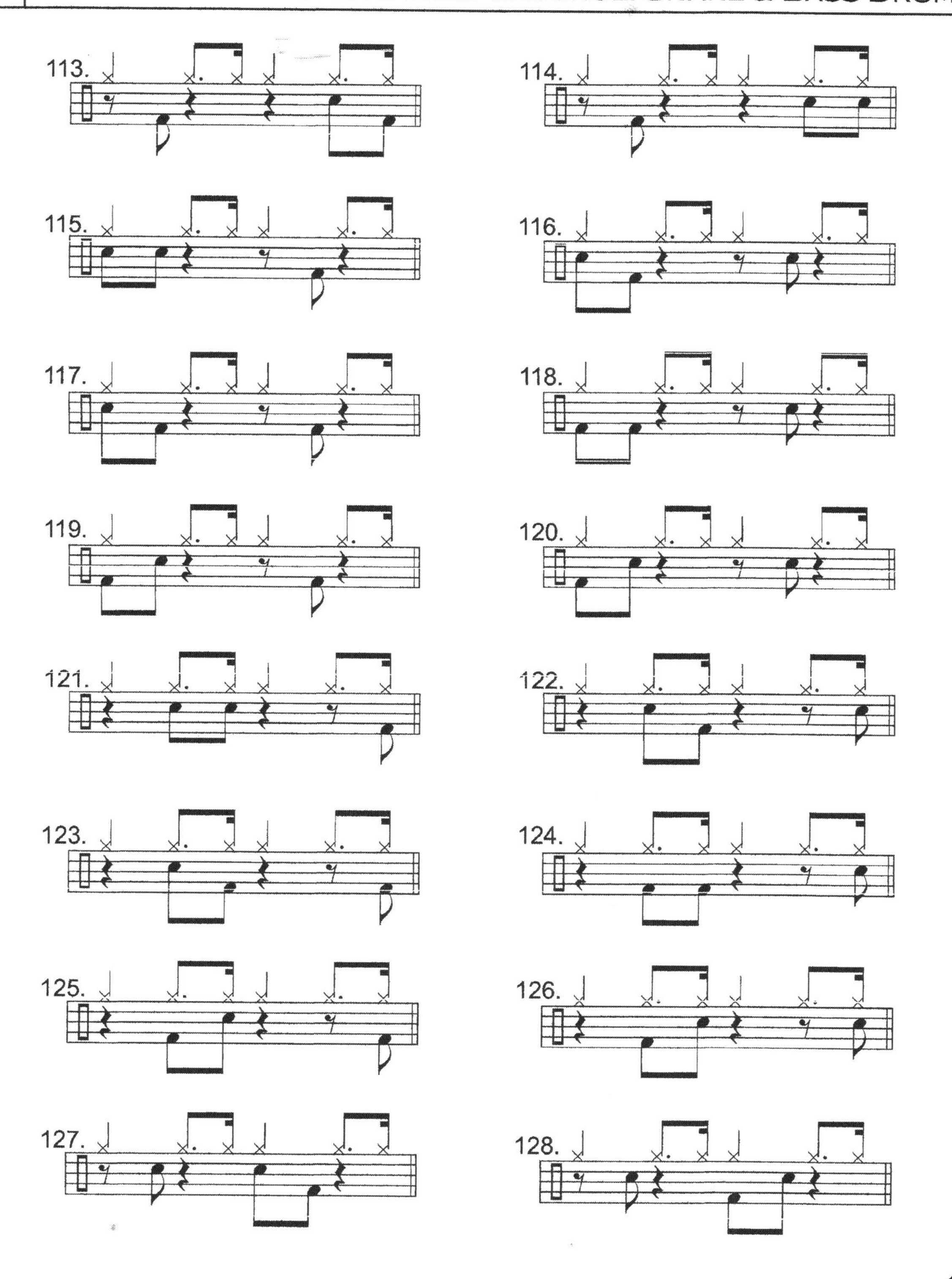
113.
114.
115.
116.
117.
118.
119.
120.
121.
122.
123.
124.
125.
126.
127.
128.

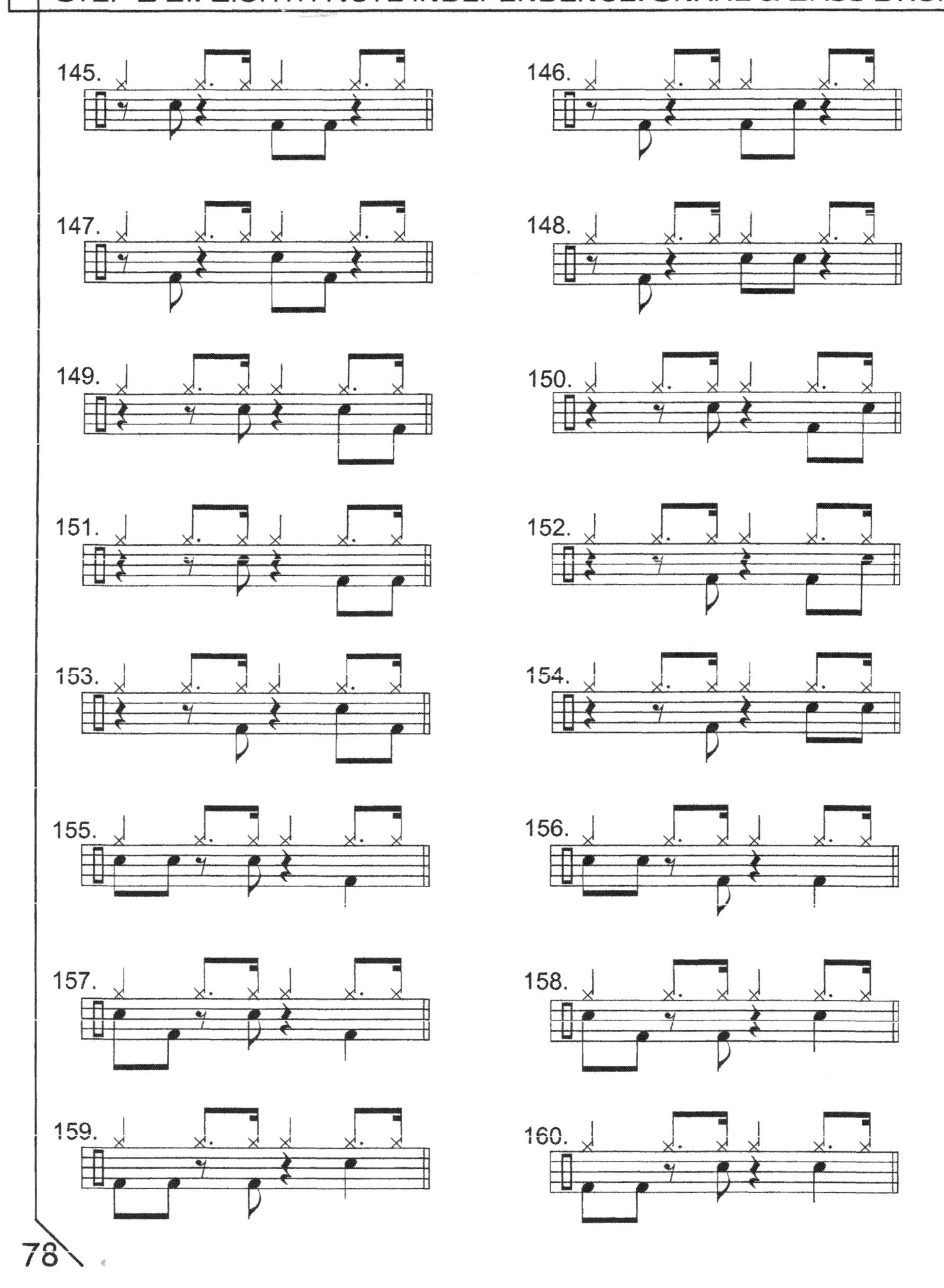
145.
146.
147.
148.
149.
150.
151.
152.
153.
154.
155.
156.
157.
158.
159.
160.

Step B 20: Keyboard Playing/Phrasing/Melody Awareness

Step B 21: Eighth Note Independence: Snare & Bass Drum

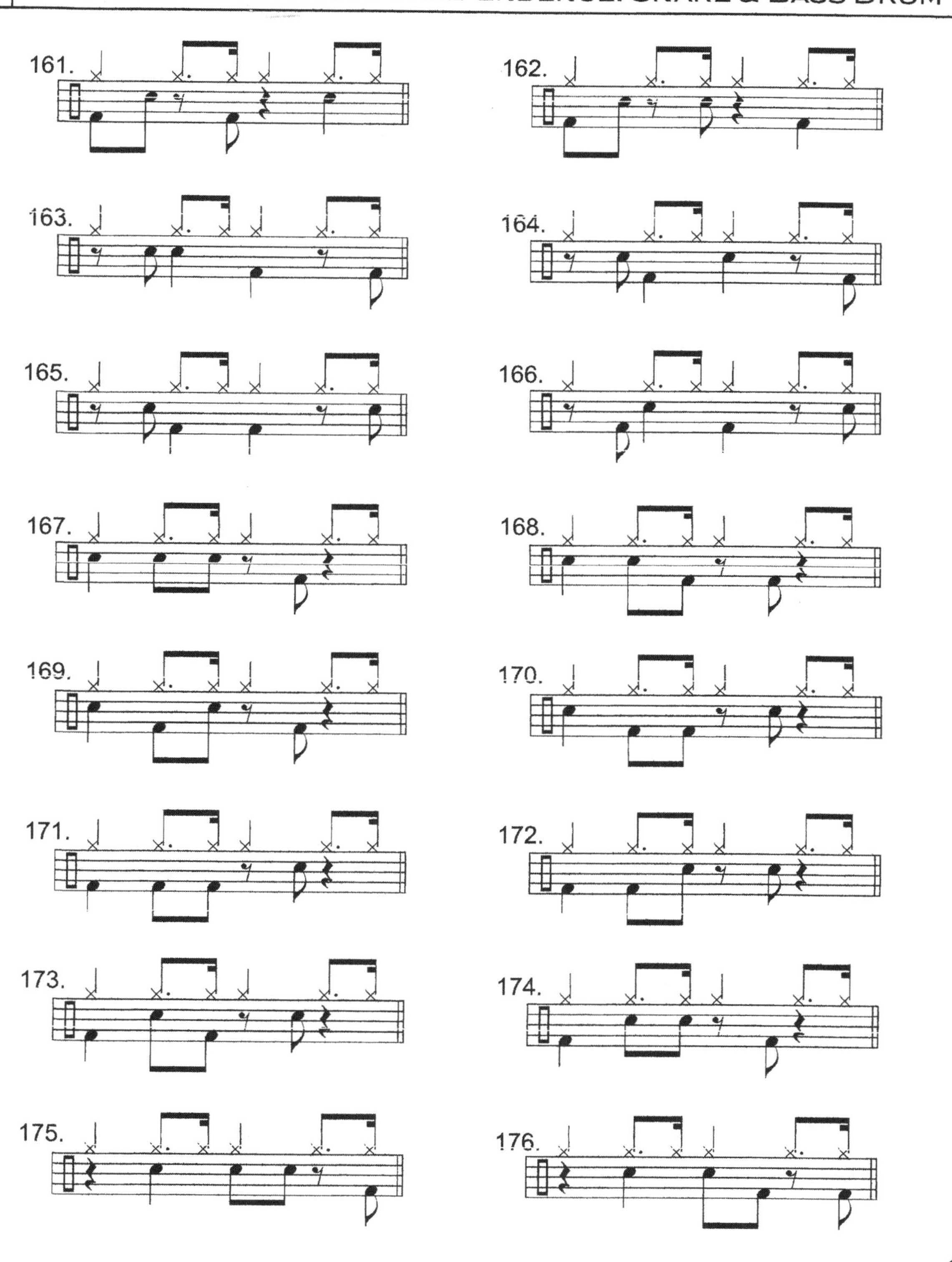

√

Step B 20: Keyboard Playing/Phrasing/Melody Awareness

Step B 21: Eighth Note Independence: Snare & Bass Drum

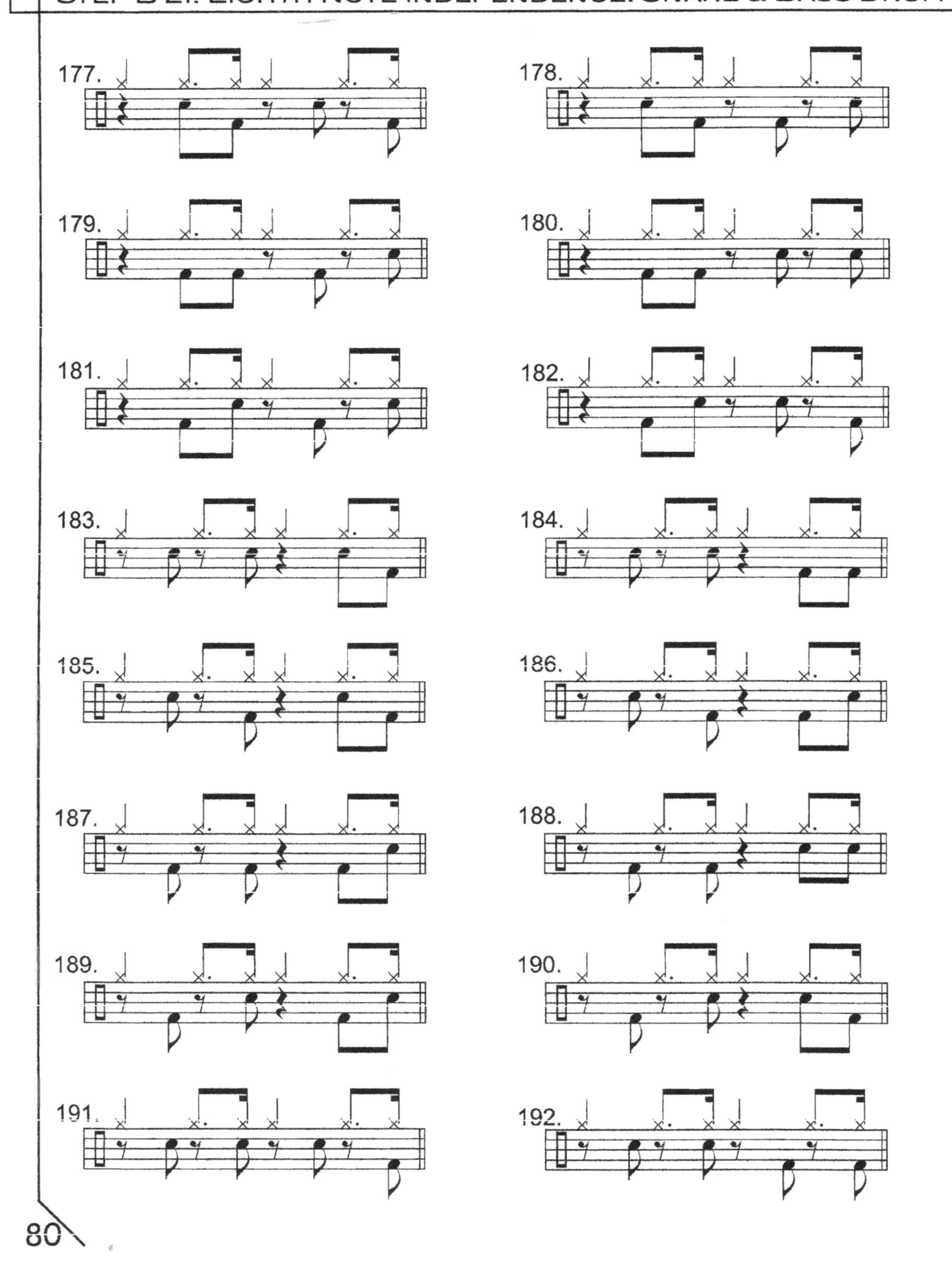

Step B 20: Keyboard Playing/Phrasing/Melody Awareness

Step B 21: Eighth Note Independence: Snare & Bass Drum

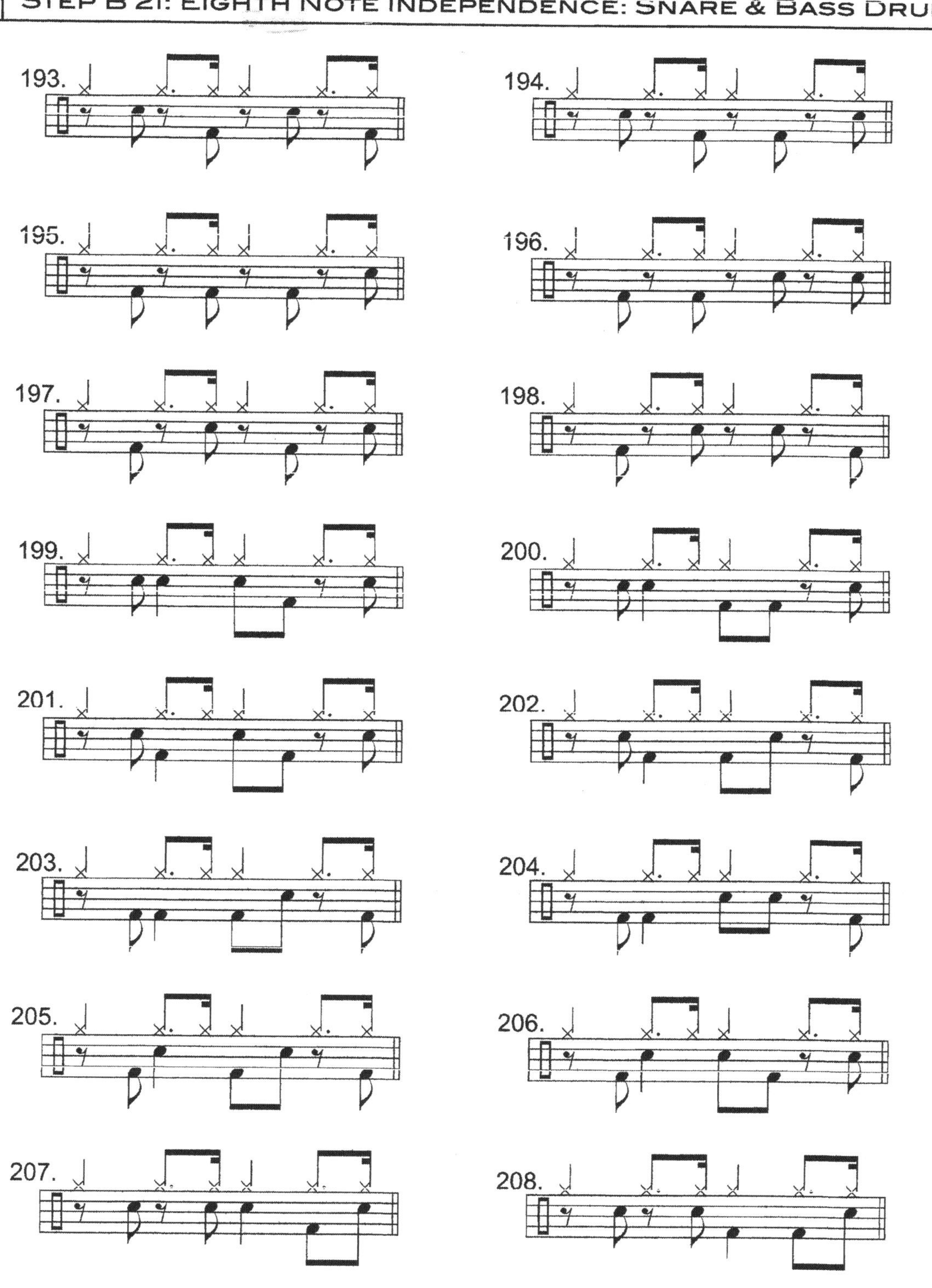

Step B 20: Keyboard Playing/Phrasing/Melody Awareness

Step B 21: Eighth Note Independence: Snare & Bass Drum

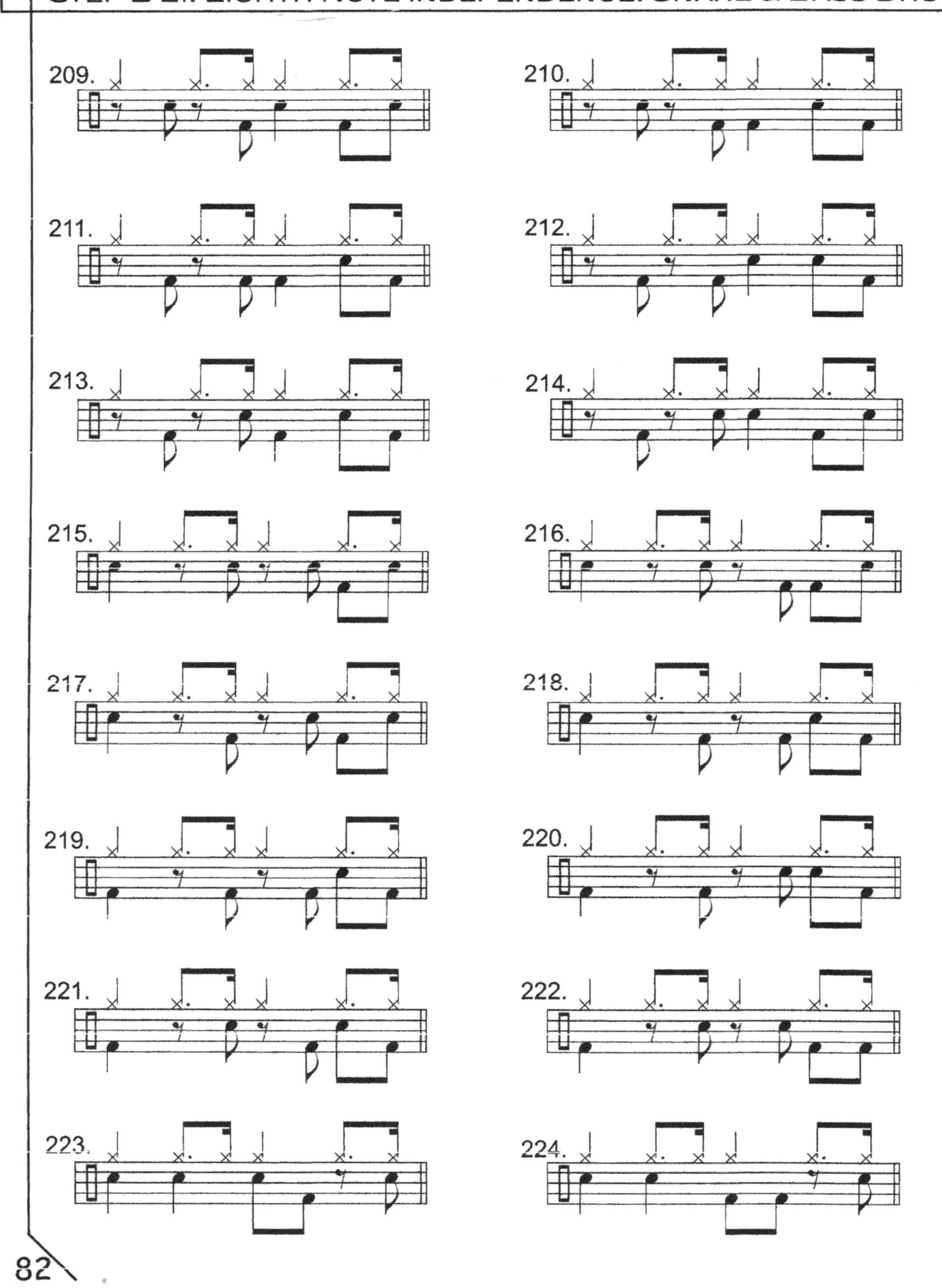

STEP B 20: KEYBOARD PLAYING/PHRASING/MELODY AWARENESS

STEP B 21: EIGHTH NOTE INDEPENDENCE: SNARE & BASS DRUM

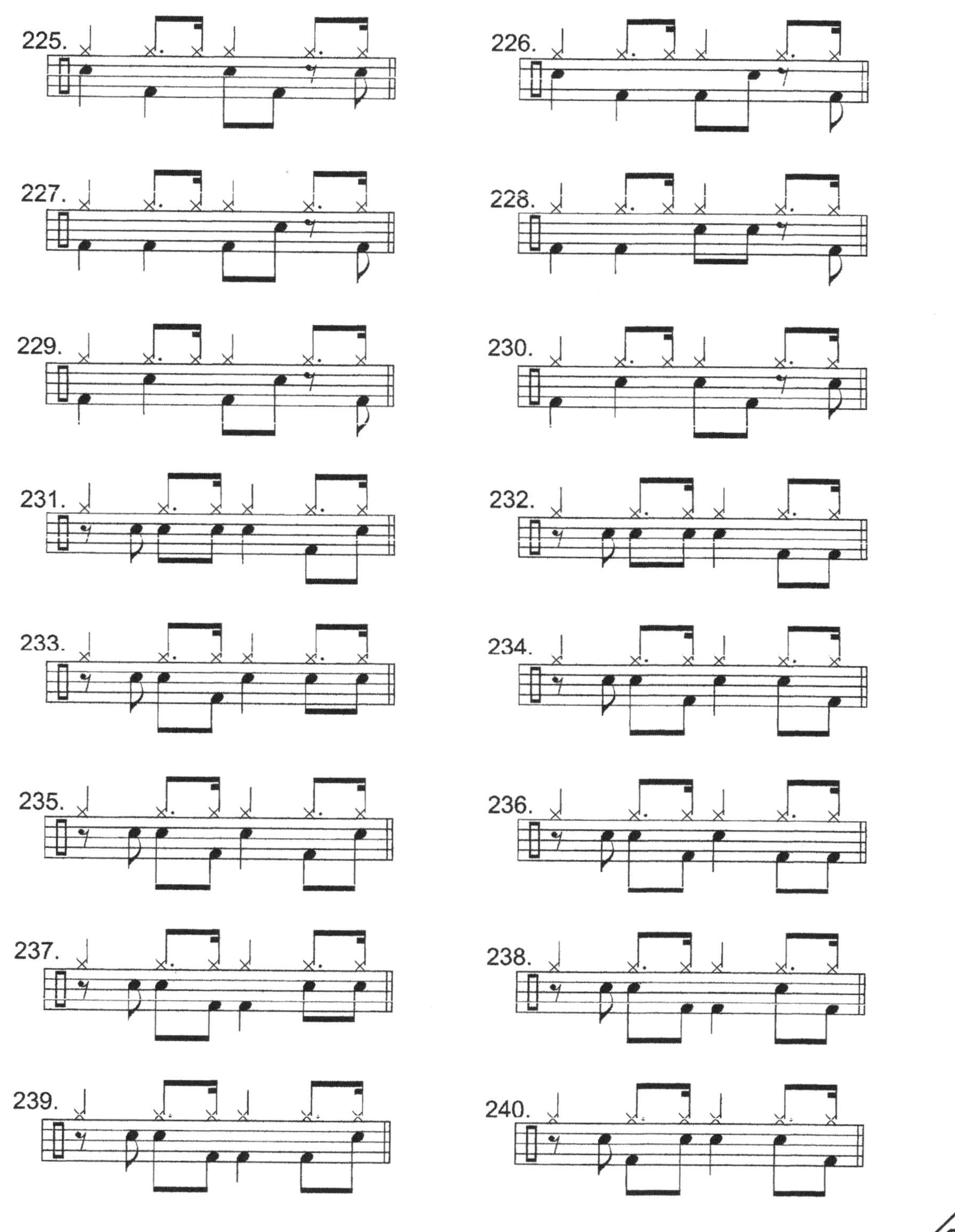

Step B 20: Keyboard Playing/Phrasing/Melody Awareness

Step B 21: Eighth Note Independence: Snare & Bass Drum

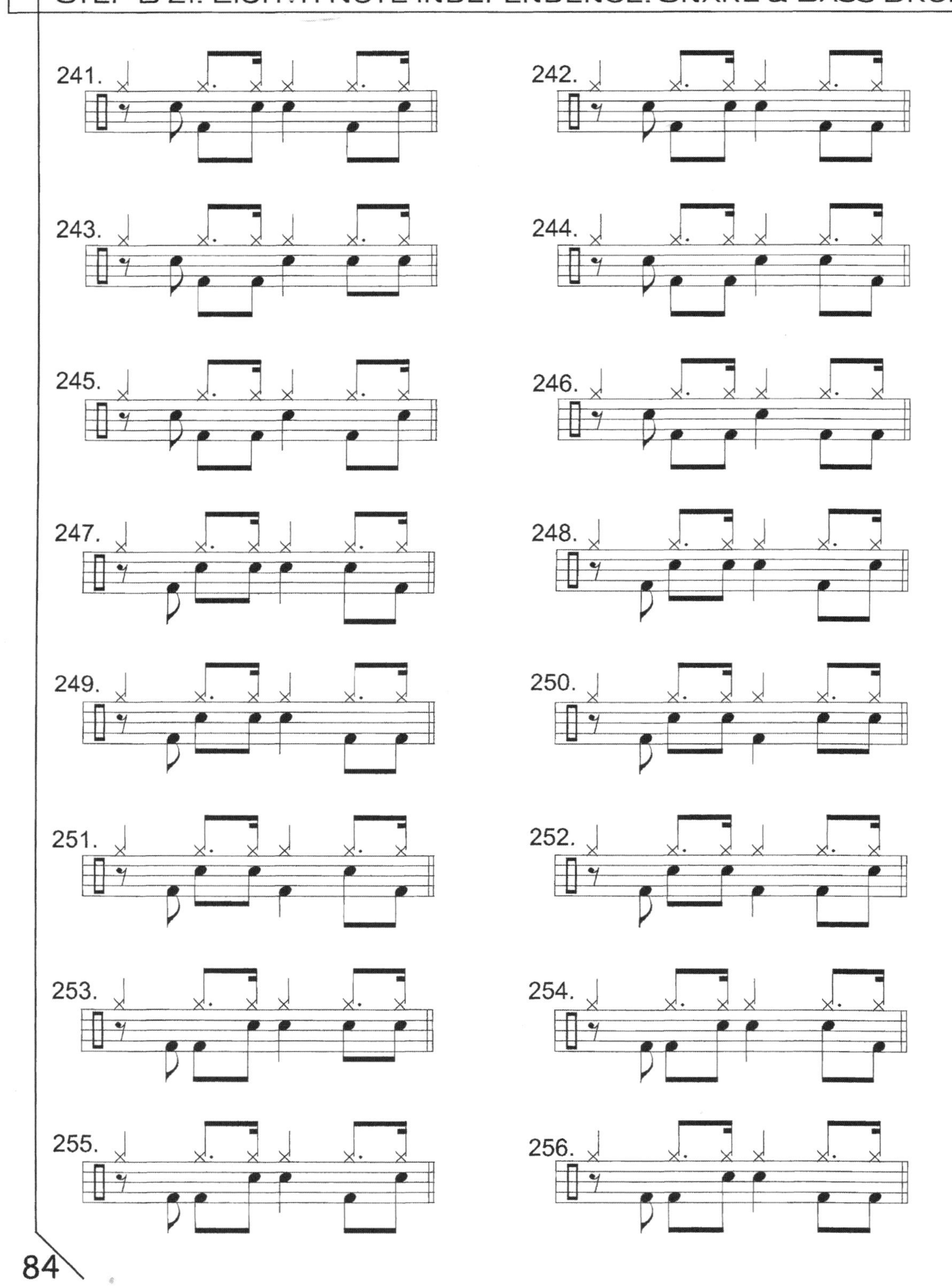

STEP B 20: KEYBOARD PLAYING/PHRASING/MELODY AWARENESS
STEP B 21: EIGHTH NOTE INDEPENDENCE: SNARE & BASS DRUM

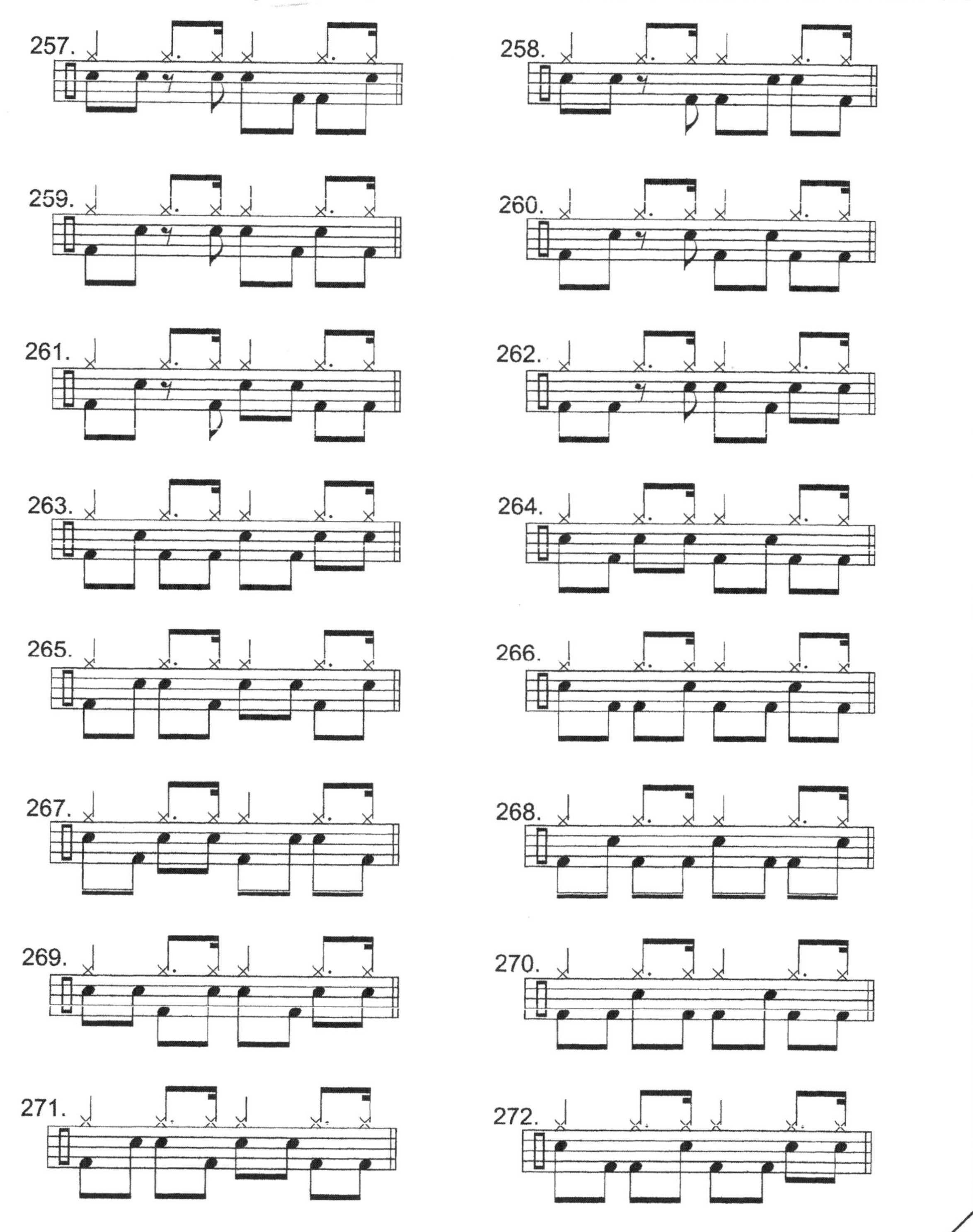

Step B 23: Keyboard Playing/Phrasing/Melody Awareness

- Follow these directions for pages 88 - 92.

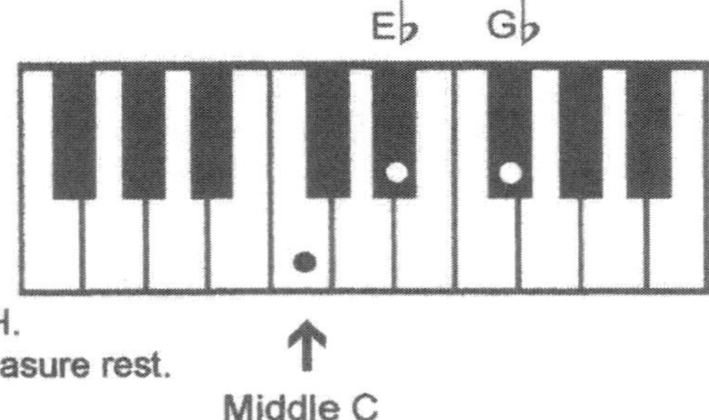

- Find the E♭ and G♭ above middle c.

- Play the **snare and bass drum rhythms** with your RH, using the G♭ for the SN part, and the E♭ for the BD. Use any two fingers of your RH. Follow each two measure exercise with a two measure rest. For example, exercise 1 looks like this:

Here's how you will play it on the keyboard:

- Sing along as you play the G♭ and E♭, using "dah." Match the pitch the best you can.

- Play each exercise twice, before moving to the next one. Thus, the playing of each exercise will be in sync with the 16 bar blues form of the CD tracks.

- Play these exercises against tracks 1 through 6 of the CD.

Space. . . The Final Frontier

I was watching an old clip of Thelonious Monk and his band go through a Monk tune, and was struck how drummer Ben Riley had quite a backstroke after hitting beats one and three on the cymbal. He was obviously using that motion between beats both as a time maintaining device as well as a technique to keep the band swinging hard. Bass player Larry Gales was doing something similar with his right hand, plunking each quarter note, with his hand recoiling away for a few inches, before coming back down for the next beat. Monk himself was, as always, making supreme use of space. We have already seen how using space judiciously was a Count Basie trademark. When you hear people discuss Joe Morello's solo in "Take Five," what do they talk about most? The rests! It would seem that how musicians use space is a strong indicator of how effective the actual notes they play are. It has everything to

(continued, next page)

STEP B 23: TWO MEASURE COMP PATTERNS: SNARE AND BD

- Follow these directions for pages 88 - 92.
- The exercises on the following pages are to be played on the SN/LH and BD/RF, against the jazz ride rhythm (RH/CYM) and HH on 2 & 4 (LF).
- As you play each exercise, sing the SN and BD part, using "bop," "tah," or "dah" for the SN, "boom" or "bom" for the BD. Follow each two measure exercise with two measures of "time" (ride cymbal and hi-hat).

  For example, exercise 1 looks like this:

  Here's how you will play it on the drumset:

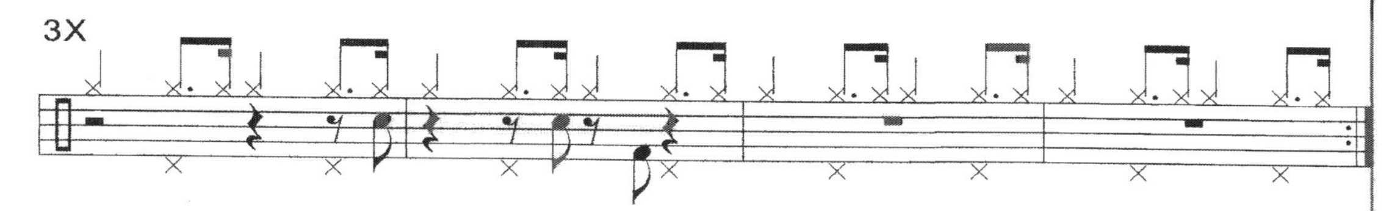

- Play each exercise twice, before moving to the next one. Thus, the playing of each exercise will be in sync with the 16 bar blues form of the CD tracks.
- Play these exercises against tracks 1 through 6 of the CD.

Space. . . The Final Frontier, continued.

do with how we keep time, articulate notes correctly, deal with phrases, view a composition, and communicate with other musicians. Which brings us to the point of this mini-essay. After over 40 years of playing and teaching drums, observing my own growth as well as my students, one thing I know to be absolutely true is this:

DRUMMERS DO NOT LIKE SPACE (OR RESTS).

It seems we drummers feel that by not being busy at times, we don't know how to deal with the above-mentioned musical concerns. Which makes the exercises on these pages all the more critical to your growth as a musician. And you do want to be known as a musician, don't you? Then make sure you do these exercises as directed, with the rests between phrases.

Step B 22: Keyboard Playing/Phrasing/Melody Awareness

Step B 23: Two Measure Comp Patterns: Snare and BD

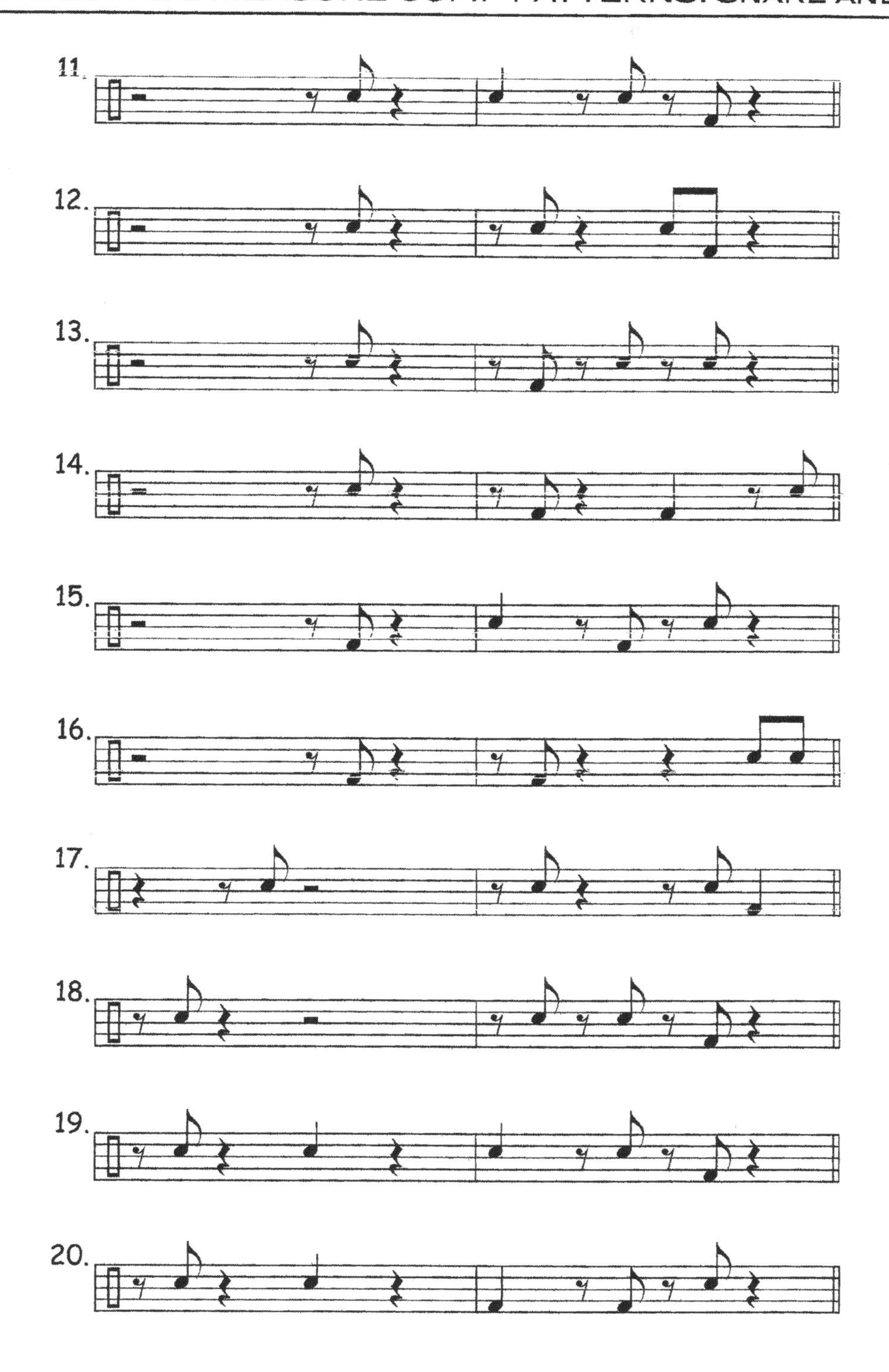
11.
12.
13.
14.
15.
16.
17.
18.
19.
20.

Step B 23: Two Measure Comp Patterns: Snare and BD

√

	STEP B 22: KEYBOARD PLAYING/PHRASING/MELODY AWARENESS
	STEP B 23: TWO MEASURE COMP PATTERNS: SNARE AND BD

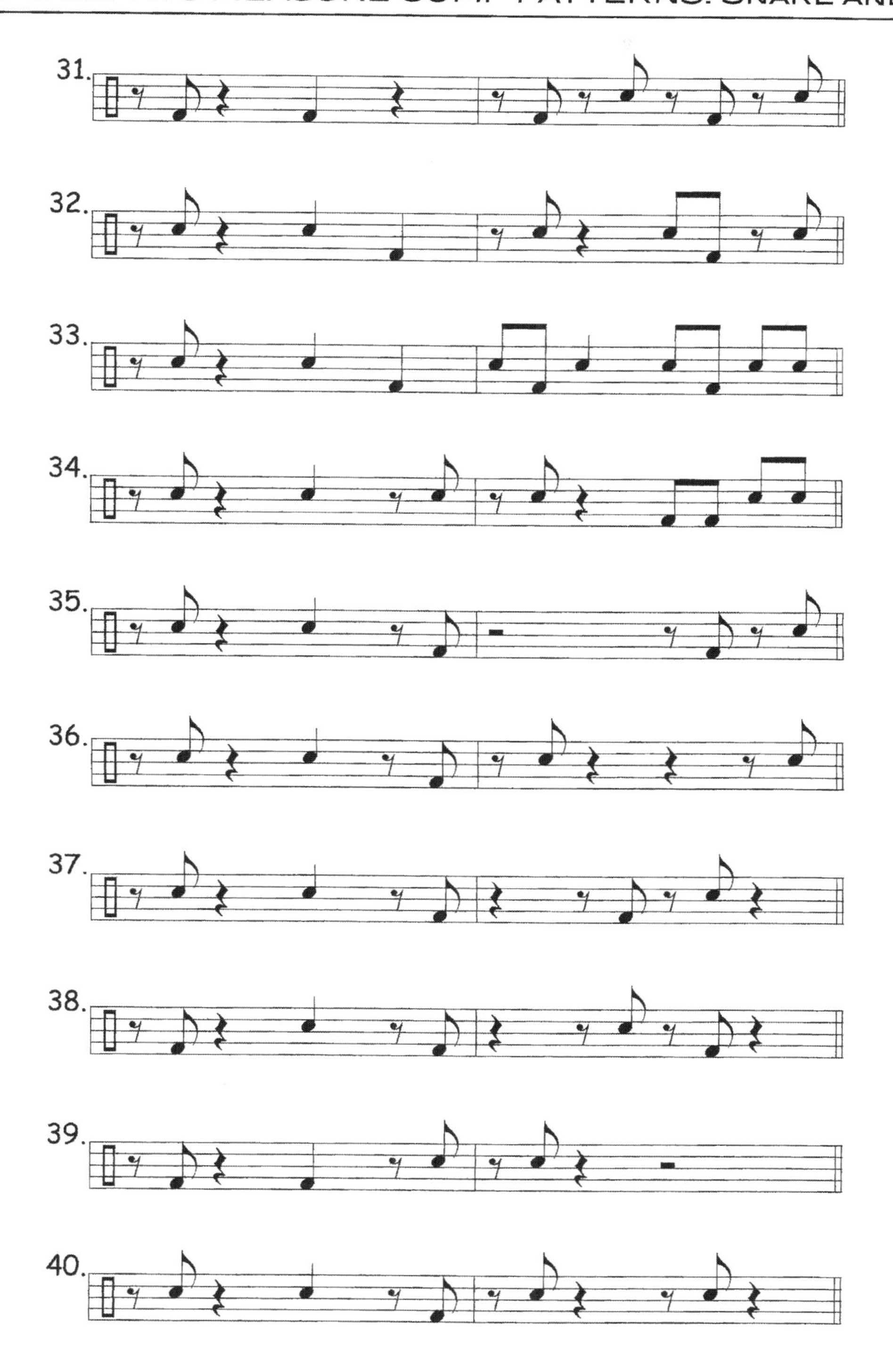

√

STEP B 22: KEYBOARD PLAYING/PHRASING/MELODY AWARENESS

STEP B 23: TWO MEASURE COMP PATTERNS: SNARE AND BD

The Need For Speed

Louie Bellson was asked his advice on how to play fast tempos. He answered with a question, "How often do you practice uptempo?" His answer illustrates the fact that while playing uptempo can indeed be intimidating (it certainly has with this writer), you can exceed your own limits by methodically applying yourself in a practice routine.

Practice playing against a click or sequenced bass line for five minutes. It is important to start this project by playing at a comfortable tempo, as you are then programming yourself correctly for the faster tempos to come. Gradually increase the tempo, and play against that tempo until you can play five minutes comfortably. Stay relaxed, even though your grip is using a combination of tension/release techniques against the cymbal, and keep your strokes lower as you increase the tempo ("fly low to the ground"). Engage your fingers more as you increase the tempo.

The faster the tempo, the more helpful it is to feel the beat in larger increments (half or whole notes instead of quarter notes). One drummer has described such playing as flying over a forest as opposed to walking through it.

Listen to uptempo recordings to get a sense of how the drumming is comping with his ride cymbal. And don't give up!

Some uptempo songs

Caldonia
Cherokee
Cotton Tail
Daahoud
Donna Lee
Giant Steps
How High The Moon
KoKo
One 'O Clock Jump
Ornithology

Drummers who played in the fast lane:

Louis Bellson
Art Blakey
Alan Dawson
Jake Hanna
Roy Haynes
Rufus Jones
Stan Levy
Sonny Payne
Buddy Rich
Max Roach
Bill Stewart
Art Taylor
Ed Thigpen
Jeff Tain Watts
Kenny Washington
Tony Williams

"Playing uptempo is just like playing slower, only faster." ☺

Brandon Mureson

The Nature Of Speed

For most midrange tempos, the ride cymbal falls into an approximate triplet underlying feel, as discussed on page 41, like this:

However, as the tempo increases, the pattern tends to "flatten out," like this:

Sticking Fluency

Earlier in the book, the importance of creativity in jazz was discussed, in that a creative musician should be able to take the simplest page of music and improvise variations on it. There are several tools, both technical (physical) and analytical (mental) that a musician employs in spontaneously creating music, and these tools need to be sharp! The drummer should possess similar skills. There is one skill specific to the drumset which I call **sticking fluency**: the ability to move fluently from one sticking to another in creating ideas. All great drummers have this facility to a high degree, and it is analogous to being able to converse spontaneously. It is obvious that one's ability to speak extemporaneously is directly proportional to one's vocabulary - the more words you know, the more choices you have. Well, the more sticking patterns you know, the more expressive choices you have. This is where you get to work in developing your sticking fluency.

This stuff is not glamorous, and can get tedious at times (one drum student of mine, in the middle of these drills, often asks me, "Can you tell me again why this is important?"). For us drummers, it is as important as the alphabet is to conversation. It will help us "talk" with our hands.

✓

Step B 25: Stick Control/Coordination

- Play RF/BD quarter notes, LF/HH on "2" & "4" throughout.
- Play each exercise on pages 96 and 97 on the snare, playing "swinging" eighth notes. Stay with each exercise until it feels smooth, relaxed, and flowing. Use the following checklist:

1	2	3	4	5	6	7	8	9	10	11	12	13	14
15	16	17	18	19	20	21	22	23	24	25	26	27	28
29	30	31	32	33	34	35	36	37	38	39	40	41	42

✓

Step B 26: Stick Control/Coordination

- Play RF/BD quarter notes, LF/HH on "2" & "4" throughout.
- Play four measures of time, using the jazz ride cymbal pattern. Then play exercise # 1 (on page 96) four times, before returning to four measures of time. Then play exercise # 2 four times, and so on, until you have played all 42 exercises. Use the following checklist:

1	2	3	4	5	6	7	8	9	10	11	12	13	14
15	16	17	18	19	20	21	22	23	24	25	26	27	28
29	30	31	32	33	34	35	36	37	38	39	40	41	42

√

☐ Step B 26: Creativity

- Play RF/BD quarter notes, LF/HH on "2" & "4" throughout.
- Play each exercise on pages 93 and 94 on the snare for four measures, playing "swinging" eighth notes. Then move around the set with each particular pattern, exploring the tonal and accenting possibilities. Keep tabs on your progress by using the following checklist:

1	2	3	4	5	6	7	8	9	10	11	12	13	14
15	16	17	18	19	20	21	22	23	24	25	26	27	28
29	30	31	32	33	34	35	36	37	38	39	40	41	42

√

☐ Step B 27: Extra Challenge/Coordination

- Play RF/BD quarter notes, LF/HH on "2" & "4" throughout.
- Create two measure sticking patterns by combining each exercise with the 41 other exercises. For example, combine exercise 1 & 2, then 1 & 3, 1& 4, etc., until you reach 1 & 42. Then proceed with combining exercise 2 with all the others. Keep going until you have combined the last exercise (# 42) with all the others.
- Since this is a rather long assignment, I suggest that you complete one combination series a day, while moving on in the book to other challenges. You can keep tabs on your progress by using the following checklist:

1	2	3	4	5	6	7	8	9	10	11	12	13	14
15	16	17	18	19	20	21	22	23	24	25	26	27	28
29	30	31	32	33	34	35	36	37	38	39	40	41	42

Stick To It

"If you want to do anything of significance, you must be willing to do the boring stuff."

8 time National League batting champion Tony Gwynn

Sticking Exercises

1. R L R L R L R L

2. L R L R L R L R

3. R R L L R R L L

4. L L R R L L R R

5. R L R R L R L L

6. L R L L R L R R

7. R L L R R L L R

8. L R R L L R R L

9. R L L R L R R L

10. L R R L R L L R

11. R R L R L L R L

12. L L R L R R L R

13. R L R L L R L R

14. L R L R R L R L

15. R L R L R R L L

16. L R L R L L R R

17. R L R L R R L R

18. L R L R L L R L

19. R L R L R L L R

20. L R L R L R R L

21. R R L L R L R L

Sticking Exercises, cont.

22. L L R R L R L R

23. R L R R L R L R

24. L R L L R L R L

25. R L R R L R R L

26. L R L L R L L R

27. R L R R L L R L

28. L R L L R R L R

29. R L L R L L R L

30. L R R L R R L R

31. R L L R R L R L

32. L R R L L R L R

33. R R L R R L R L

34. L L R L L R L R

35. R R R L R R R L

36. L L L R L L L R

37. R L L L R L L L

38. L R R R L R R R

39. R R L R R R L R

40. L L R L L L R L

41. R L R R R L R R

42. L R L L L R L L

STEP B 29: INTERACTIVE PHRASING: EIGHTH NOTES

The exercises in this step relate to the eighth note sticking patterns on page 96 and 97. Each pattern will be expressed as a rhythmic phrase on ther drumset, as follows.

- Play two measures of jazz time.

- Play each sticking exercise for two measures on the set, with each "R" on RH/CYM and RF/BD simultaneously, and each "L" on the LH/SN. LF/HH plays on "2" and "4."

  Exercise one on page 94 looks like this:

  and should be played like this:

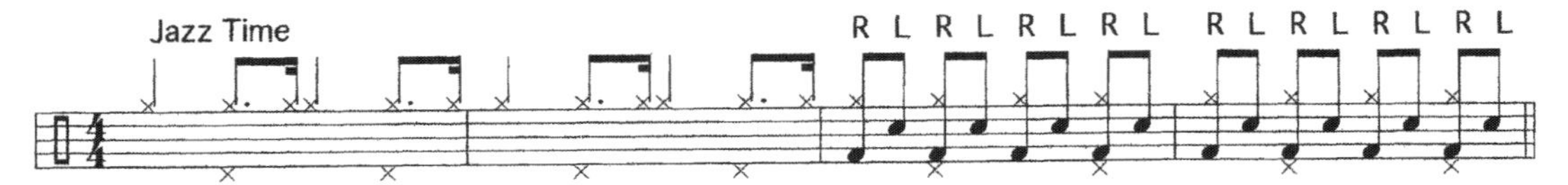

- For those patterns that feature three successive underlined L's, substitute "L R L" on the snare in its place. For example, exercise 36 looks like this:

  and should be played like this:

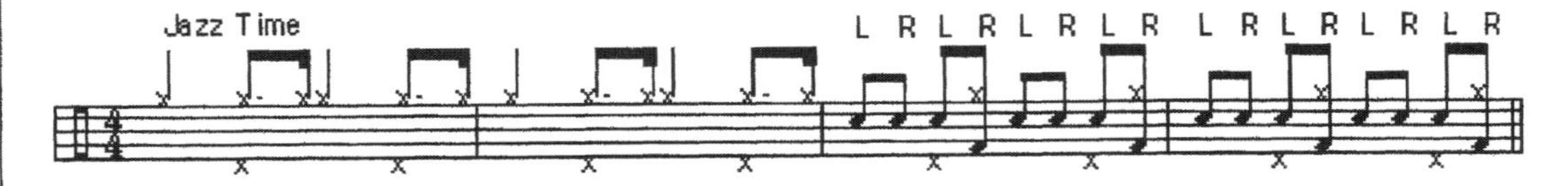

- Play against CD tracks 1 - 6.

- For your convenience, the 42 patterns are presented on the next page. Checklist below:

1	2	3	4	5	6	7	8	9	10	11	12	13	14
15	16	17	18	19	20	21	22	23	24	25	26	27	28
29	30	31	32	33	34	35	36	37	38	39	40	41	42

STICKING PATTERNS FOR STEP C 19

1. R L R L R L R L
2. L R L R L R L R
3. R R L L R R L L
4. L L R R L L R R
5. R L R R L R L L
6. L R L L R L R R
7. R L L R R L L R
8. L R R L L R R L
9. R L L R L R R L
10. L R R L R L L R
11. R R L R L L R L
12. L L R L R R L R
13. R L R L L R L R
14. L R L R R L R L
15. R L R L R R L L
16. L R L R L L R R
17. R L R L R R L R
18. L R L R L L R L
19. R L R L R L L R
20. L R L R L R R L
21. R R L L R L R L
22. L L R R L R L R
23. R L R R L R L R
24. L R L L R L R L
25. R L R R L R R L
26. L R L L R L L R
27. R L R R L L R L
28. L R L L R R L R
29. R L L R L L R L
30. L R R L R R L R
31. R L L R R L R L
32. L R R L L R L R
33. R R L R R L R L
34. L L R L L R L R
35. R R R L R R R L
36. L L L R L L L R
37. R L L L R L L L
38. L R R R L R R R
39. R R L R R R L R
40. L L R L L L R L
41. R L R R R L R R
42. L R L L L R L L

The Properties Of Sound

It was a dark and stormy night. Suppose you heard a sound in the middle of the night that was later connected to a crime. A detective comes to interview you, and quickly senses your value as a witness.The interview goes like this:

Q. About what time did you hear the noise, sir?
A. It was exactly 2:15 in the morning.

Q. How can you be so sure about the time?
A. I had my practice pad in bed, and was going for five minutes of paradiddles, so my eye was on the clock when I heard that sound.

Q. So what did you hear, exactly?
A. Well, I would say it sounded like a scream.

Q. A scream?
A. A scream.

Q. Was it a man or woman screaming?
A. Definitely a woman screaming.

Q. How could you tell?
A. Well, by the pitch and timbre.

Q. I beg your pardon?
A. I'm sorry, I'm so used to talking with musicians, that the terminology just slipped in. By pitch I meant the relative highness or lowness of the voice, and by timbre I meant the quality of the voice.

Q. Very good, sir. Was it a loud scream?
A. Yes, indeed. It had the intensity of the scream that was in the shower scene in the movie *Psycho*.

Q. Would that be the earlier *Psycho* or the later remake?
A. Oh, definitely the first one by Hitchcock. They should never have tried to remake a masterpiece. Wasn't Hitchcock the master of suspense?

Q. Yes, indeed. But back to the scream. Was it a long or short scream?
A. Quite a long one, I would say. Easily worth a whole note or two.

Pitch
The relative highness or lowness of a sound.

Timbre
(TAM-burr). The quality of a sound. Sometimes called tone color.

The detective refers back to his notes.

Q. So what I've got so far, sir, is this: At 2:15 in the morning you heard a woman's high pitched scream (not unlike the shower scene scream in Hitchcock's *Psycho*), that could also be described as long and loud. Would that best describe what you heard?

A. That's it.

The detective closes his notebook, and puts that and his reading glasses in the inside pocket of his long, brown coat.

"Well thank you, sir, you've been most helpful."

"No problem, detective. By the way, what was the crime?"

A sad looked crossed the detective's face. It was then that he looked his age.

"I've been on the force twenty years, but I've never had anything like this come my way."

"Oh, no what was it, a murder?"

"No, nothing like that. The singer down the streetwas rehearsing for a Yoko Ono tribute concert."

Now it's our turn to play detective. What facts about sound can we derive from the above literary masterpiece (there are usually truths to be found in great literature).There are four basic characteristics of sound, and here they are:

1. **Volume**: the relative loudness or softness of the sound.

2. **Duration**: the length of the sound.

3. **Pitch**: the relative highness or lowness of the sound.

4. **Timbre** (pronounced TAM-burr): the quality of the sound, sometimes referred to as "tone color." Technically it is the spectrum of frequencies any sound generates that distinguishes itself uniquely. It is also the way you can tell the difference between a guitar and a trumpet. Or a trombone and your mother-in-law. All these sounds have unique characteristics that make them distinct and recognizable.

What does all this new information have to do with you as a drummer? Plenty, as you will see in the following pages. As your powers of perception develops as a musician, you will be able to interact with other musicians at a much deeper level. It bears repeating: your ears are as important as your hands.

"I had to find a way to play the music instead of playing the drums."

One of the most recorded and sought after jazz drummers of all time: Billy Higgins

THE SHAPE OF EACH NOTE

On the previous page you learned of the four basic properties of sound: volume, duration, pitch, and timbre. In music, each note can have additional characteristics,
which can give any given phrase its uniqueness. Some of these expressive devices are:

attack (how a note begins; the opposite of release)
release (how a note ends; the opposite of attack)
accent (an accented note is played louder than its neighbors)
staccato (notes that are separated; the opposite of legato)
legato (notes which are smoothly connected; the opposite of staccato)
vibrato (fluctuation of a tone's pitch)
tremolo (fluctuation of a tone's volume)
pitch bending (altering a pitch at the beginning, middle, or end of a sound)

In addition to improvisation and syncopation, early jazz musicians employed the above techniques in their phrasing. This non-traditional approach to soloing gave jazz a unique sound that set it apart from other forms of music.

Good Vibrations

"When you work with Dave [Tough], it's like being on a magic carpet after the first chorus. Everything becomes so easy."

Vibraphonist Lionel Hampton

"Billy [Higgins] fits into any situation. He always listens and responds to what you're doing."

Vibraphonist Bobby Hutcherson

"Roy [Haynes] had just given us a master class in what great drummers do. From the first beat, we knew he was in charge and we wouldn't have to worry about a thing. He always make you sound like a million dollars."

Vibraphonist Gary Burton

Step B 32: Ear Training, Phrasing

- Play this exercise against track 7 of the CD.
- Find the E♭ above middle c.
- On the CD track, a bass line is played. A two measure phrase is played on the piano. You will listen carefully, and copy that phrase on your keyboard, using the E♭ on the following two measures. Listen carefully to each phrase, and try to perceive the shape of each note, and the feel of the phrase itself. There will be a new phrase each time, so stay sharp until each phrase is mastered.

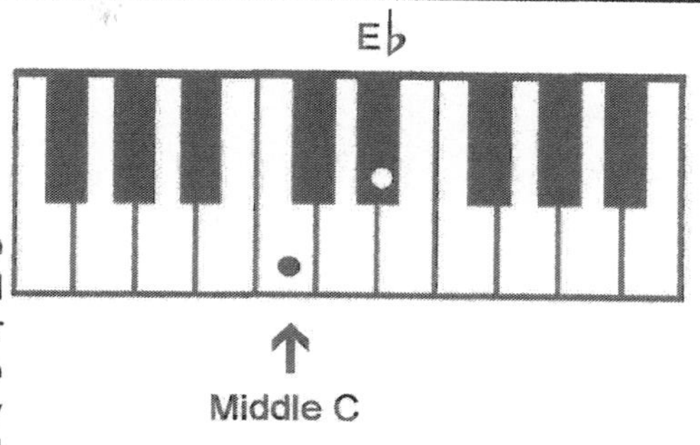

As an example, the first phrase will be like this:

piano (you listen) keyboard (you play the same phrase)

- Sing along with each phrase as you play it.

Step B 33: Ear Training, Phrasing

- Play this exercise against track 8 of the CD.
- Find the E♭ and D♭ above middle c.
- On the CD track, a bass line is played. A two measure phrase is played on the piano, using two pitches now, the E♭ and the D♭. You will listen carefully, and copy that phrase on your keyboard, using the E♭ and D♭ on the following two measures. The phrases played are using two pitches now, so use your ears! Stay with this exercise until each phrase is mastered.

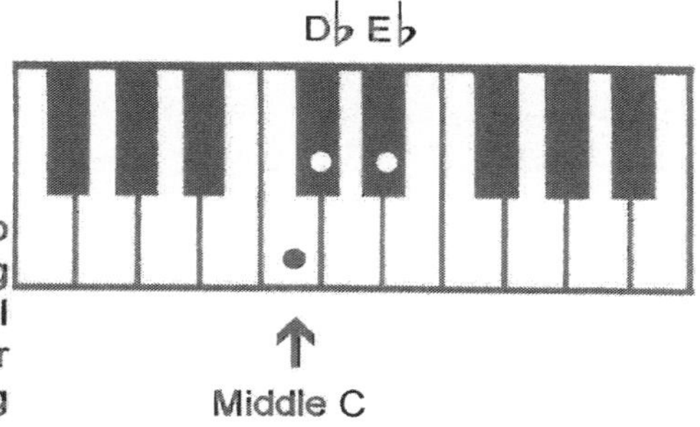

As an example, the first phrase will be like this:

piano (you listen) keyboard (you play the same phrase)

- Sing along with each phrase as you play it.

STEP B 34: EAR TRAINING, PHRASING

- Play this exercise against track 9 of the CD.
- Find the D♭, E♭, and G♭ above middle c.
- On the CD track, a bass line is played. A two measure phrase is played on the piano, using three pitches now, D♭, E♭, and G♭. You will listen carefully, and copy that phrase on your keyboard, using those three pitches on the following two measures. The phrases played are using three pitches now, so use your ears! Stay with this exercise until each phrase is mastered.

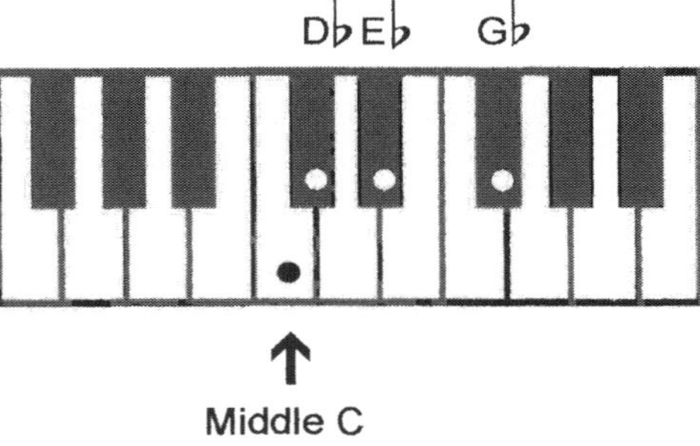

As an example, the first phrase will be like this:

piano (you listen) keyboard (you play the same phrase)

- Sing along with each phrase as you play it.

STEP B 35: EAR TRAINING PHRASING

- Play this exercise against track 10 of the CD.
- Find the B♭, D♭, E♭ , and G♭ above middle c.
- On the CD track, a bass line is played. A two measure phrase is played on the piano, using four pitches now, B♭ , D♭ , E♭ , and G♭. You will listen carefully, and copy that phrase on your keyboard, using those four pitches on the following two measures. The phrases played are using four pitches now, so use your ears! Stay with this exercise until each phrase is mastered.

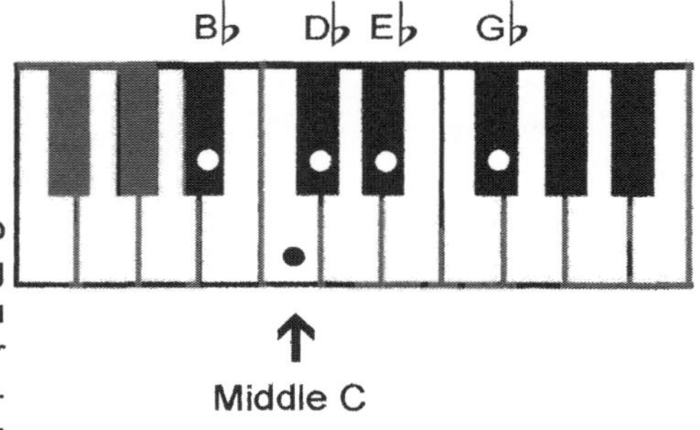

As an example, the first phrase will be like this:

piano (you listen) keyboard (you play the same phrase)

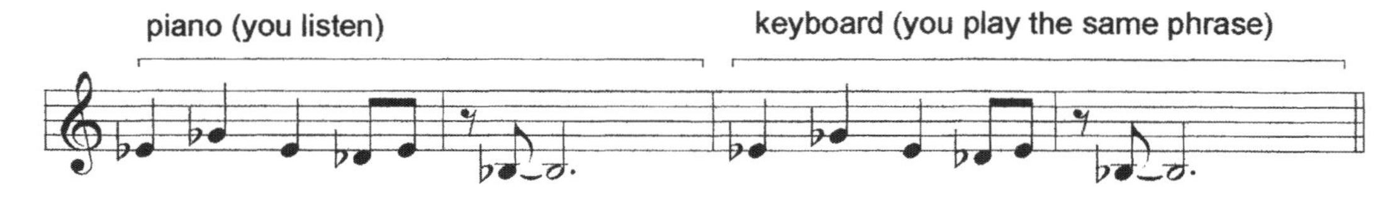

- Sing along with each phrase as you play it.

STEP B 36: COMPING/CREATIVITY

Follow these directions for pages 48-54.

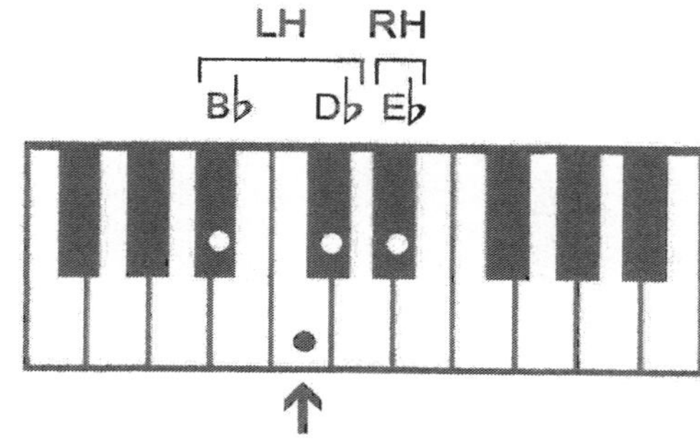

- Find the E♭ above middle c. You will be playing this note with the right hand.
- Find the D♭ above middle c, and the B♭ below middle c. You will be playing these two notes **together** with your left hand.
- Play these exercises against tracks 1-6 of the CD..
- Play the snare rhythms with your RH, using the E♭ . On the following measure, "answer" that rhythm with your own comping pattern with your LH, using the D♭ and B♭ together as a chord. Play this sequence four times for each exercise.

Chord
Two or more pitches sounded together.

Think for a minute about what you are doing. Your right hand has a "target" to hit: the written rhythm. Your left hand fills in around that target rhythm, as you create your own comping patterns. Each hand has a separate task. In our own little way, we are trying to think like a jazz pianist thinks.

For example. exercise 1 looks like this:

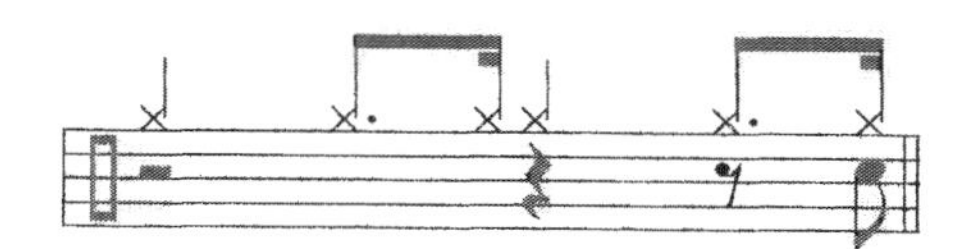

Here's how you will play it on the keyboard:

Turn the page for some comping ideas.

Cross Training

"Art Blakey was a pianist before he became a drummer, and I also played the piano on some dates."

Max Roach

Here are some comping ideas for your LH chord:

Comping, like soloing, is not a static endeavor. Not all the above examples will mesh with all the written exercises. Here's a general rule to follow. Leave a little "space" between the last note of the "melody" (your RH playing the written exercise) and the comping pattern (your LH playing the chord). For example, exercise 1 would not go well with comp idea #4:

Awkward:

Comp idea # 2 would be a better choice:

Comping is Cool

One way of learning how a jazz pianist thinks is to listen to him comp, as he solos or backs another soloist. Here are some pianists you may want to check out: Count Basie, Dave Brubeck, Bill Evans, Red Garland, Herbie Hancock, Wynton Kelly, Oscar Peterson, Bud Powell, McCoy Tyner, and Joe Zawinul. It would also be helpful to listen to how pianists back up and comp behind jazz singers. You will become a more sensitive drummer by doing this.

Be Bop
Builders of Bop
Bop Drummers
Bop Standards
Triplet Snare Independence
Triplet Bass Drum Independence
Broken Triplets: Snare & Bass
Triplet Comp Patterns

✓ STEP C 1: READ "BEBOP"

BEBOP

The commercial appeal of the big bands faded after World War II, when the wartime economy and the public's changing tastes put many bands out of business. Their decline coincided with a new style of jazz, "bebop" (or "bop"), an onomatopoetic coining. The **era of bebop was in effect the era of the soloist**, for just as Louis Armstrong expanded the strictures of New Orleans jazz with his improvisational skill, so also a new generation of soloists (many from the ranks of former big bands) now elaborated on the foundation of the swing bands. Indeed, the earlier improvisations of saxophonist Lester Young (with Count Basie) and guitarist Charlie Christian were forerunners of the bebop era.

Like swing, bebop was characterized by improvisations over the chord changes, but more so than ever before. In fact, **improvisation was a major feature** of bebop. The songs were generally played at **faster tempos**, and the chord progressions and solos involved a more chromatic appoach. Bebop was usually played in much **smaller groups**. Bebop never attained the commercial appeal of big band swing, and this is partially explained by the music and its performers. Improvisation is in one sense a self examination of one's skills, and with this new focus on extended solos (some artists would solo for 45 straight minutes), some critics viewed bebop as an exercise in self-indulgence, while adherents saw bebop as an exciting vehicle for new heights of creativity. Bebop was also perceived by some as being indifferent to its audience, and this perception was perhaps personified by the way trumpeter Miles Davis sometimes performed, with his back to the audience. Bebop was uncompromising, and had to be accepted on its own terms.

By far the dominant musician on the bop scene was alto saxophonist **Charlie "Bird" Parker**, whose creativity seemed inexhausible. His ability to improvise melodies that were related in unorthodox ways to the chord structure set the standard for all future soloists. In fact, his solos are still studied and analyzed today as models of improvisation. Other influential figures on the bop scene included **Earl "Bud" Powell** and trumpeter **John Birks "Dizzy" Gillespie**, both frequent collaborators with Parker, and pianist **Thelonious Monk**, noted for his original style.

Chromatic

Relating to the alteration of scale tones, chords, and solos by using half-steps. The word is derived from a Greek word meaning "color," so a chromatic melody might be inferred to be more colorful or with unexpected steps.

Half-steps

On the keyboard, a half-step is the distance from any one note to its adjacent neighbor, up or down, black or white key. A whole step consists of two half-steps. Scales are constructed using different combinations of whole and half-steps.

BUILDERS OF BOP

Here are short biographies of the four men who created this new form of jazz.

Charlie Parker

Bird. Charlie Parker was born in Kansas City, Kansas, on August 29, 1920. His first musical instruction came by playing the saxophone in high school, and by listening to bands in the local bars. By age 16, Parker had dropped out of school, was already married, with a child, and a drug addict. His early influences were Count Basie (whose band was based in Kansas City), and Basie's star tenor saxophonist, Lester Young. While on tour with Jay McShann's band, he often sat in at jam sessions at a club called Minton's Playhouse in New York (often called the birthplace of bop music). In 1945, he made his first recording under his own name, with Dizzy Gillespie and the young trumpeter Miles Davis.

Later that year, he toured Los Angeles. While in California, he suffered a nervous breakdown and spent six months at Camarillo State Hospital. In 1947, he returned to New York, and formed his famous quintet, which included Miles Davis and drummer Max Roach. Ironically, at the same time he was becoming the most influential jazz musician in the world (his followers would tape record his live performances to later transcribe), he was beset by employment (his New York cabaret card was revoked) and mental problems. He gigged out-of-town more frequently, and attempted suicide twice in 1954. His last appearance was March 5, 1955, at Birdland, the club named after him. One week later he was dead. He was only 34.

The Flying Cymbal (or You've Got To Pay Your Dues. . .)

Largely self-taught but full of ambition, a young Charlie Parker dared to sit in with members of Count Basie's band. The beginner was having so much trouble playing a fluent solo, that drummer Jo Jones did his version of the Gong Show, throwing his cymbal at the feet of the youngster (Parker: "They laughed me off the bandstand, laughed at me so hard I had to leave the club."). He began a practice regimen that included playing and soloing in all 12 keys. One of the laughing musicians, Eddie Barefield, recounted: "I was in Kansas City when he first came out to play. He sounded so bad that we wouldn't let him play. He went down to Oklahoma and stayed about six months with Buster Smith, who really taught him a lot about his playing. And he came back and JUST WASHED EVERYBODY OUT." There are two morals to this story: (1) all the giants of jazz that we want to emulate were all struggling beginners at one time, and (2) practice and persistence do pay off.

What They Said About Bird

"The first time I heard Bird play, it hit me right between the eyes." John Coltrane

"He was the other half of my heartbeat." Dizzy Gillespie

"Bird's mind and fingers work with incredible speed. He can imply four chord changes in a melodic pattern where another musician would have trouble inserting two." Leonard Feather

"Louis Armstrong, Charlie Parker." Miles Davis summing up the history of jazz.

Birdsongs

Charlie Parker compositions which became part of the jazz repertoire: "Anthropology," "Billie's Bounce," "Ornithology," "Ko Ko," "Donna Lee," "Parker's Mood," and "Yardbird Suite."

Something To Think About: What Informs Your Playing?

Here's something amazing: Fifty years after Charlie Parker's death, musician's are still studying and analyzing his solos. His ability to put forth idea after new idea at impossibly fast tempos still astounds listeners today. Yet is wasn't the speed of his playing that was significant, it was his ideas. Oftentimes Parker would place quotes in his solos that came from sources that indicate a very broad musical base. It is obvious that Parker was an insatiable student of all types of music. The music of his predecessors, traditional folk songs, opera, modern orchestral composers (especially Stravinsky), and the pop songs of the day all colored and influenced his playing. Which brings us to the question: How broad is your musical base? How many types of music do you listen to? Which stations are preset in your car radio? How many styles of music does your CD collection reflect? Maybe its time to step out of your musical "comfort zone" and go exploring. The results can only be positive and helpful.

Dig Deeper

"The Essential Charlie Parker" (Polygram Records #517173/ASIN: B0000IE03). A collection of Parker gems from the late '40s to early '50s, and a kind of "best of" CD that makes this valuable to anyone new to Parker. Songs include: "Now's The Time," "Confirmation," "Just Friends," "I Got Rhythm," "K.C. Blues," "April In Paris," "Okiedoke," and others. Released in 1992.

Quote

To interject a phrase from another composition into one's own solo.

Dizzy. One of the premier ambassadors of bebop, and jazz in general, John Birks Gillespie was born on October 21, 1917, in Cherraw, South Carolina. While a young teenager, Gillespie and his family moved to Philadelphia. Gillespie played in bands there for two years before moving to New York. Like his fellow boppers, it was in New York where he developed and honed his style, eventually becoming an in-demand trumpet player, noted for his fresh soloing ideas. He toured Europe with the Teddy Hill Orchestra, and upon his return, joined the Cab Calloway Orchestra. Gillespie regarded the job a prime gig, and stayed with Calloway for nearly three years. Following an infamous misunderstanding over a spitball, Gillespie left the band in 1941, and joined the Earl "Fatha" Hines band the following year. The gig was especially propitious in that Charlie Parker joined the band about the same time. Soon, the two were in a musical partnership. Gillespie later wrote, "I guess Charlie Parker and I had a meeting of the minds, because both of us inspired each other." A gig with Billy Ekstine put him on 52nd Street, which became known as the training ground for the new music soon to be called bebop.

Dizzy Gillespie

In 1944, Gillespie finally had his own quintet, which at turns included Charlie Parker on alto sax, Bud Powell on piano, and Max Roach on drums. In 1953 Gillespie took his group to Toronto to play Massey Hall. The concert was recorded by bassist Charles Mingus, who was subbing for regular bassist Oscar Pettiford. Some critics called the recording "the greatest jazz concert ever." It certainly was instrumental in presenting modern jazz to other musicians as well as lay people.

Gillespie also popularized the blending of latin and jazz elements by using a conga player and employing Latin rhythms, producing an exciting Afro-Cuban style of jazz. Many awards and accomplishments later, Gillespie, at an age when most people slow down, kept up a tremendous pace of gigs all over the world. Gillespie died in his sleep on October 6, 1993 at the age of 75.

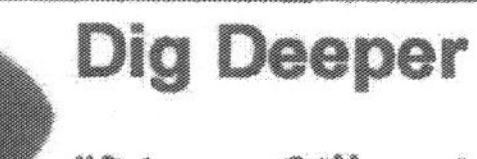

Dig Deeper

"Dizzy Gillespie - Greatest Hits" (RCA #68499/ ASIN: B000003G31). The title is what it is, including "Night In Tunisia," a song every jazz musician must be familiar with. Also recommended: "Oscar Peterson & Dizzy Gillespie (Pablo #2310740/ ASIN: B000000XJO). Two great musicians play and respond to each other with incredible spontaneity. "Con Alma," "Caravan," "Autumn Leaves," more.

Dizzy's Horn and Cheeks

The horn: someone sat on it at a party. Dizzy liked the bent angle and had another made just like it. The cheeks: years of intense playing gave his cheeks a ballooning effect.

Monk. When musicians and critics describe the playing and compositions of Thelonious Monk, words like angular, strange, choppy, and unexpected are used. Back in the days when bop was new to the jazz world, Monk was even more misunderstood. Even some of his bebop peers didn't understand him or his music. Some thought he had bad technique and his songs had "wrong" notes. Yet today his music is played and appreciated with the same degree of esteem musicians have for any other jazz legend, like Louis Armstrong or Duke Ellington. Though he is associated historically with Charlie Parker and Dizzy Gillespie, his music sounds quite different from theirs. His compositions seem to have their own logic. One thing is sure: his music grows on you.

Monk's Dream

Thelonious Monk was born in Rocky Mount, North Carolina on October 10, 1917. His family moved to New York when he was four years old. Early musical experiences included playing in church, at Harlem parties, and playing piano for a traveling medicine man show. While in his 20s, he was a working sideman and the house pianist at Minton's, the bop training ground. In 1947, Monk began recording for Blue Note Records, and the first period of compositions emerged. In 1951, he was busted for drugs (it is said that he took the rap for his friend Bud Powell) and his cabaret card was taken away - he could not play New York's clubs for six years. He occasionally performed elsewhere and continued to record. He returned to the New York scene in 1957 with a new quartet that featured saxophonist John Coltrane. By the early '60s, Monk and his music were more accepted, and he toured throughout the United States, Japan, and Europe. In 1964, he even made the cover of *Time* magazine (only five musicians have done so).

In the late '60s and early '70s, Monk's appearances were more intermittent, with periods of inactivity. Long known for his eccentric behavior, we now understand more the mental illness he was suffering from. He made appearances at the Newport Jazz Festival, and his last public appearance in July of 1976. After suffering a stroke, he died in February 17, 1982.

Monk's piano style was unique in that it was at odds with the prevailing bop piano style of the day. Instead of rapidly flowing lines, Monk's playing was often punctuated by silence. His phrasing was intensely rhythmical, with shifting accents, he used notes that clashed with each other, and often would lay out completely during another musician's solo.

Sideman

A musician who plays a supporting role in a musical performance. An analogy: think of a supporting actor's role in a play or movie.

Lay out

To not play.

What They Said About Monk

"Everything I learned about jazz back then I learned from Dizzy and Monk." Miles Davis

"He had his own style of playing and his own technique, just as he had his own style of harmonic usage of time relationships, of dress, speech, walk, and mannerism. He was a total individualist and as a friend of mine remarked to us after the concert, 'It sounds as if that music is coming right out of his head into the piano.'" David Amram

"Thelonious Monk is not only the greatest of modern jazz. . . he is the greatest composer since Bartok" A Berlin newspaper, quoted in the Criss-Cross sleeve notes

"A Monk tune is so profound that you have to be thinking about every note that you play. The whole tune is compositionally tight. Each little inflection - where Monk places an eighth note on one side of the beat or another - means something. Improvising on a Monk tune is like an extension of the composition, because that's the way Monk plays, and that's the way he writes. So, your improvisation grows out of the piece itself." Fred Hersch

Monk's Music

"'Round Midnight," "Straight No Chaser," "Blue Monk," "Ruby My Dear," "In Walked Bud," "Well, You Needn't," and "Epistrophy" are among his many original compositions. Monk also applied his unique style to the music of others: He did an album of Duke Ellington music, and redid standards such as "Just A Gigolo."

Dig Deeper

Monk's Dream (see box previous page - Sony #63536/ASIN: B00006G099, released in 1963). Monk in great form with a great band: tenor Charlie Rouse, bassist John Ore, and drummer Frankie Dunlap had been together for two before recording this. **Brilliant Corners** (Original Jazz Classics #26/ASIN: B000000Y1H, released in 1956). Earlier recording with drummer Max Roach, trumpeter Clark Terry, and the intense Sonny Rollins on tenor sax. **Thelonious Monk With John Coltrane** (Original Jazz Classics #39/ASIN: B000000Y2F). Released one year after Brilliant Corners, and with a new band that featured of course John Coltrane, with bassist Wilbur Ware, and drummer Shadow Wilson. CD also features outtakes from an octet with Coleman Hawkins.

If You Can't Say Something Nice About Someone. . .

Bassist Al McKibbon went on tour with Monk, and let's just say there were some awkward moments: "In about three months Monk said maybe two words. I mean, literally, maybe two words. He didn't say 'Good morning,' 'Goodnight,' 'What time?' Nothing. Why, I don't know. He sent word back after the tour was over that the reason he couldn't communicate was that Art Blakey and I were so ugly."

Bud. Earl "Bud" Powell was to bop piano what Charlie Parker was to the saxophone. Born in New York in 1924, Powell was trained as a classical pianist (he maintained a lifelong veneration for Bach) and was playing by the age of six. With the encouragement of Thelonious Monk, Powell began developing a bop piano style that became the model for hundreds of other pianists. Just as jazz drumming evolved from a strict two-beat feel into a flowing, swinging, looser, four-beat feel, Powell moved away from the time-keeping chord punching function of the left hand to a sparser, more intermittent comping, not unlike what bop drumming comping became with the snare and bass drum. His right hand solo lines were extremely creative, fast and forceful, reminiscent of the lines of Bird and Dizzy. Powell moved to Paris, and formed a trio with Kenny Clarke, another expatriate, and stayed there from from 1959 to 1962. Mental and physical problems made later appearances sporadic and erratic, and he died in 1966.

✓

STEP C 3: READ "BOP DRUMMERS"

BOP DRUMMERS

Two drummers that were pioneers in the development of bebop:

Kenny Clarke. Kenny Clarke was born in Pittsburgh in 1914, to a musical family. He was playing drums from boyhood, and was playing jazz by the time he was 17. He moved to New York in 1935, and played with many bands and tours. His break came when he was asked to manage the house band at Minton's. The jam sessions there were critical to the development of bop. Clarke had been experimenting with the timekeeping role of the drummer, and developed a style that placed the pulse on the cymbal, with the bass drum taking the role of a "third hand," with the snare and bass drum creating a continous non-repetitive conversation, interacting with the soloist as well as a comping device. Some musicians were put off by Clarke's new approach (he lost more than one job because of it). Clarke would respond, "If you are playing, the tempo should be in your head. Don't depend on me."

Kenny Clarke
A true pioneer

Max Roach
The Professor

Max Roach. Max Roach was born in Brooklyn, New York in 1925. His first theater gig was subbing for Duke Ellington's drummer, Sonny Greer, at the Paramount Theater, when he was 18. By 1945, he was an established bop drummer, recording with Charlie Parker, and later with Dizzy Gillespie and Miles Davis. In 1953, he was part of the legendary Massey Hall Concert. His ability to handle the breakneck tempos other bop musicians favored, and his sense of lyricism to his comping and soloing made him a favorite model among drummers. A composer and educator as well, Roach had many laurels, but never rested on them. Roach died August 16, 2007, in Manhatten.

Other bop drummers of the time: Joe Harris, Tiny Kahn, Don Lamond, Roy Haynes, Osie Johnson, Denzil Best, and Shadow Wilson.

Bop Standards

Here are some bop standards which have stood the test of time. In time, you should be familiar with all of them.

A Night in Tunisia
Anthropology
Billie's Bounce
Blue Monk
Bouncin' With Bud
Confrmation
Donna Lee`
Groovin' High
In Walked Bud
Ko Ko
Lester Leaps In
Misterioso
Monk's Dream
Off Minor
Ornithology
'Round Midnight
Salt Peanuts
Scrapple From The Apple
Shaw 'Nuff
Straight, No Chaser
Well You Needn't
Yardbird Suite

Lean On Me:

James Moody and Dizzy Gillespie supporting the legendary Miles Davis for a photo-op.

"I know there must be dozens of James Moody stories, but here's mine. About 10 years ago I stopped by Moody's house to borrow some photos for a jazz drum book I had been working on [this book]. Moody greeted me with a bear hug, told me he was practicing the flute. 'My flute chops are so bad, I have to start with the basics again,' he explained. Oh yeah, I thought. Before his wife Linda arrived to help me with the photos, he tried like the most enthusiastic waitress in the world to serve me. I asked if I drank coffee (I did, he didn't), so he literally tore the pantry apart to find the drink. He gave me a banana, and told me it was good for me. I cannot remember Moody not smiling, and I'm sure everyone else who knew him felt the same."

Letter to Downbeat, April, 2010

Eighth Note Triplet Snare Independence

We are now going to apply these concepts of independence to eighth note triplets. Remember that the jazz ride rhythm and most jazz melodies have an underlying triplet feel. There are six parts to this section:

Keyboard Playing/Phrasing
Triplet Independence: Snare
Two measure comp patterns: Snare
Triplet Independence: Bass Drum
Triplet Independence: Snare and Bass Drum
Two measure comp patterns: Snare and Bass Drum

Follow the instructions carefully for best results.

Step C 4: Keyboard Playing/Phrasing

Follow these directions for pages 118 - 122.

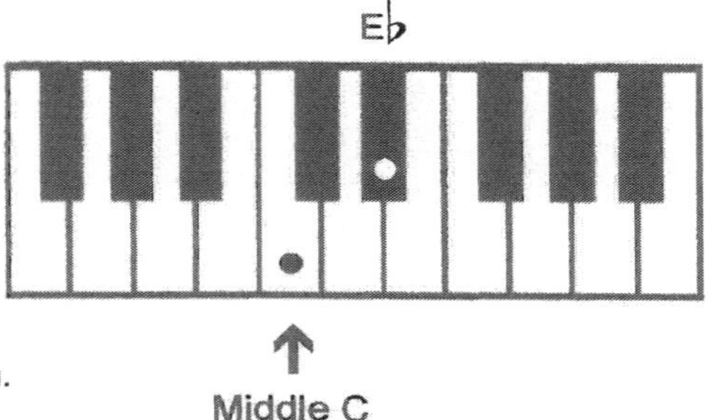

- Find the E♭ above middle c.
- Play Track 1 of the CD.
- Play the **snare rhythms** with your RH, using the E♭. Use any finger of your RH. Play each exercise with a **measure rest** in between. Repeat this sequence for each exercise. For example, exercise 1 looks like this:

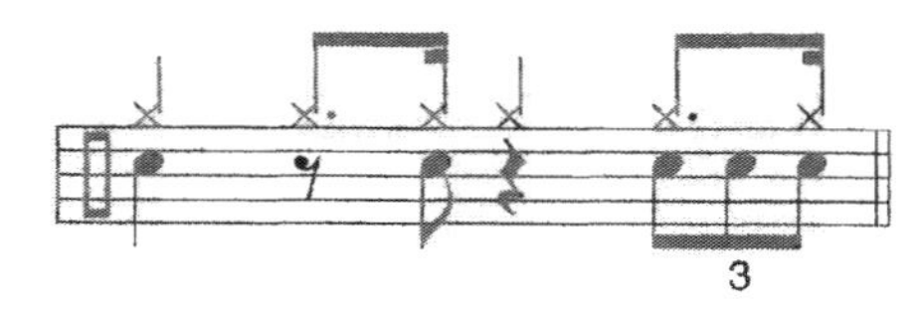

Here's how you will play it on the keyboard:

- Sing along as you play the E♭, using "tah." Match the pitch the best you can.
- Repeat this exercises against tracks 2 through 6 of the CD.

STEP C 5: TRIPLET INDEPENDENCE: SNARE

Follow these directions for pages 118 - 122.

- The exercises on the following 5 pages are to be played on the snare with the LH, against the jazz ride rhythm (RH/CYM) and hi-hat of 2 & 4 (LF).
- Even though it is not notated, keep **very light** quarter notes on the bass drum.
- As you play each exercise, sing the snare part, using "bop," "tah," or "dah." Play each exercise with a **measure of "time"** in between. Repeat this sequence for each exercise. For example, exercise 1 looks like this:

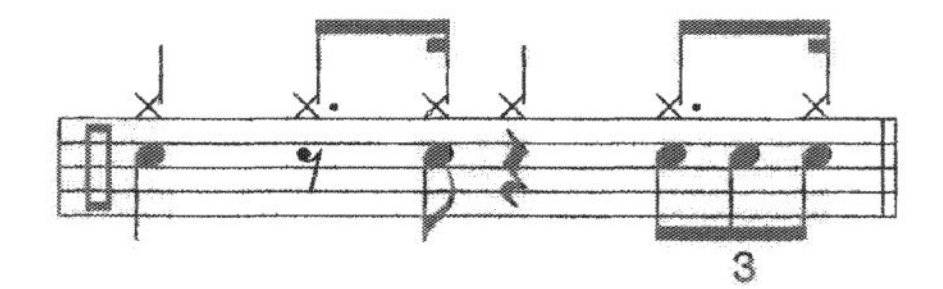

Here's how you will play it on the drumset:

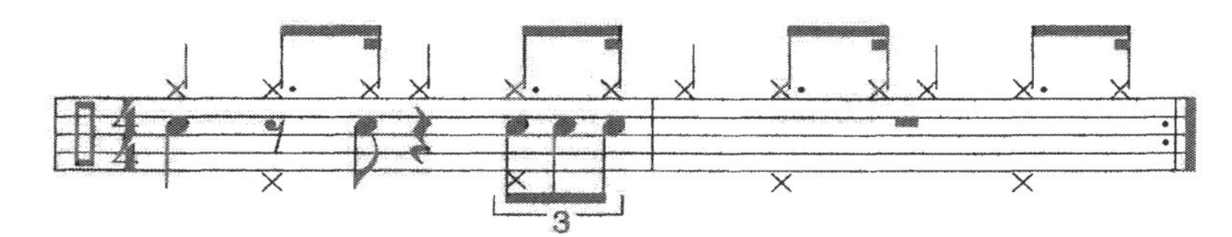

- Play these exercises against tracks 1 through 6 of the CD.

Can One Note Swing?

"A band can really swing when it swings easy. When it can play along like cutting butter. Even a single note can swing."

Count Basie
Ken Burns Jazz, Volume 6

"Swing is a matter of coordination. So when Count Basie says that he can make one note swing, what he means is that the whole preparation and everything in the rhythm and the feeling of the note is coordinated. Louis Armstrong is the master of that, but the Count, just the way he sat at the piano, you could tell before he came in he was going to swing. The way he lifted his hand before he hit the note, he was already swingin'. So bing! When he would hit it. . . you would know we were in for a treat tonight."

Wynton Marsalis
Ken Burns Jazz, Volume 6

Step C 4: Keyboard Playing/Phrasing

Step C 5: Triplet Independence: Snare

1.

2.

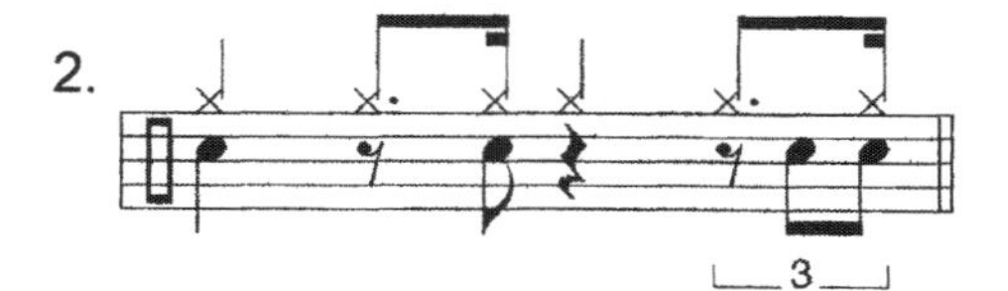

3.

4.

5.

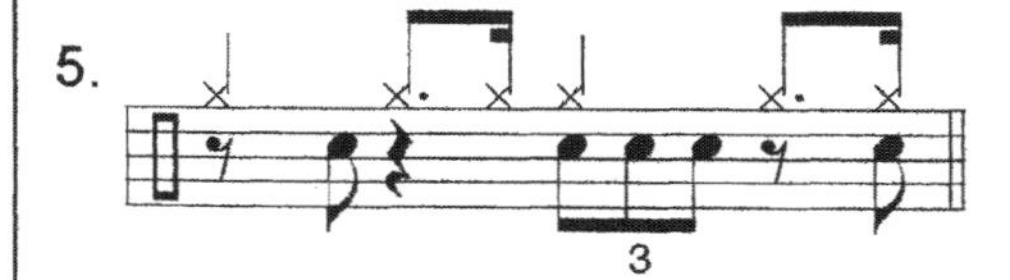

6.

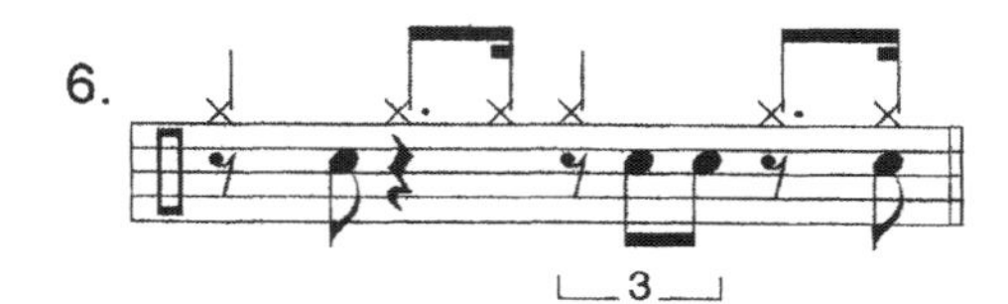

7.

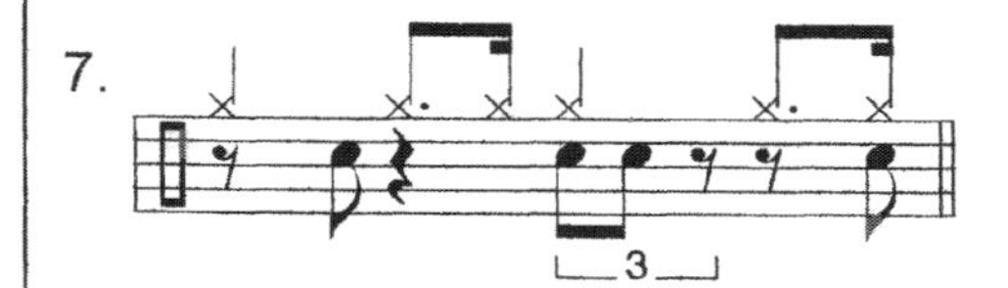

8.

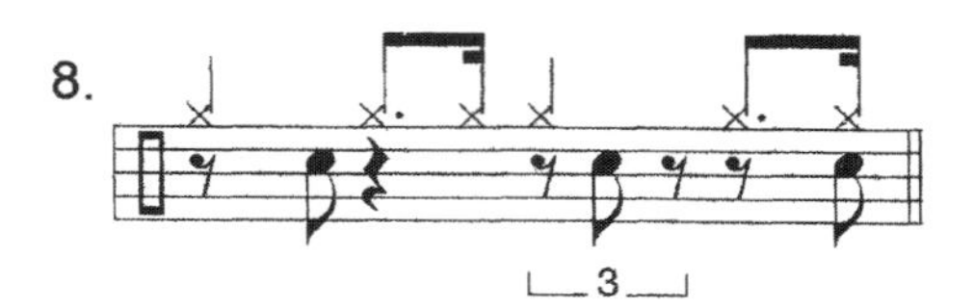

9.

10.

11.

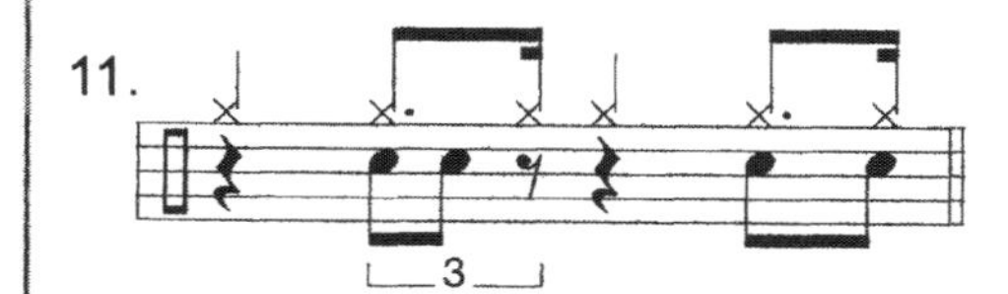

12.

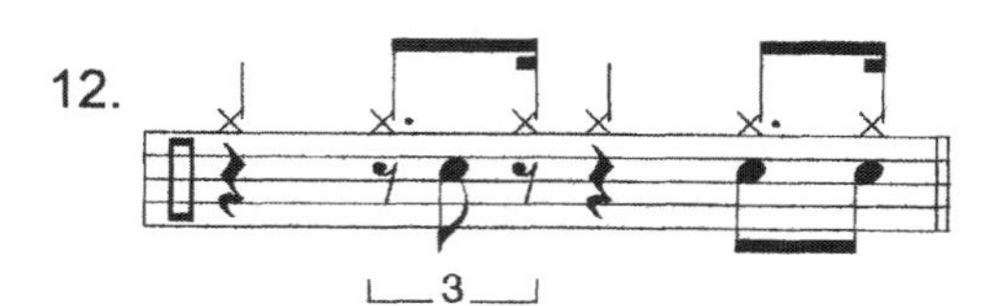

13.

14.

15.

16.

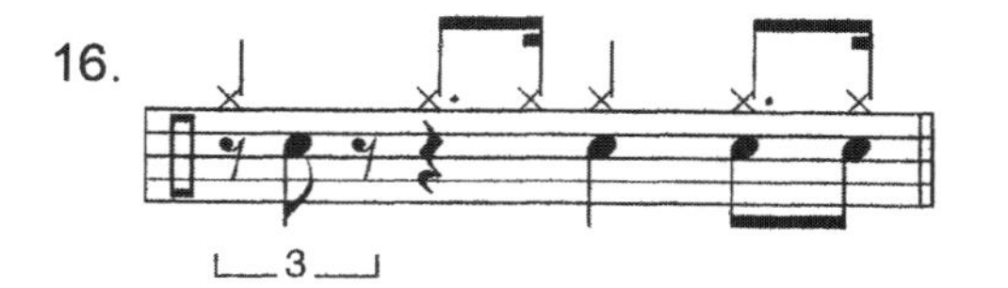

✓

	STEP C 4: KEYBOARD PLAYING/PHRASING
	STEP C 5: TRIPLET INDEPENDENCE: SNARE

17. 

18. 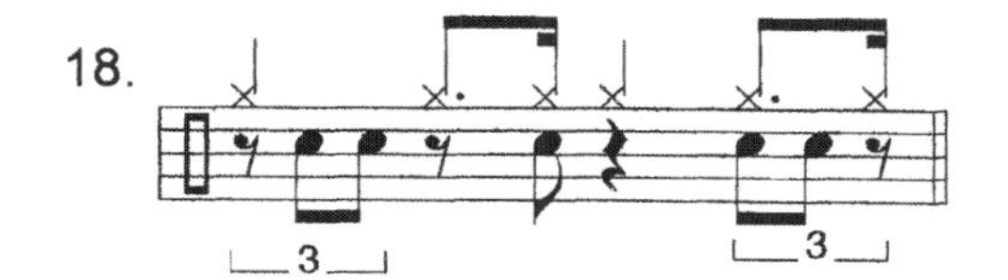

19. 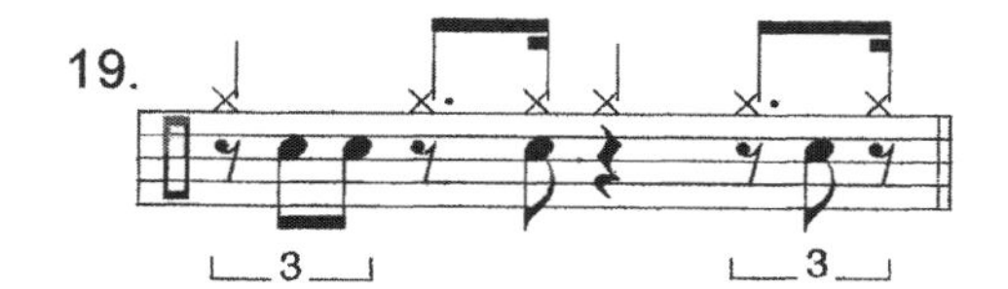

20. 

21. 

22. 

23. 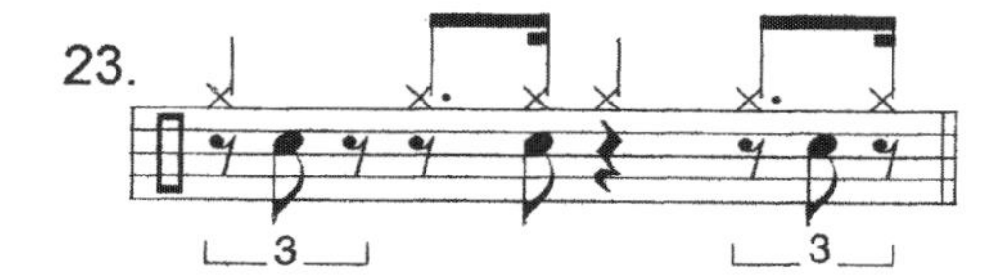

24. 

25. 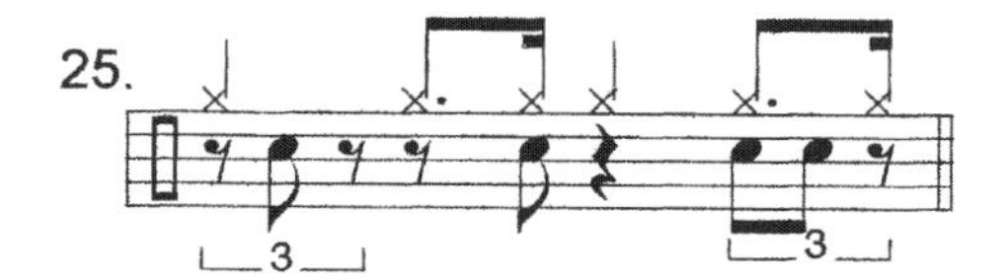

26. 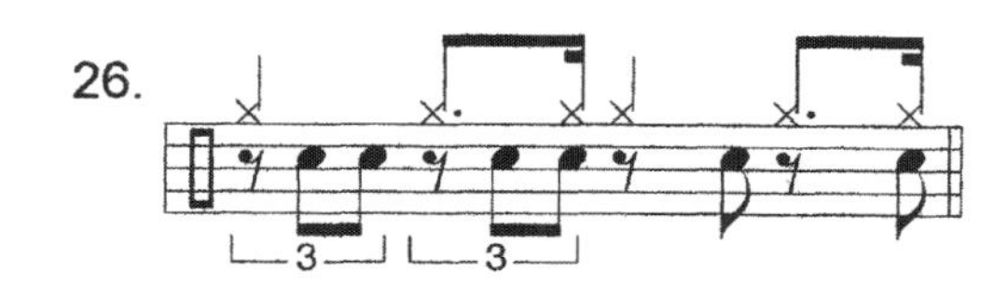

27. 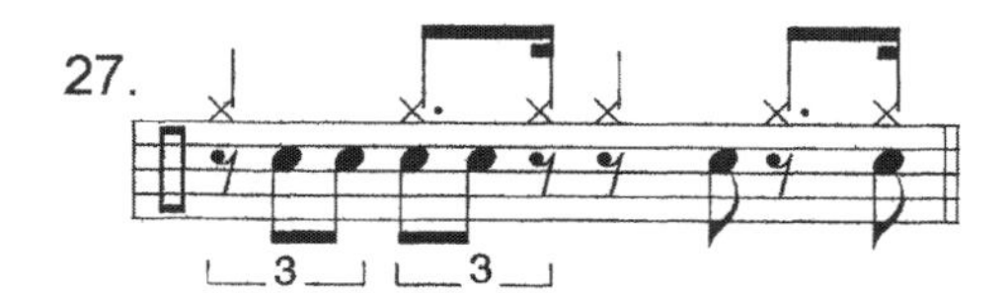

28. 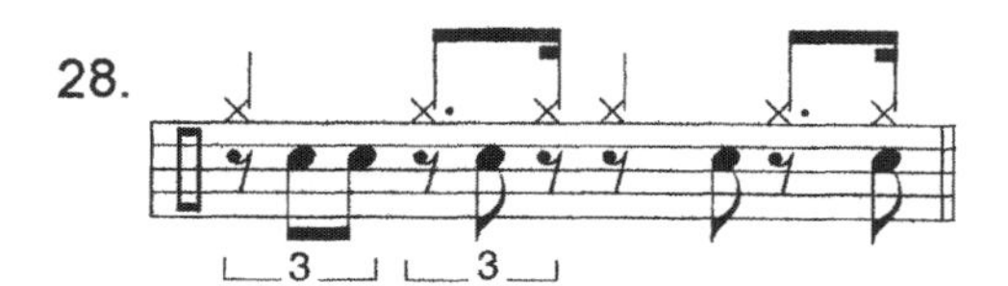

29. 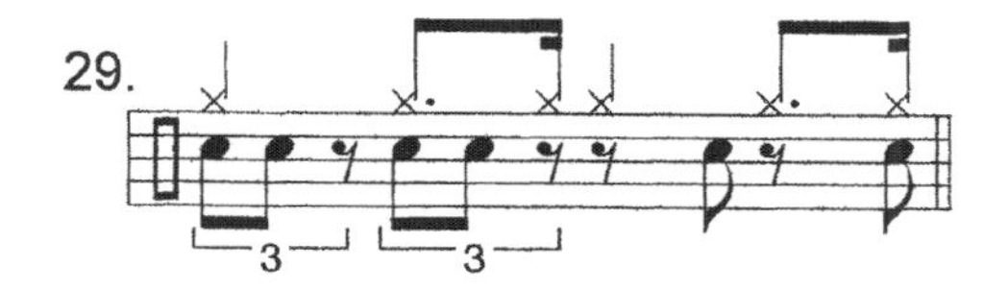

30. 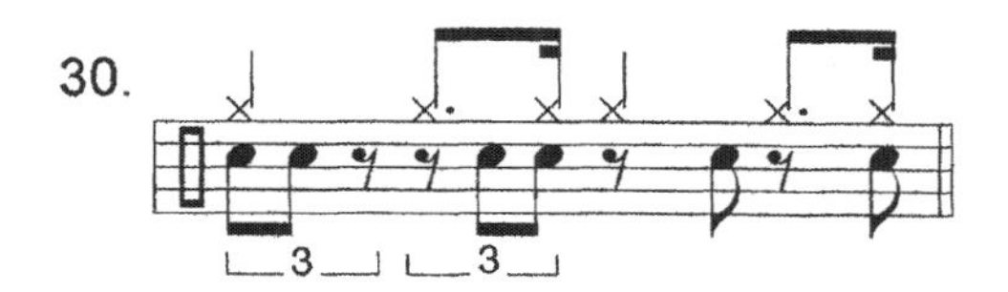

31. 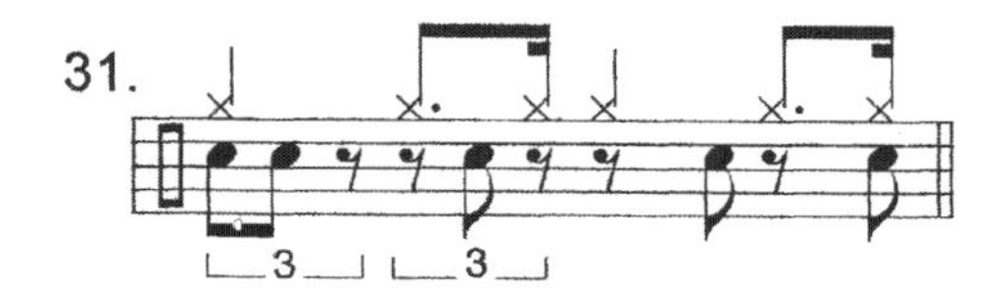

32. 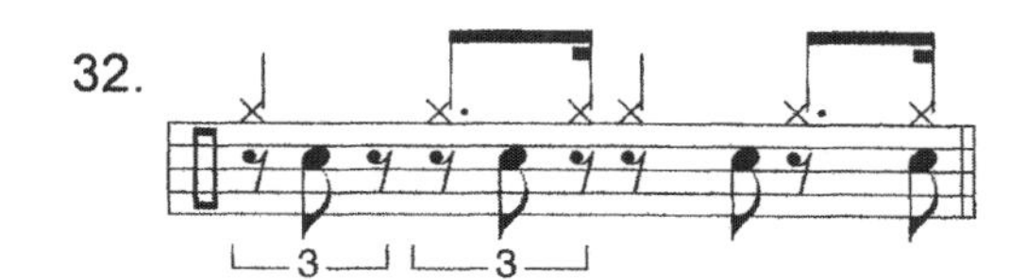

33.
34.
35.
36.
37.
38.
39.
40.
41.
42.
43.
44.
45.
46.
47.
48.

✓

	STEP C 4: KEYBOARD PLAYING/PHRASING
	STEP C 5: TRIPLET INDEPENDENCE: SNARE

49.
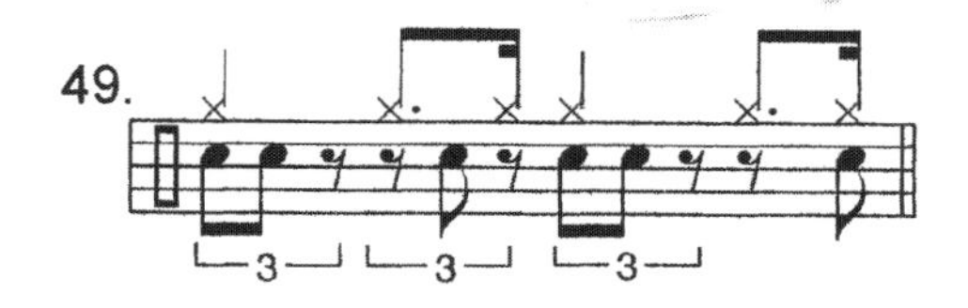

50.
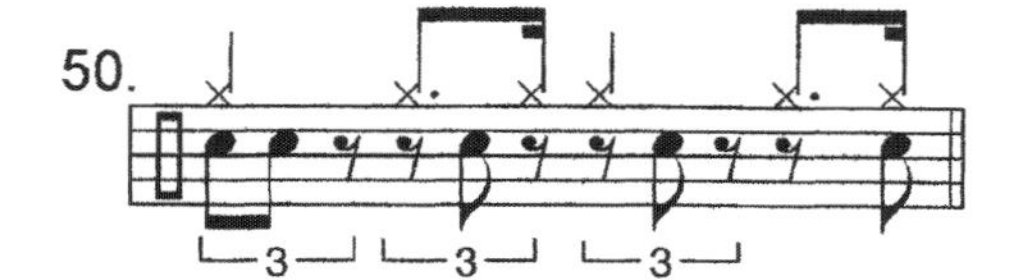

51.
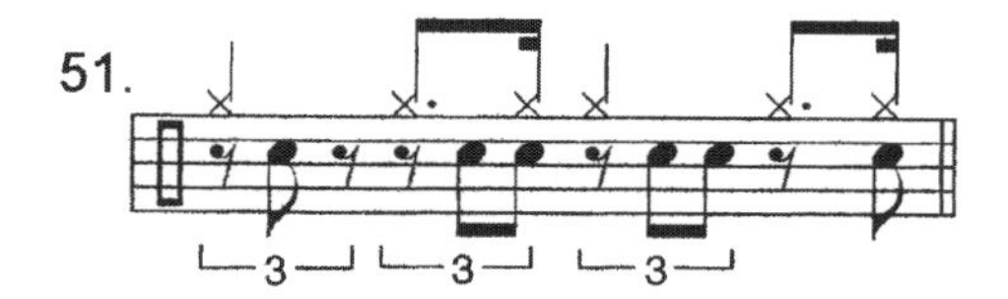

52.
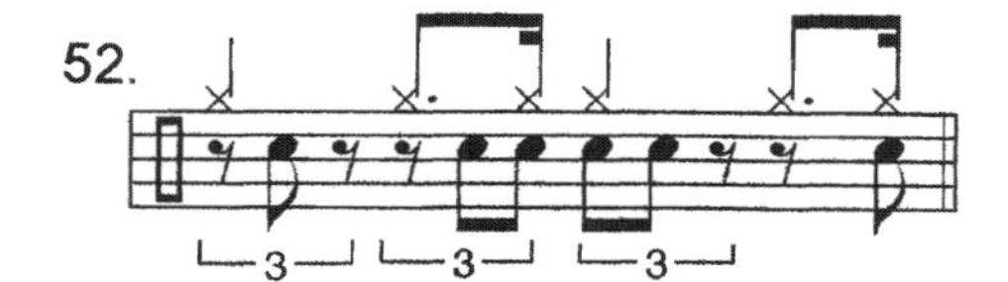

53.
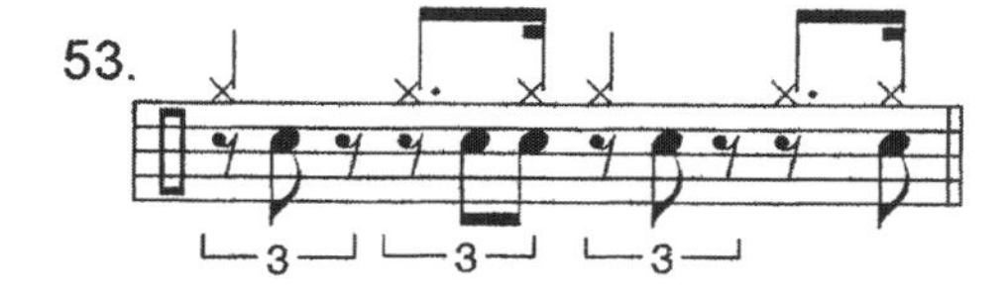

54.

55.

56.
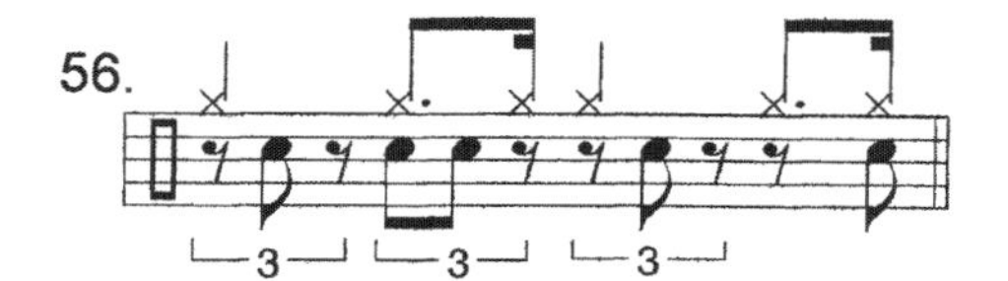

57.
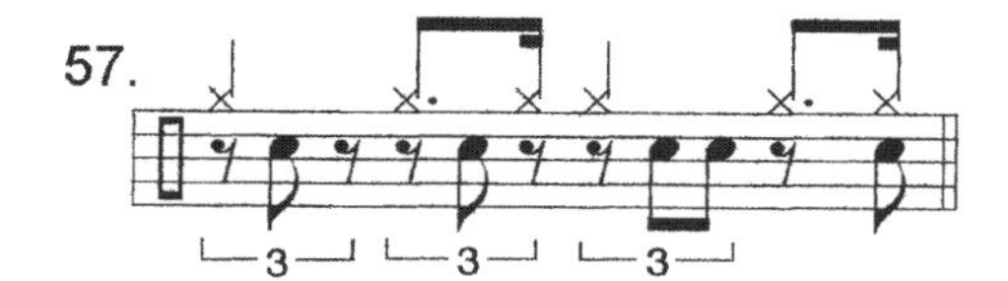

58.
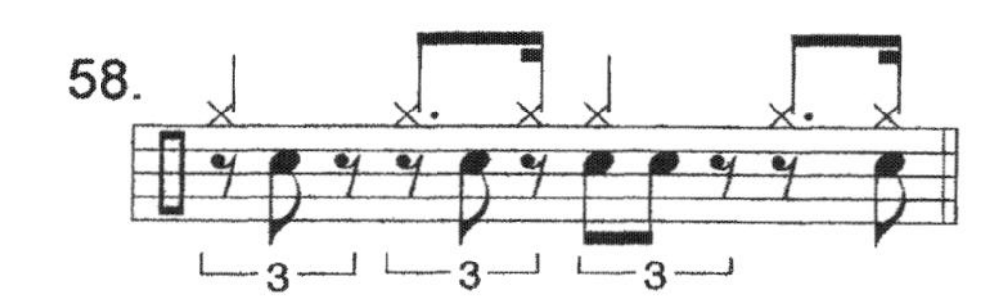

59.

60.
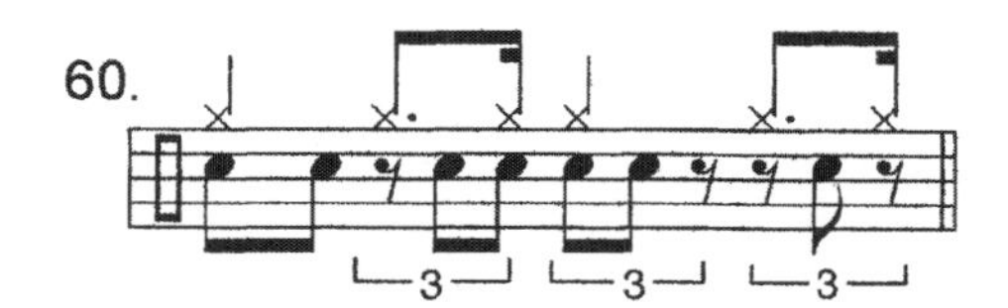

61.
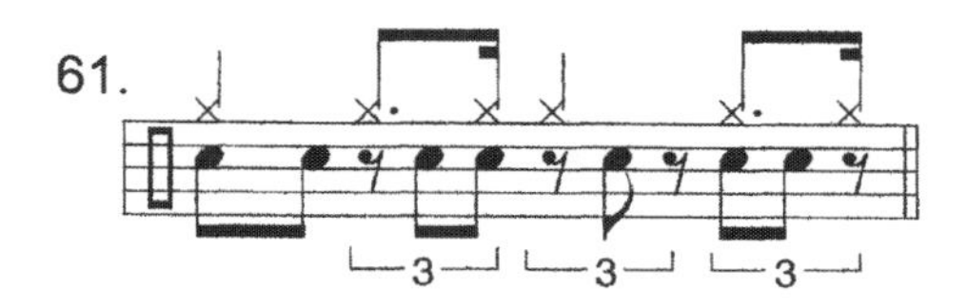

62.
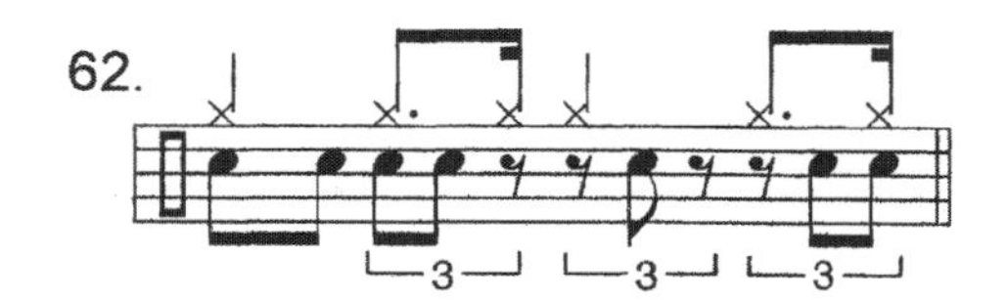

63.

64.
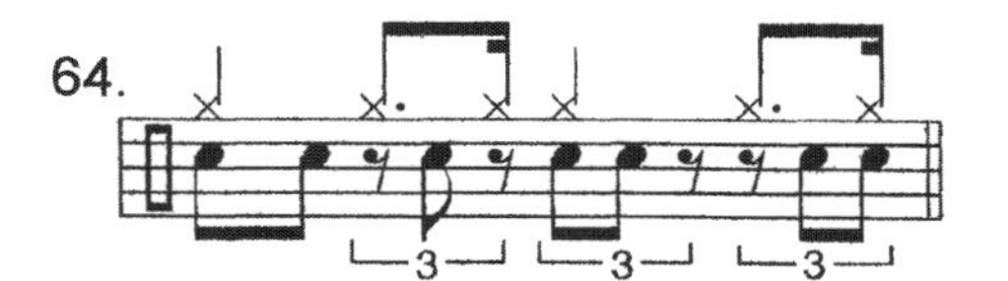

Step C 4: Keyboard Playing/Phrasing

Step C 5: Triplet Independence: Snare

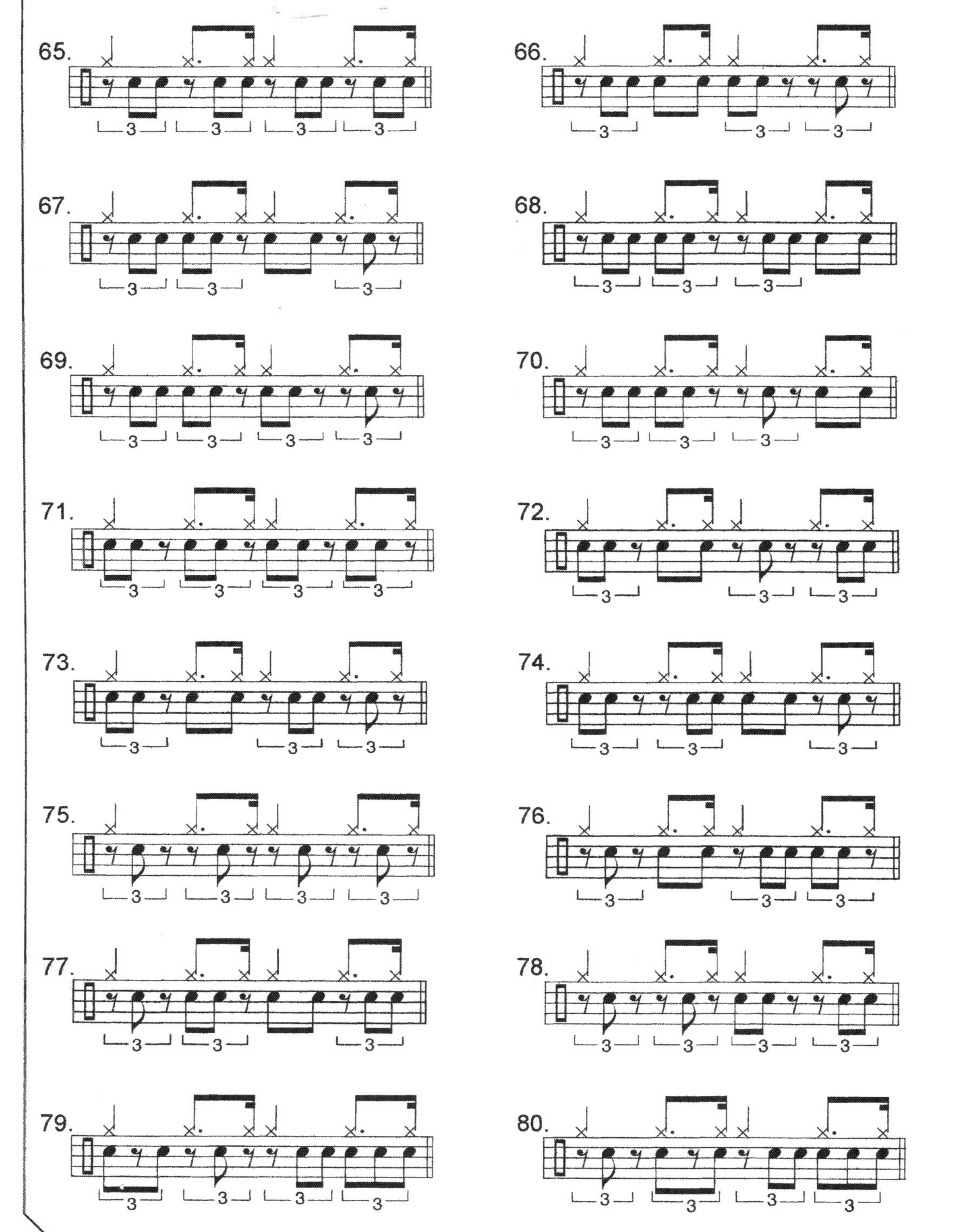

✓

STEP C 6: TRIPLET INDEPENDENCE: BASS DRUM

Follow these directions for pages 124 - 127.

- The exercises on the following four pages are to be played on the BD with the RF, against the jazz ride rhythm (RH/CYM) and hi-hat on 2 & 4 (LF).
- As you play the two exercises, sing the BD part, using "boom" or "bom," and the SN part, using "bop," "tah," or "dah." Play each exercise with a **measure of "time"** in between. Repeat this sequence for each exercise. For example, exercise 1 looks like this:

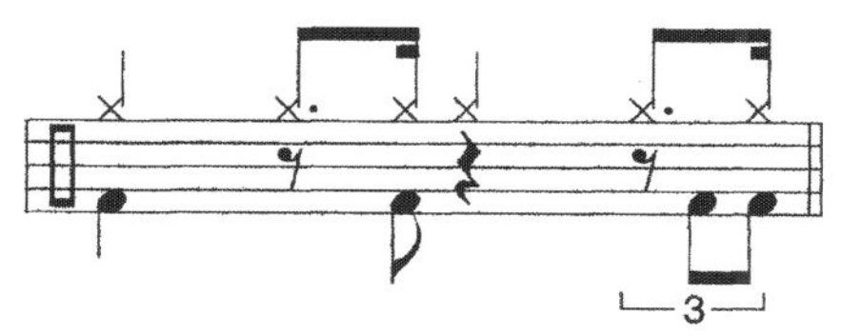

Here's how you will play it on the drumset:

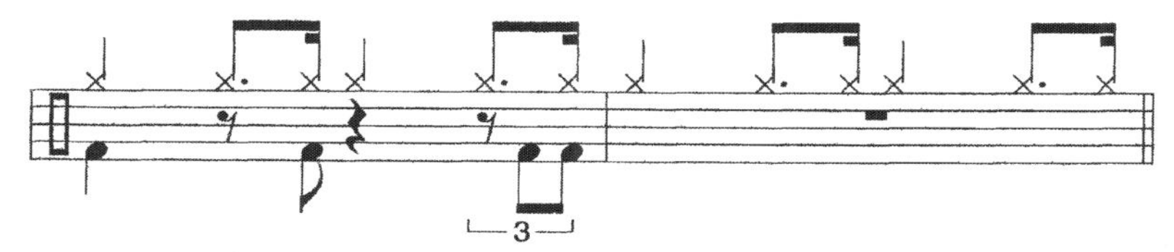

- Play these exercises against tracks 1 through 6 of the CD.

WHAT'S WITH THE BASS DRUM?

There is sometimes confusion about the role of the bass drum in jazz. This is partly due to the changing role of the bass drum in the history of jazz. From the early days of jazz and throughout the big band era, the bass drum's role was that of a palpable keeper of the beat (before bebop, jazz was music to dance to, like much of pop music). With the pioneering drumming of Jo Jones, and the groundbreaking work of Kenny Clarke and Max Roach, the bass drum became what some have described as a "third hand," with the bass drum providing ongoing commentary and comping, much like the snare drum. Many drummers have also developed a hybrid style, with the bass drum keeping light quarter notes, falling out to hit a comp figure or ensemble hit, and then falling back in to light quarter notes. The choice as to which bass drum technique to use is generally based on some concurrent factors: the size of the ensemble (big band, small combo, something in between), style of jazz being played (big band swing, be bop, traditional New Orleans, ballad, etc.), the venue of the performance (recital hall or the local lounge), how the bass player is playing, and the personnel of the group. Also to be considered is the drummer's personal style. Some drummers are comfortable with their right foot maintaining a light pulse around the comp hits and punches - it fits in with their sense of balance and is part of their overall "dance" on the set. Other drummers tend to use the right foot as a "third hand" almost exclusively.

STEP C 6: TRIPLET INDEPENDENCE: BASS DRUM

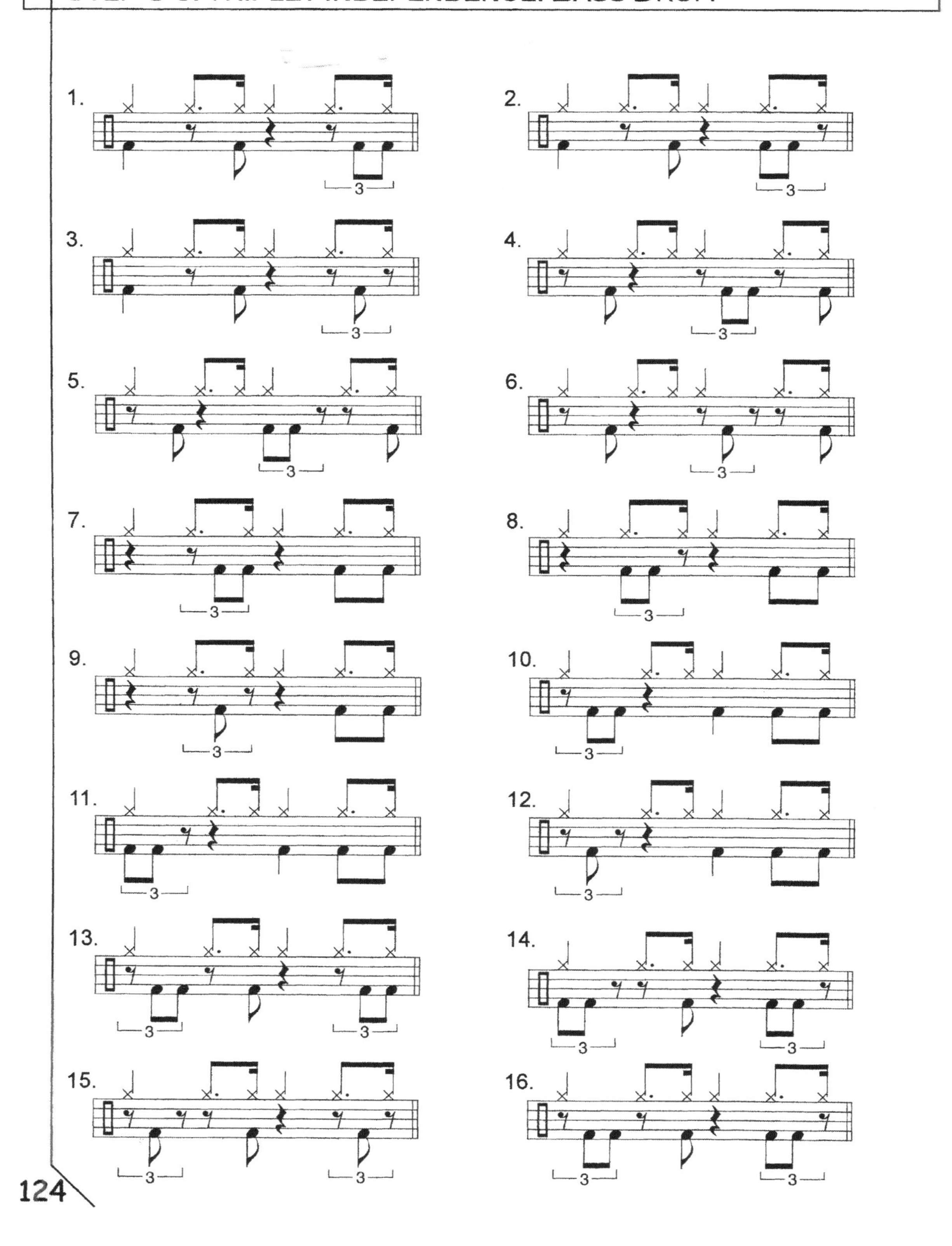

STEP C 6: TRIPLET INDEPENDENCE: BASS DRUM

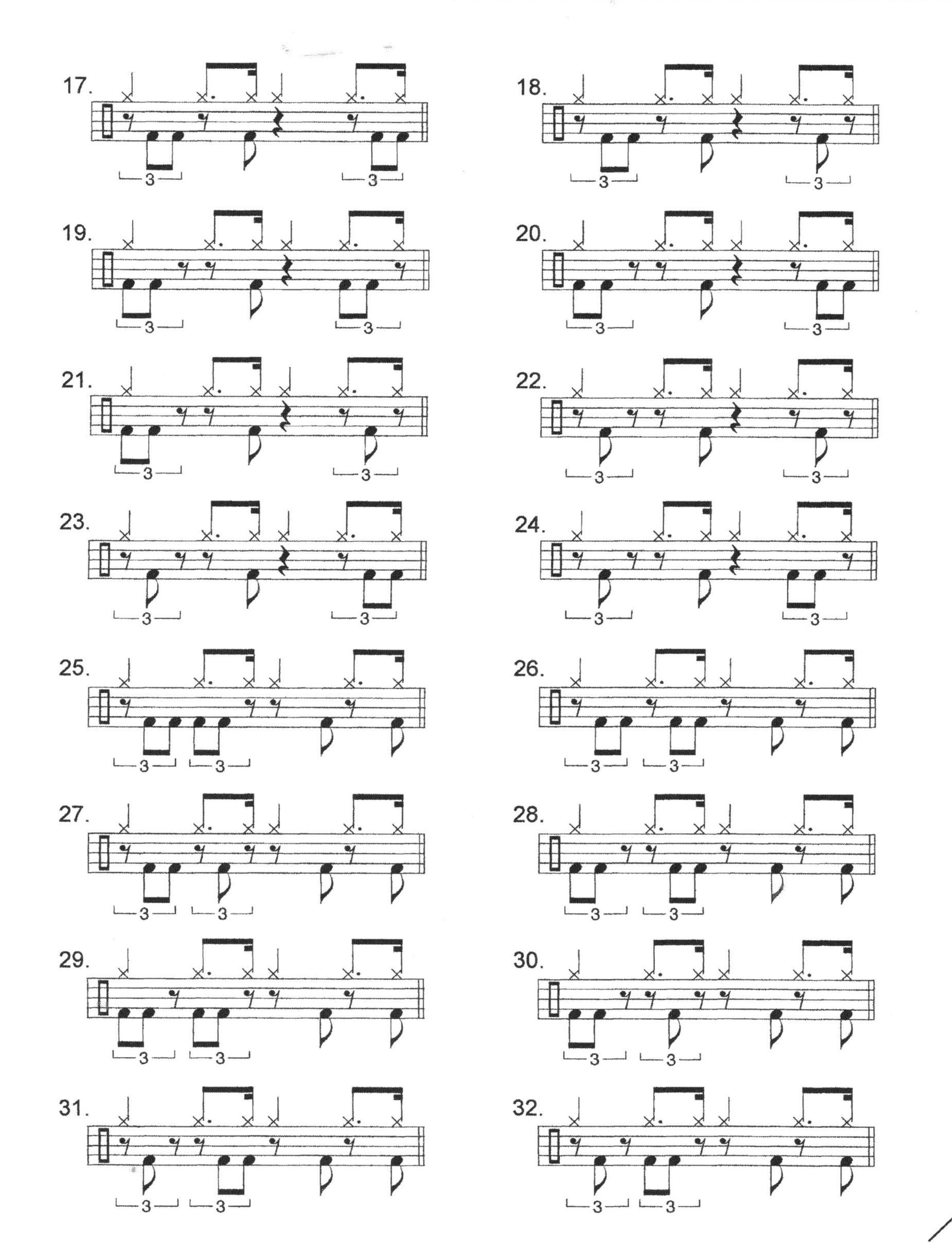

Step C 6: Triplet Independence: Bass Drum

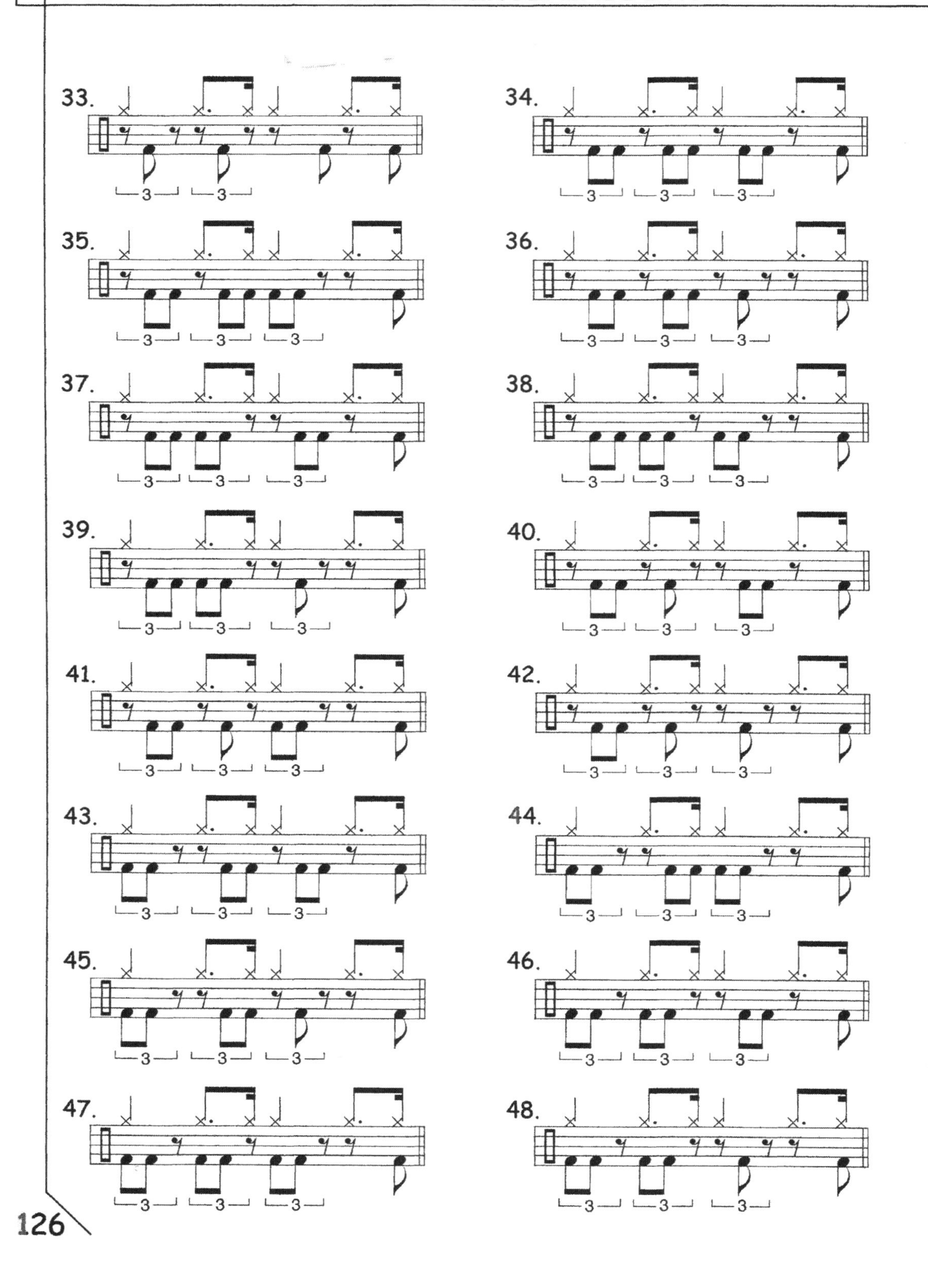

STEP C 6: TRIPLET INDEPENDENCE: BASS DRUM

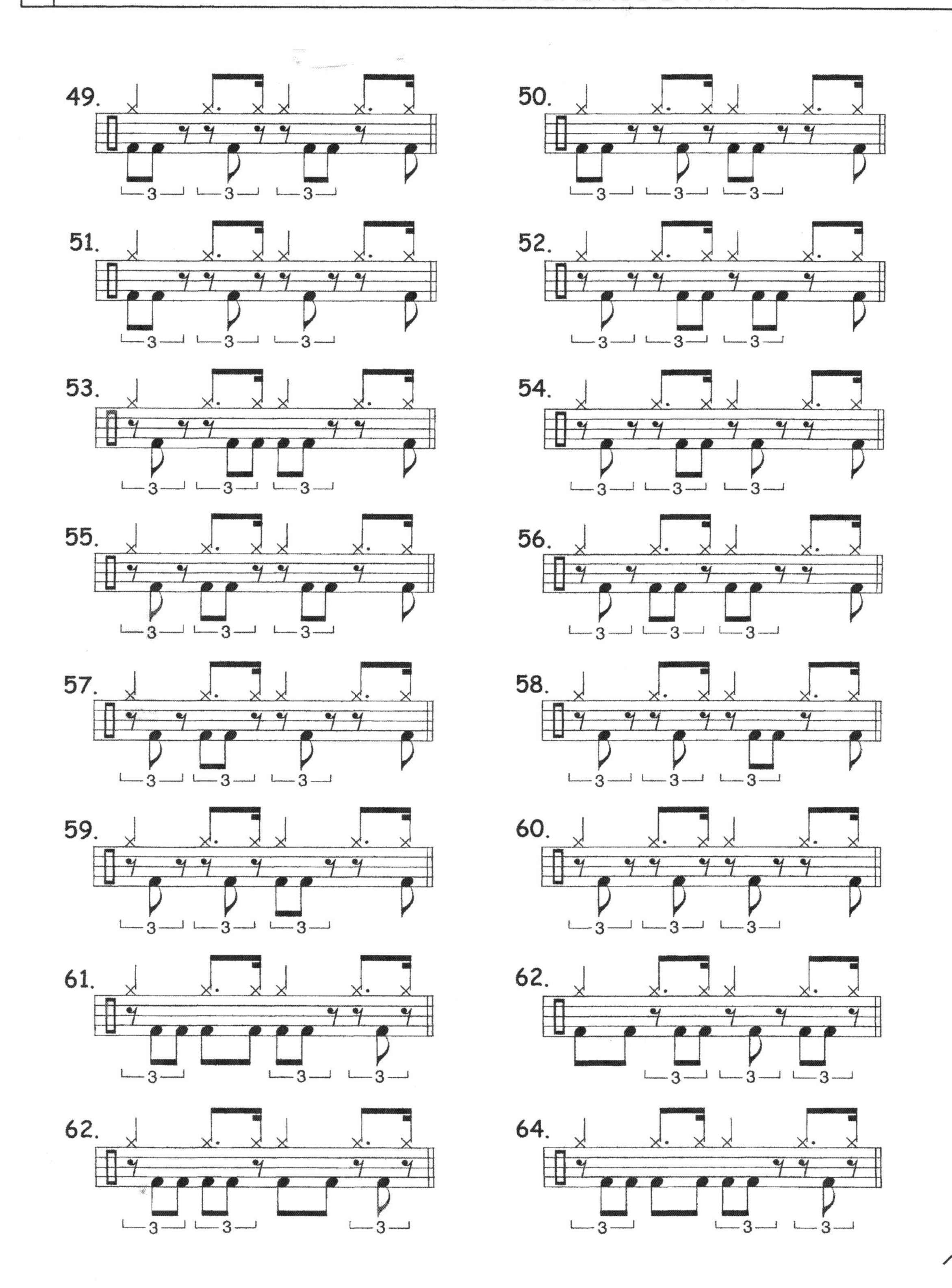

STEP C 7: KEYBOARD PLAYING/PHRASING/MELODY AWARENESS

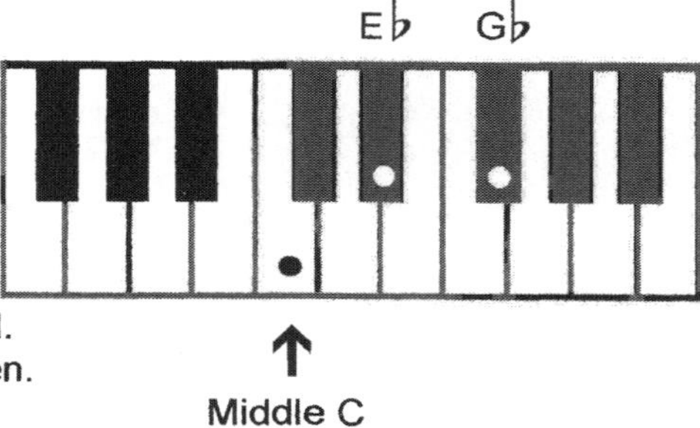

- Follow these directions for pages 129 - 146.
- Find the E♭ and G♭ above middle c.
- Play the **snare and bass drum rhythms** with your RH, using the G♭ for the SN part, and the E♭ for the BD. Use any two fingers of your RH. Play each exercise with a **measure rest** in between. Repeat this sequence for each exercise. For example, exercise 1 looks like this:

Here's how you will play it on the keyboard:

- Sing along as you play the G♭ and E♭, using "dah." Match the pitch the best you can.
- Play these exercises against tracks 1 through 6 of the CD.

STEP C 8: TRIPLET INDEPENDENCE: SNARE AND BASS DRUM

- The exercises on the following pages are to be played on the SN/LH and BD/RF, against the jazz ride rhythm (RH/CYM) and HH on 2 & 4 (LF).
- As you play each exercise, sing the SN and BD part, using "tah" or "dah" for the SN, 'boom" or "bom" for the BD. Play each exercise with a **measure of "time"** in between. Repeat this sequence for each exercise. For example, exercise 1 looks like this:

Here's how you will play it on the drumset:

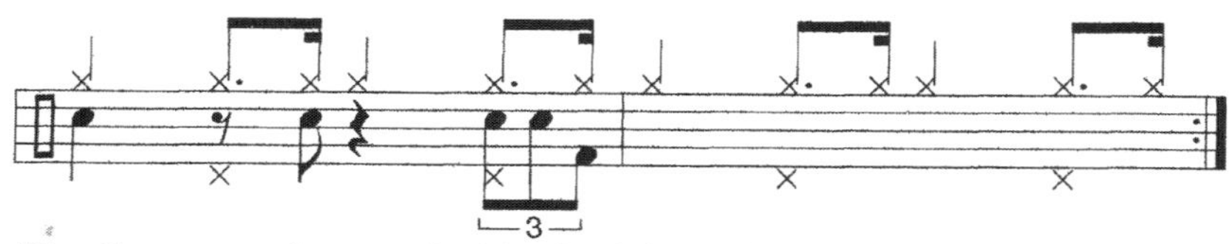

- Play these exercises against tracks 1 through 6 of the CD.

STEP C 8: TRIPLET INDEPENDENCE: SNARE & BASS DRUM

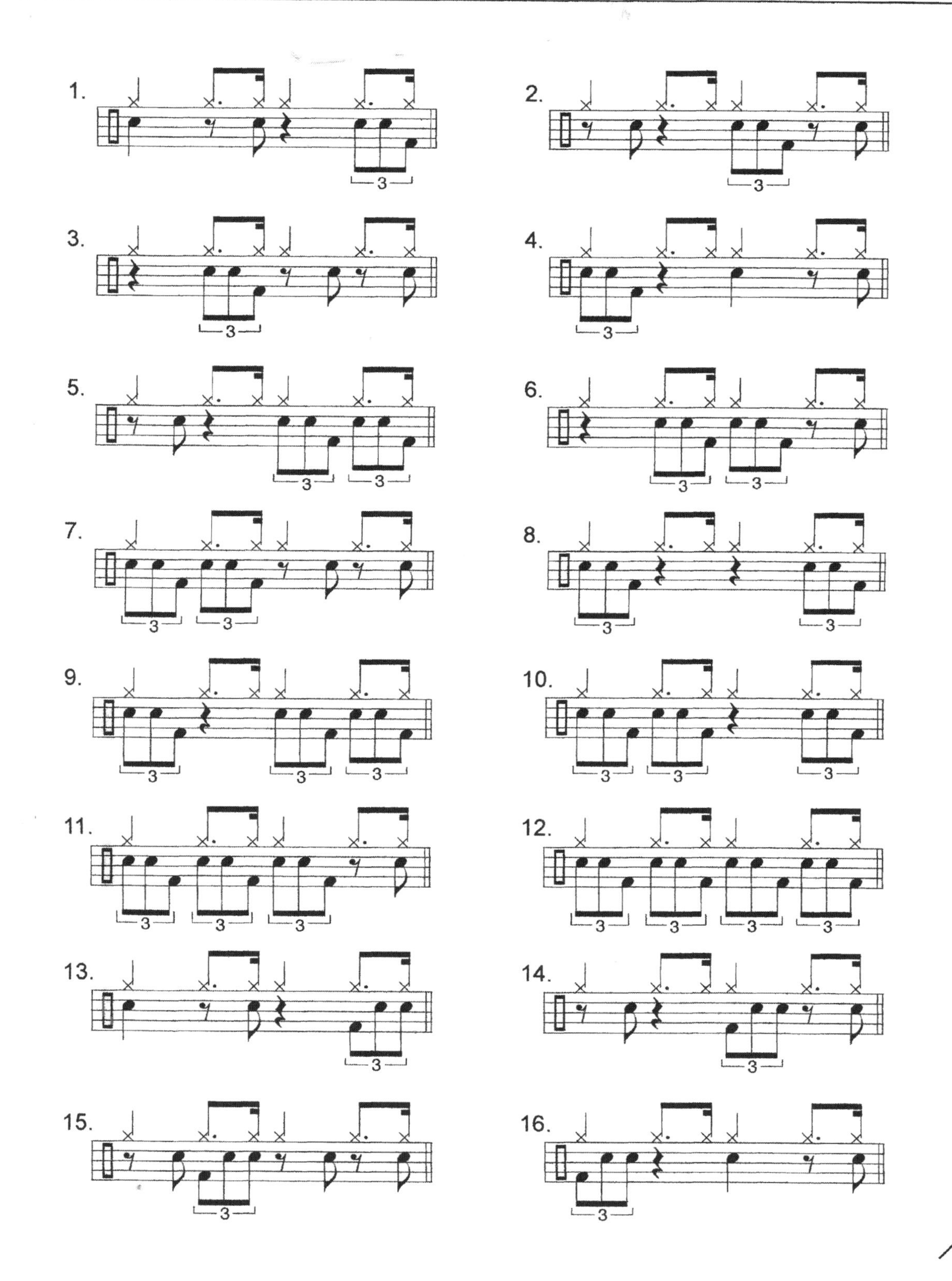

Step C 8: Triplet Independence: Snare & Bass Drum

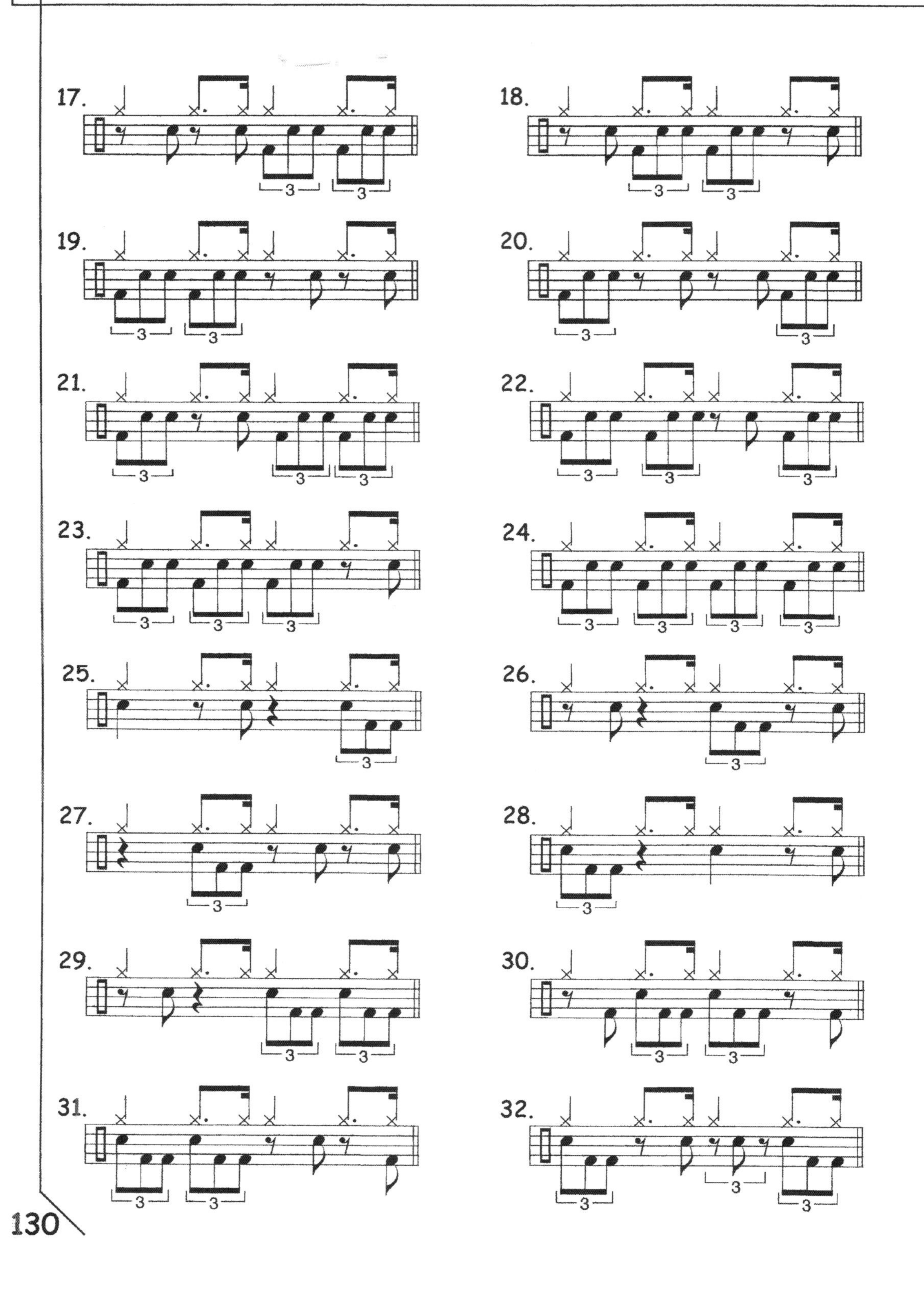

Step C 8: Triplet Independence: Snare & Bass Drum

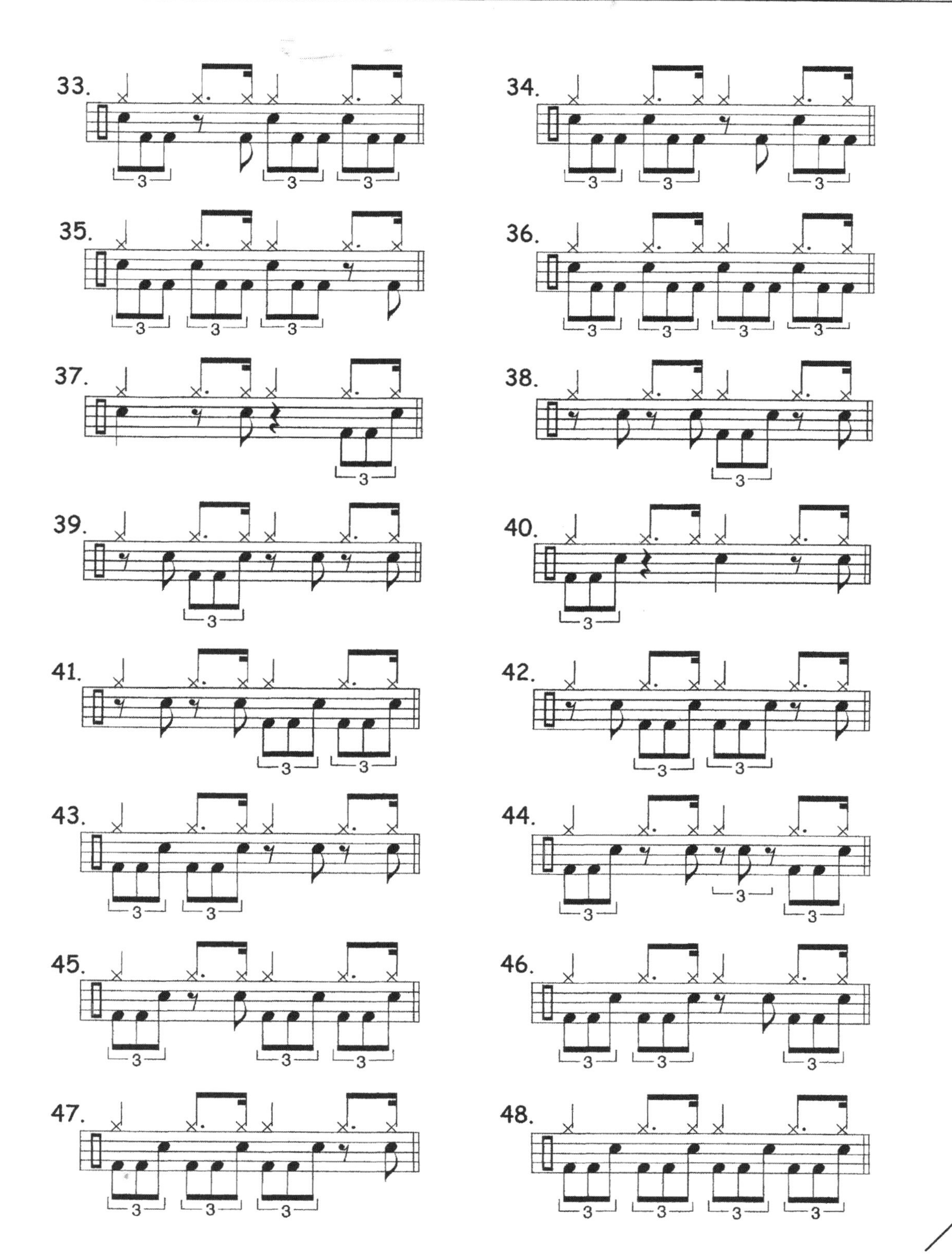

STEP C 8: TRIPLET INDEPENDENCE: SNARE & BASS DRUM

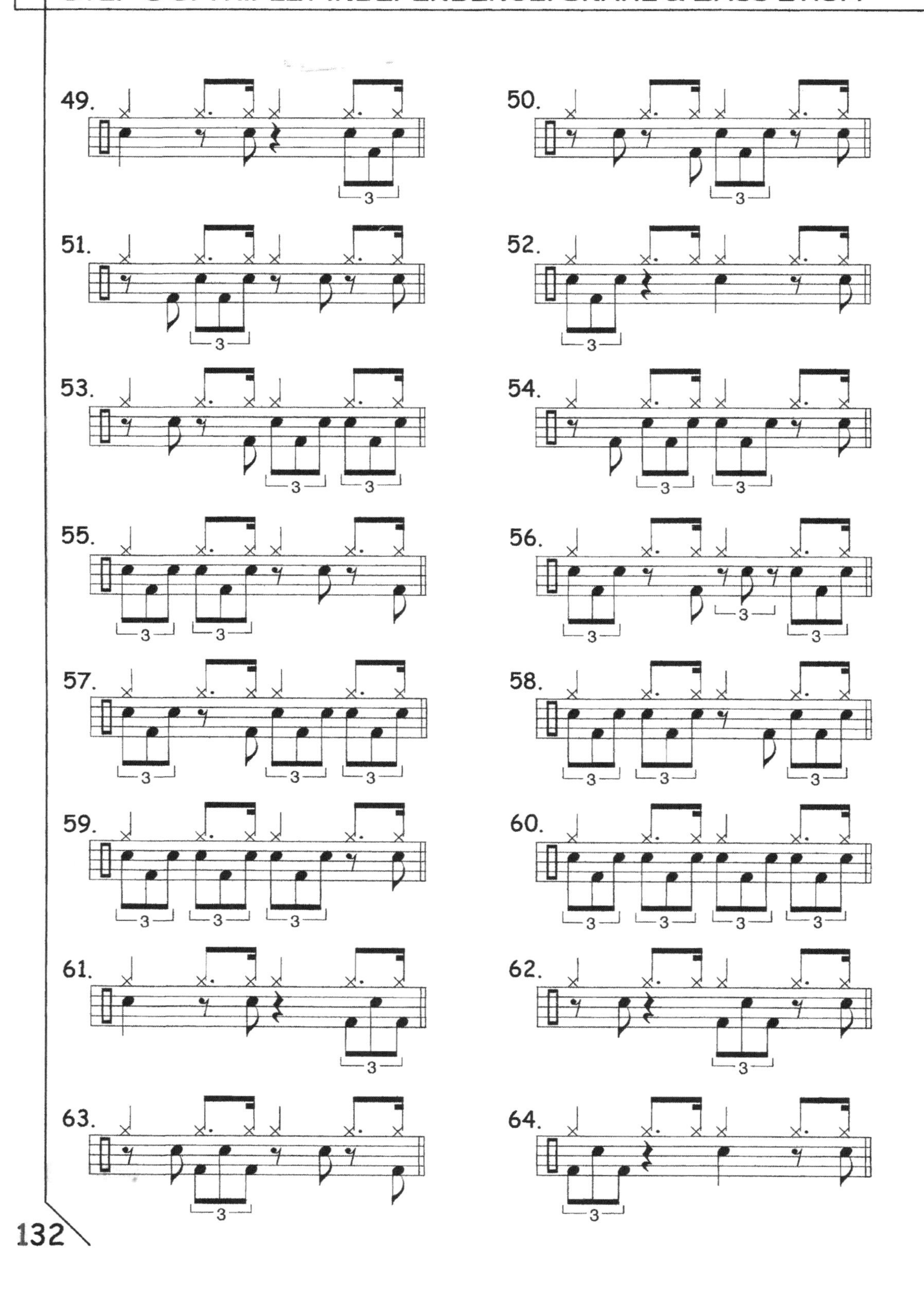

STEP C8 : TRIPLET INDEPENDENCE: SNARE & BASS DRUM

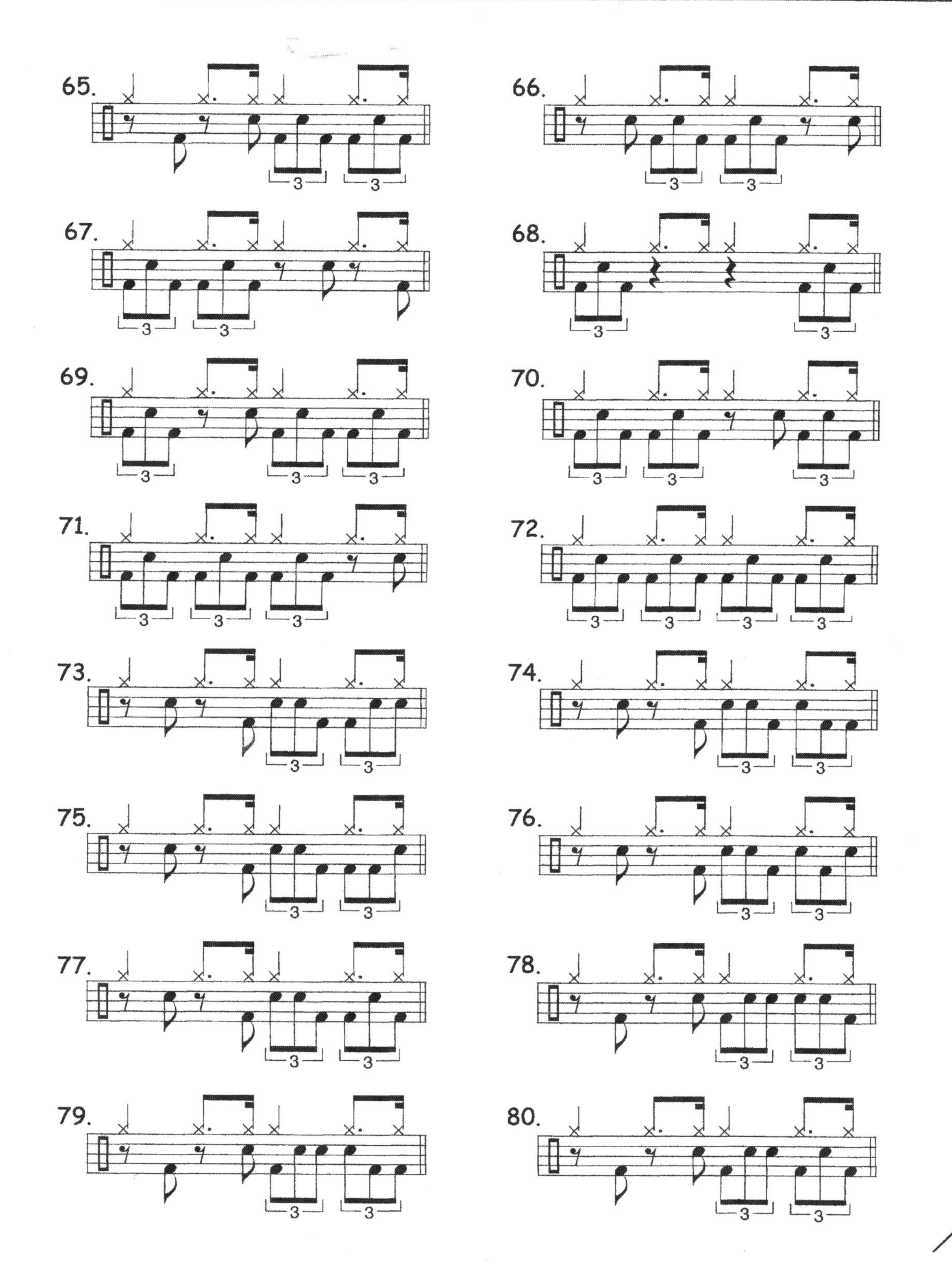

STEP C 8: TRIPLET INDEPENDENCE: SNARE & BASS DRUM

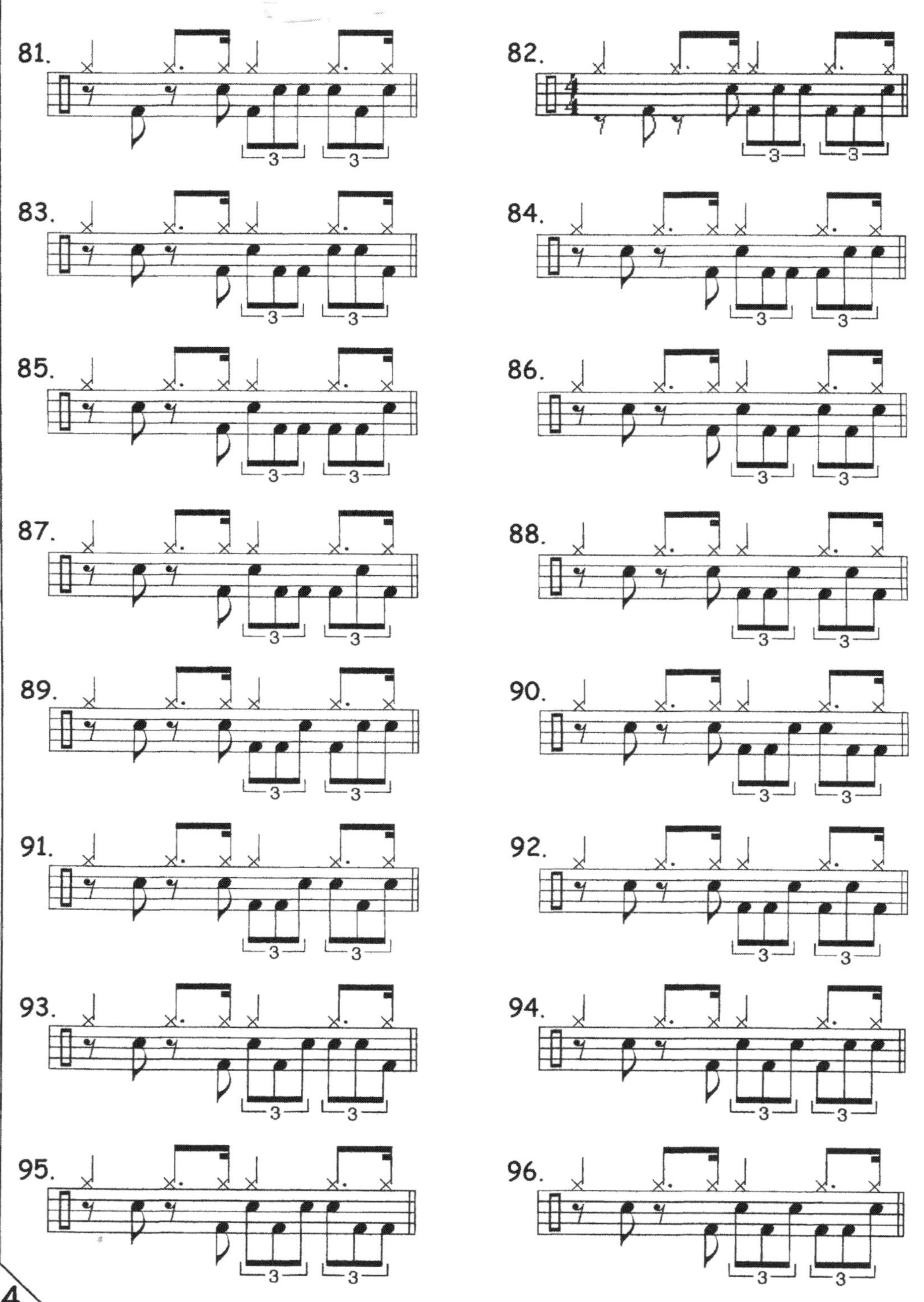

STEP C 8: TRIPLET INDEPENDENCE: SNARE & BASS DRUM

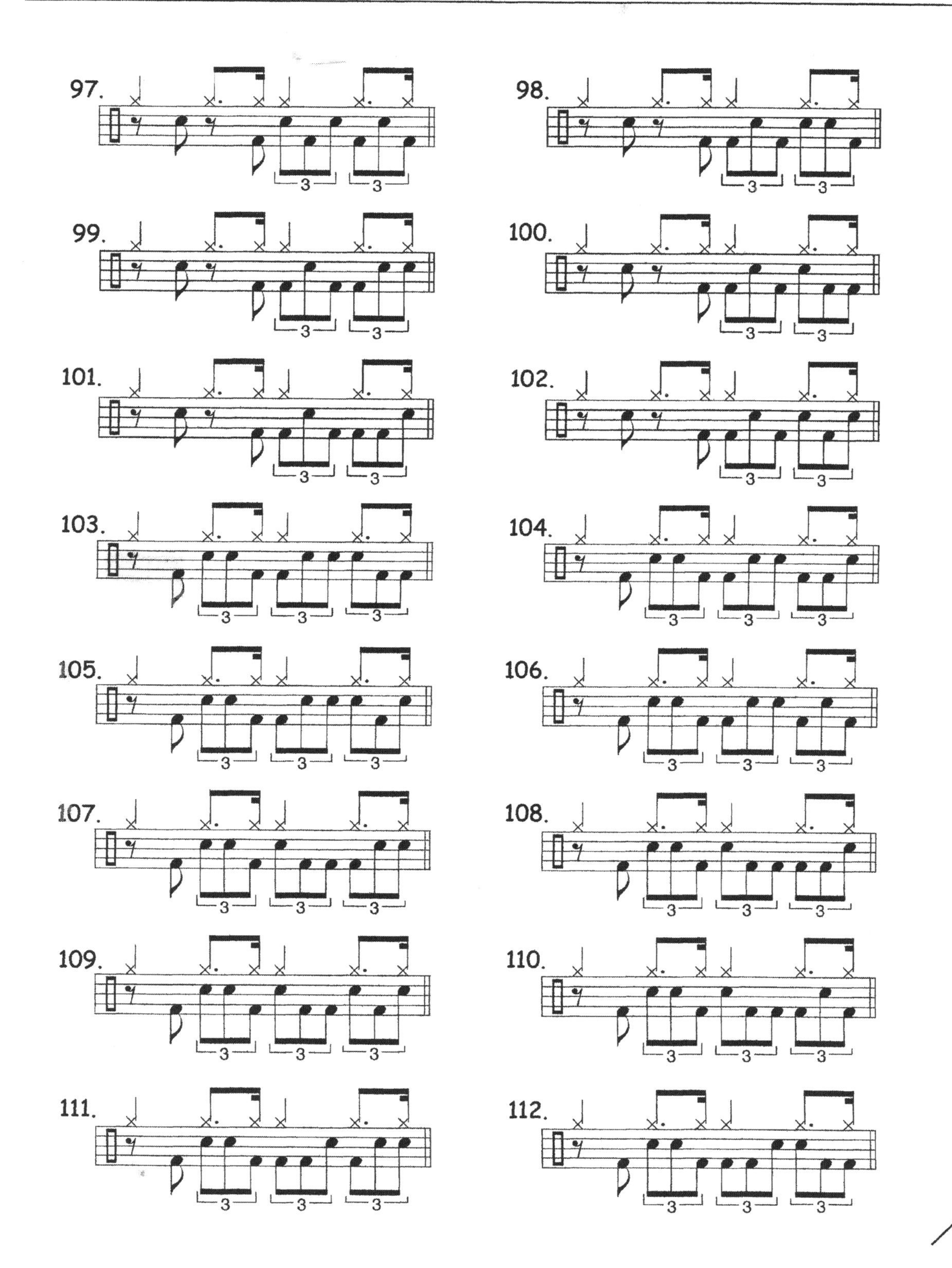

Step C 8: Triplet Independence: Snare & Bass Drum

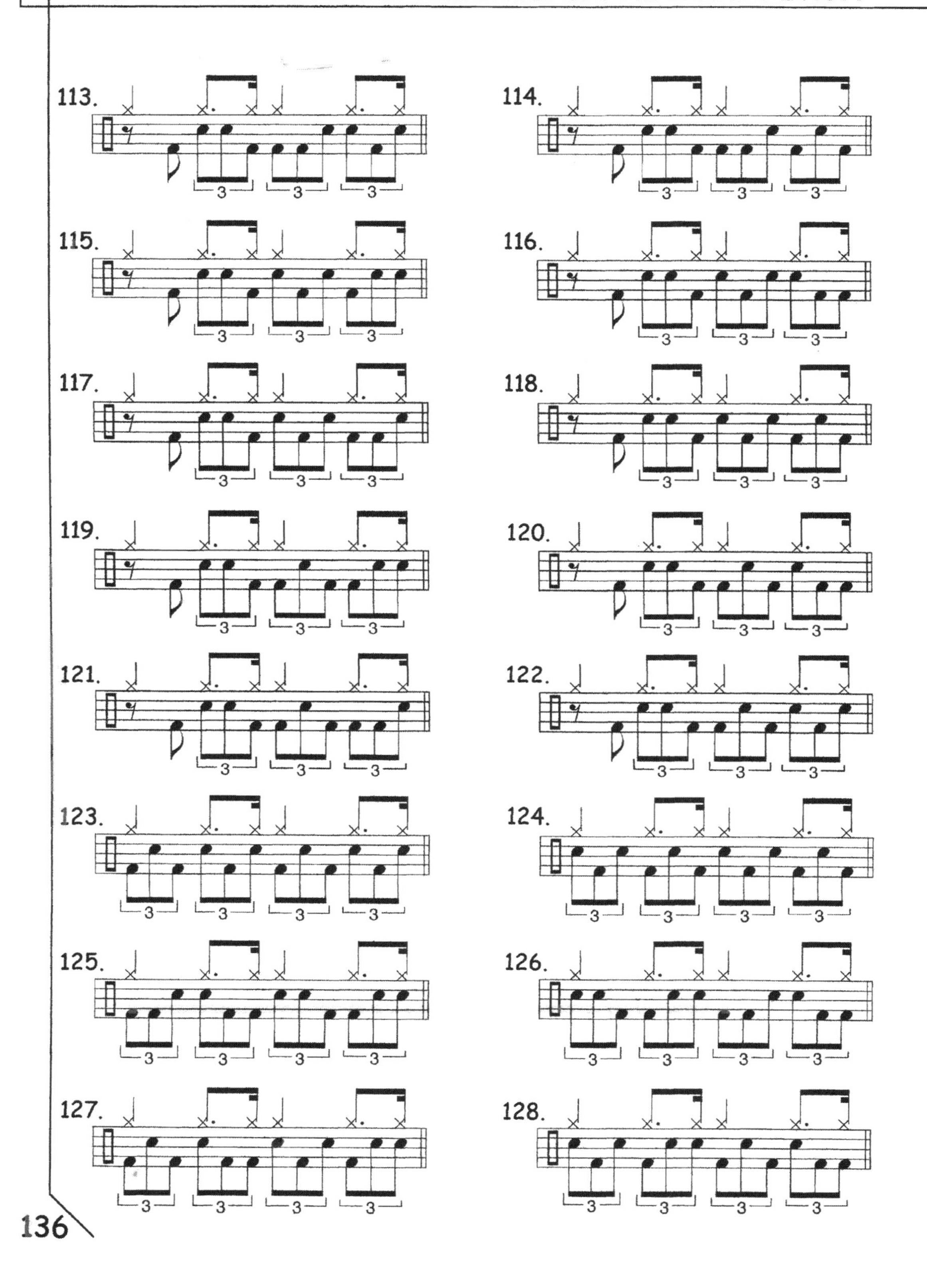

✓

Step C 8: Triplet Independence: Snare & Bass Drum

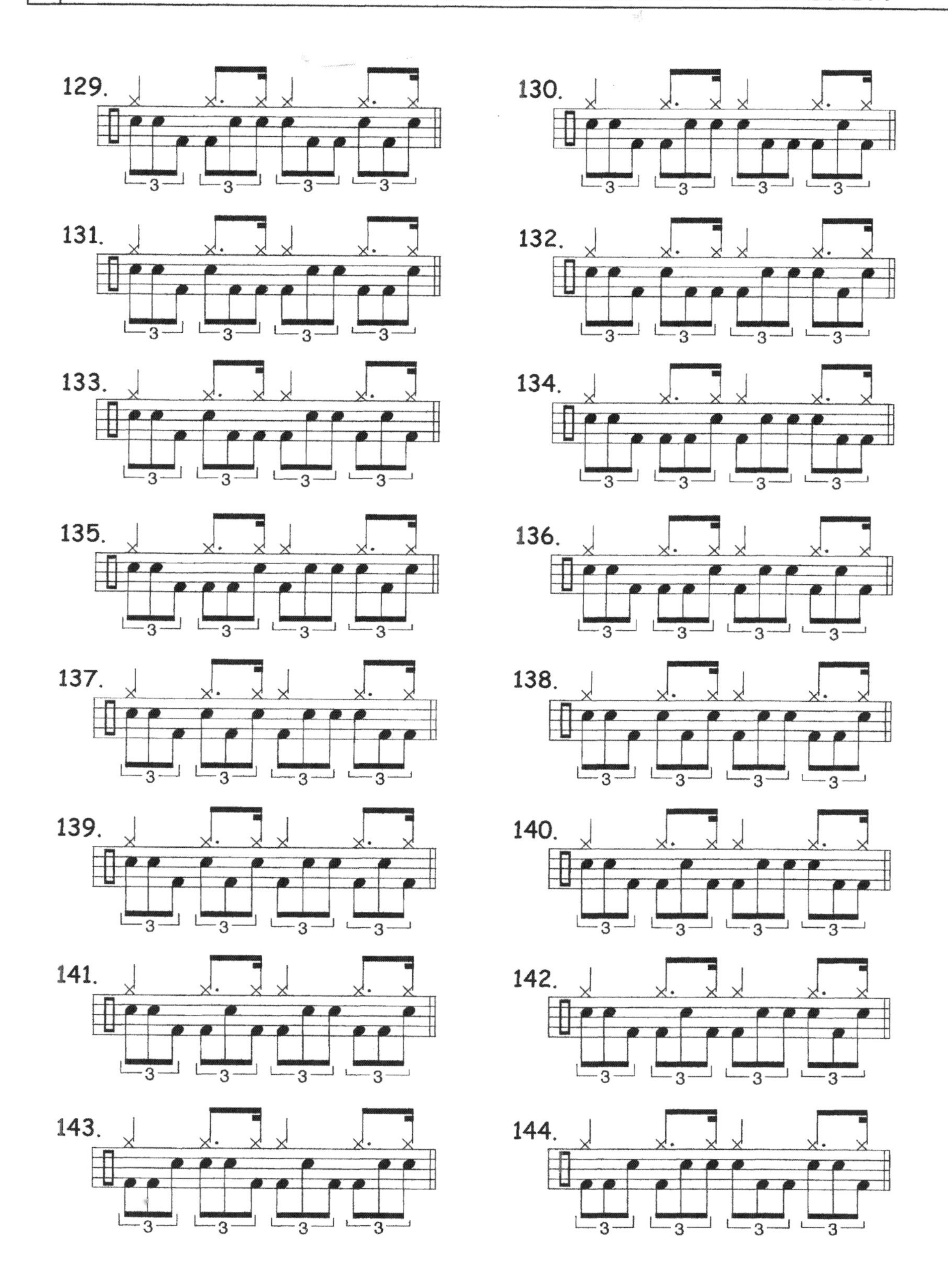

STEP C 8: TRIPLET INDEPENDENCE: SNARE & BASS DRUM

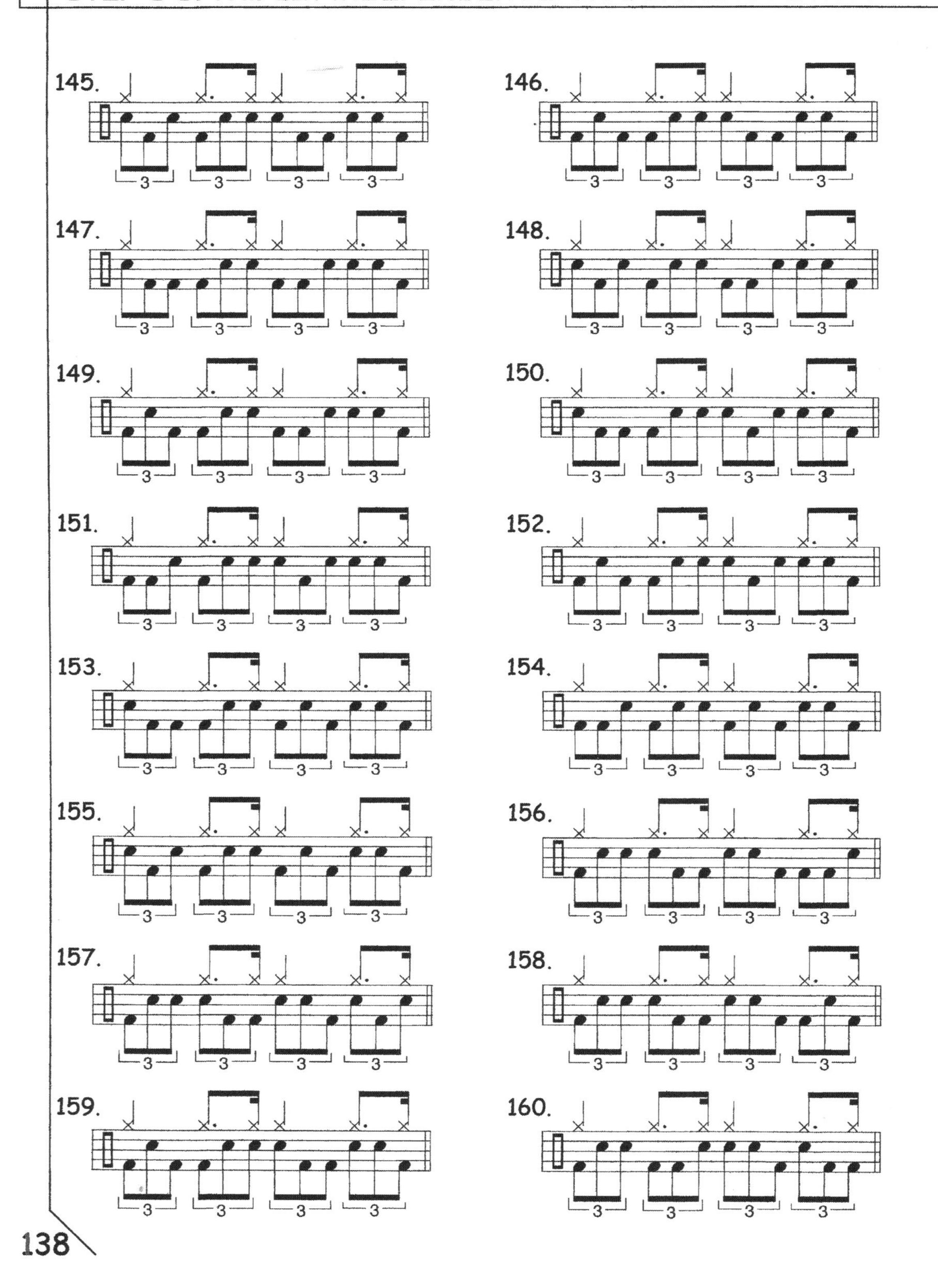

STEP C 8: TRIPLET INDEPENDENCE: SNARE & BASS DRUM

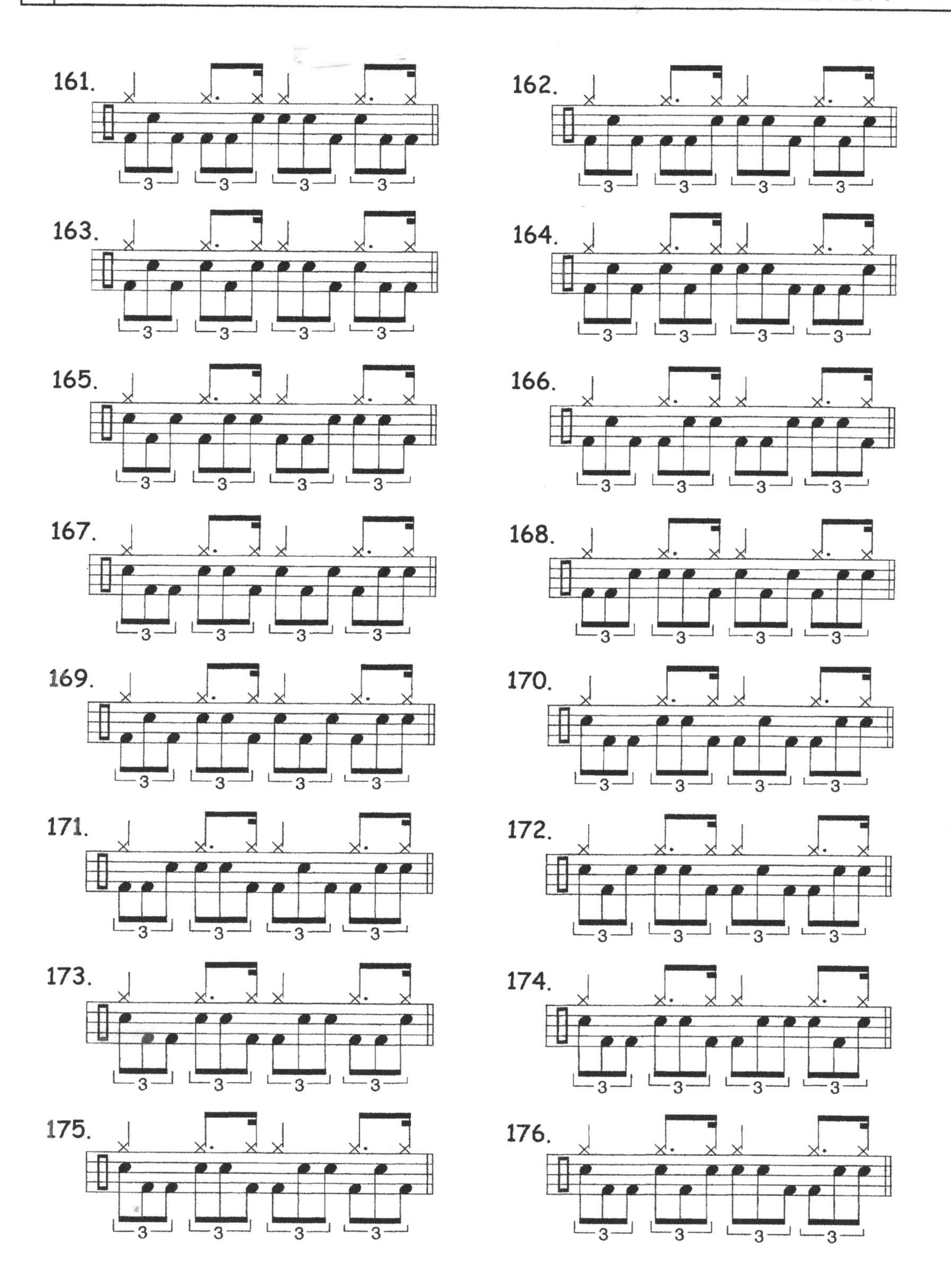

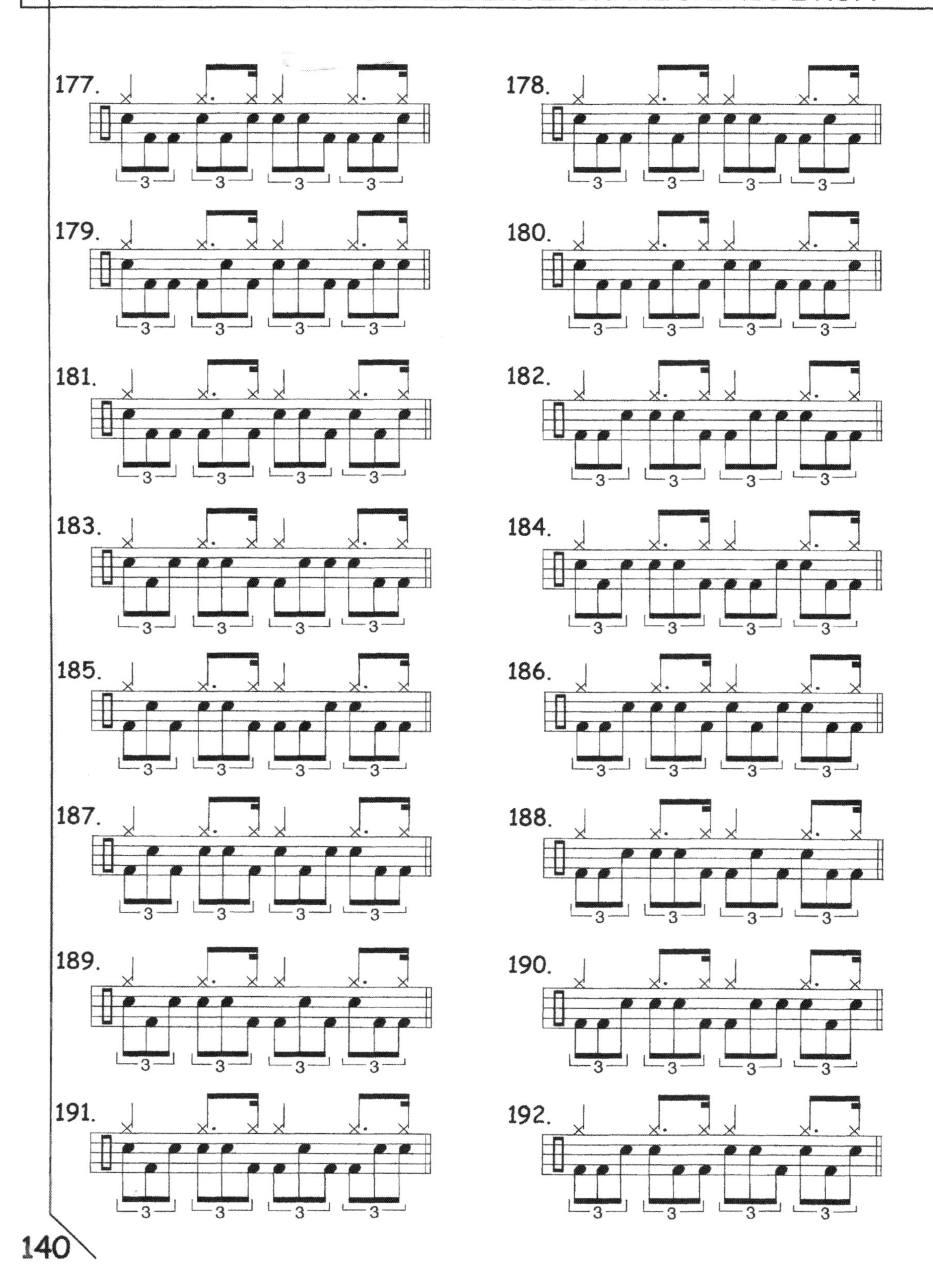
177.
178.
179.
180.
181.
182.
183.
184.
185.
186.
187.
188.
189.
190.
191.
192.

STEP C 8: TRIPLET INDEPENDENCE: SNARE & BASS DRUM

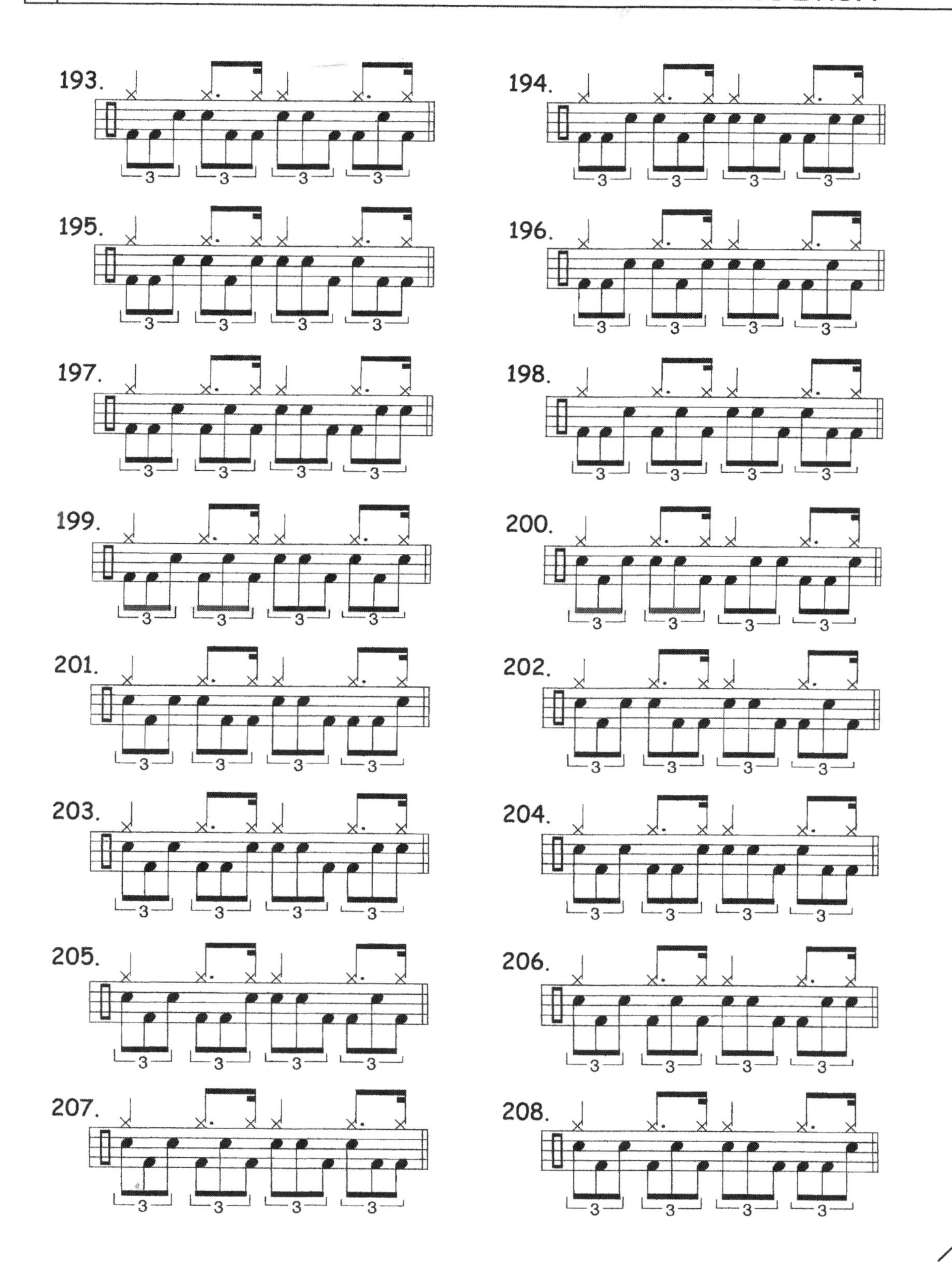

STEP C 8: TRIPLET INDEPENDENCE: SNARE & BASS DRUM

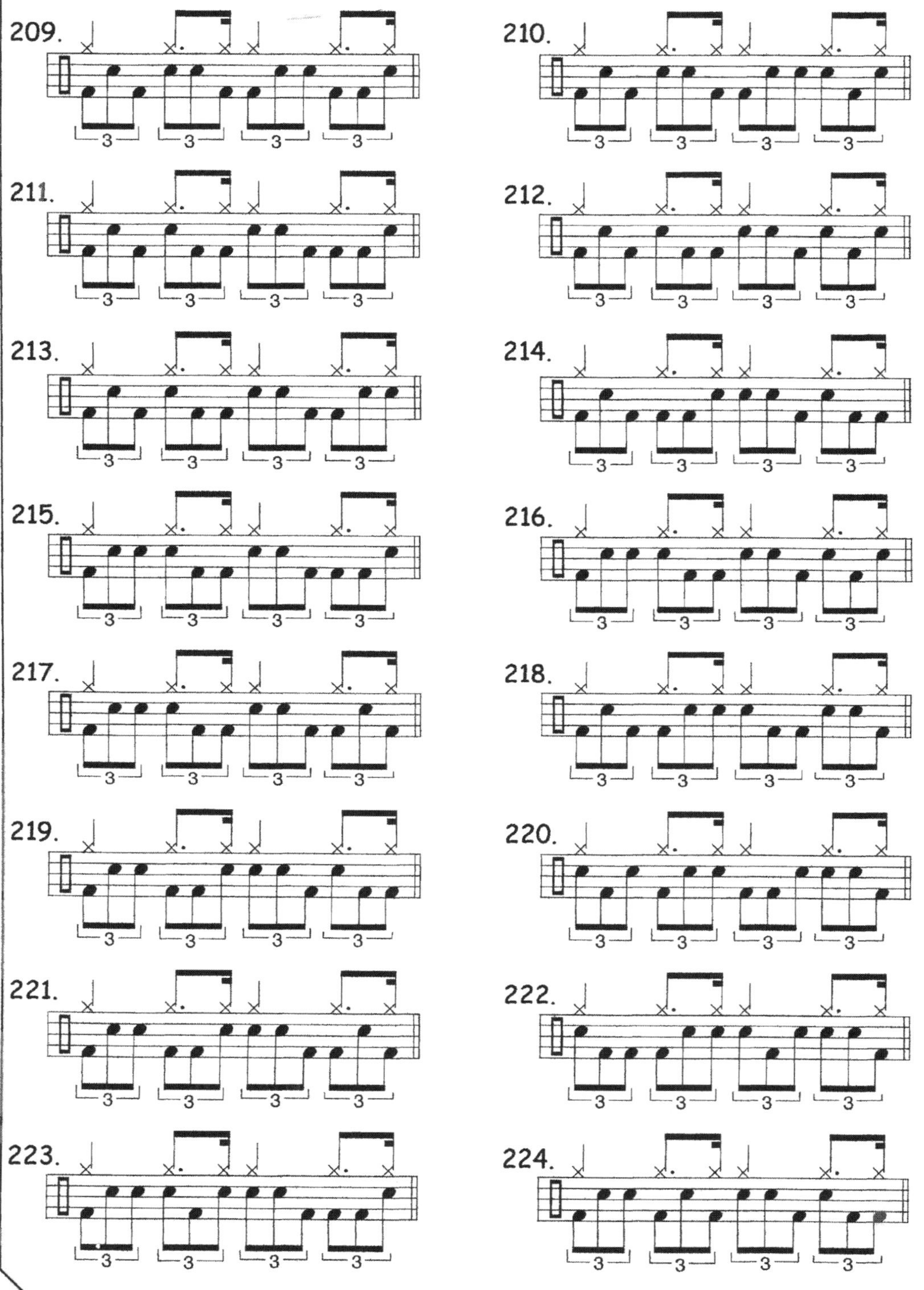

STEP C 8: TRIPLET INDEPENDENCE: SNARE & BASS DRUM

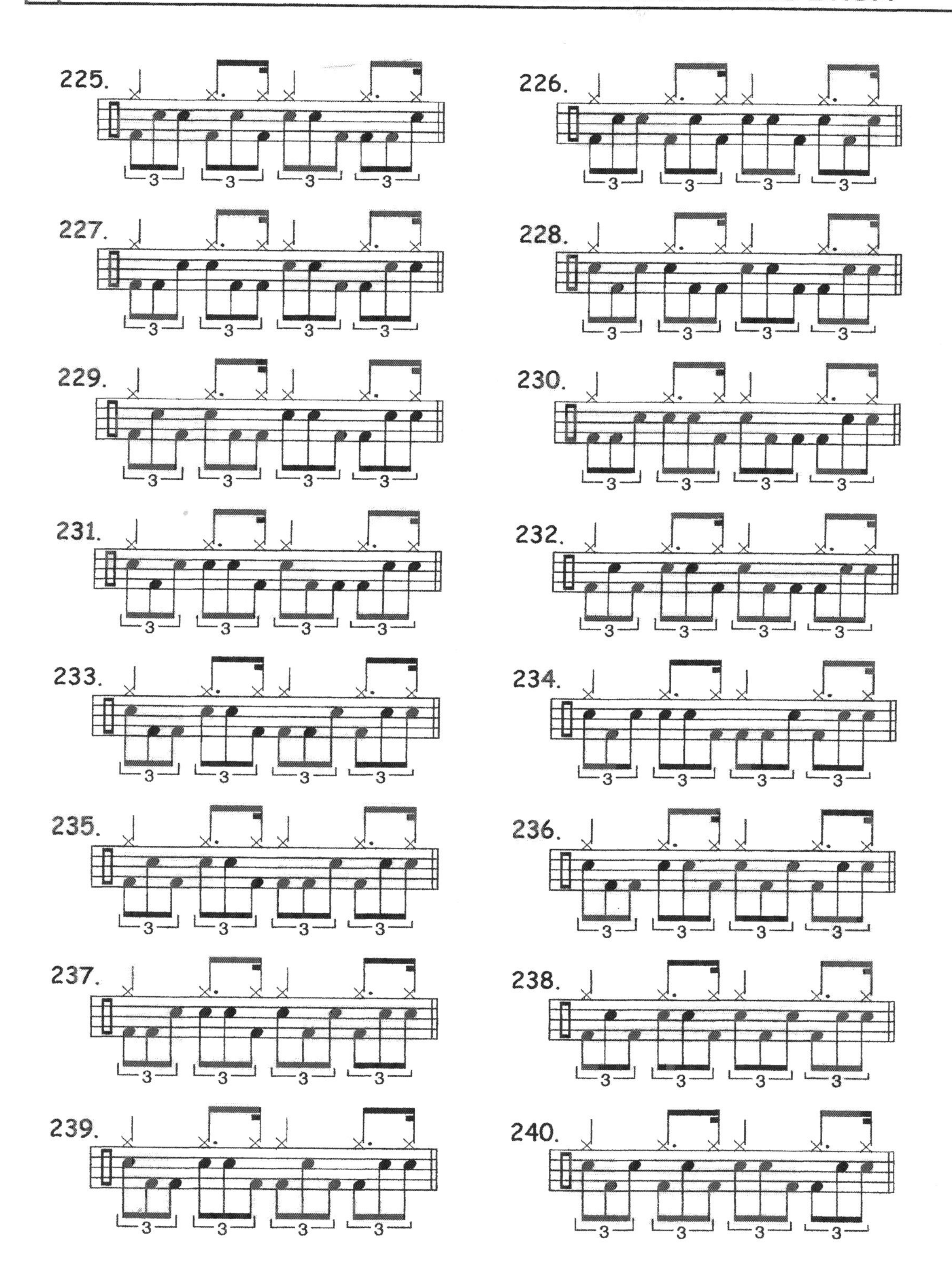

STEP C 8: TRIPLET INDEPENDENCE: SNARE & BASS DRUM

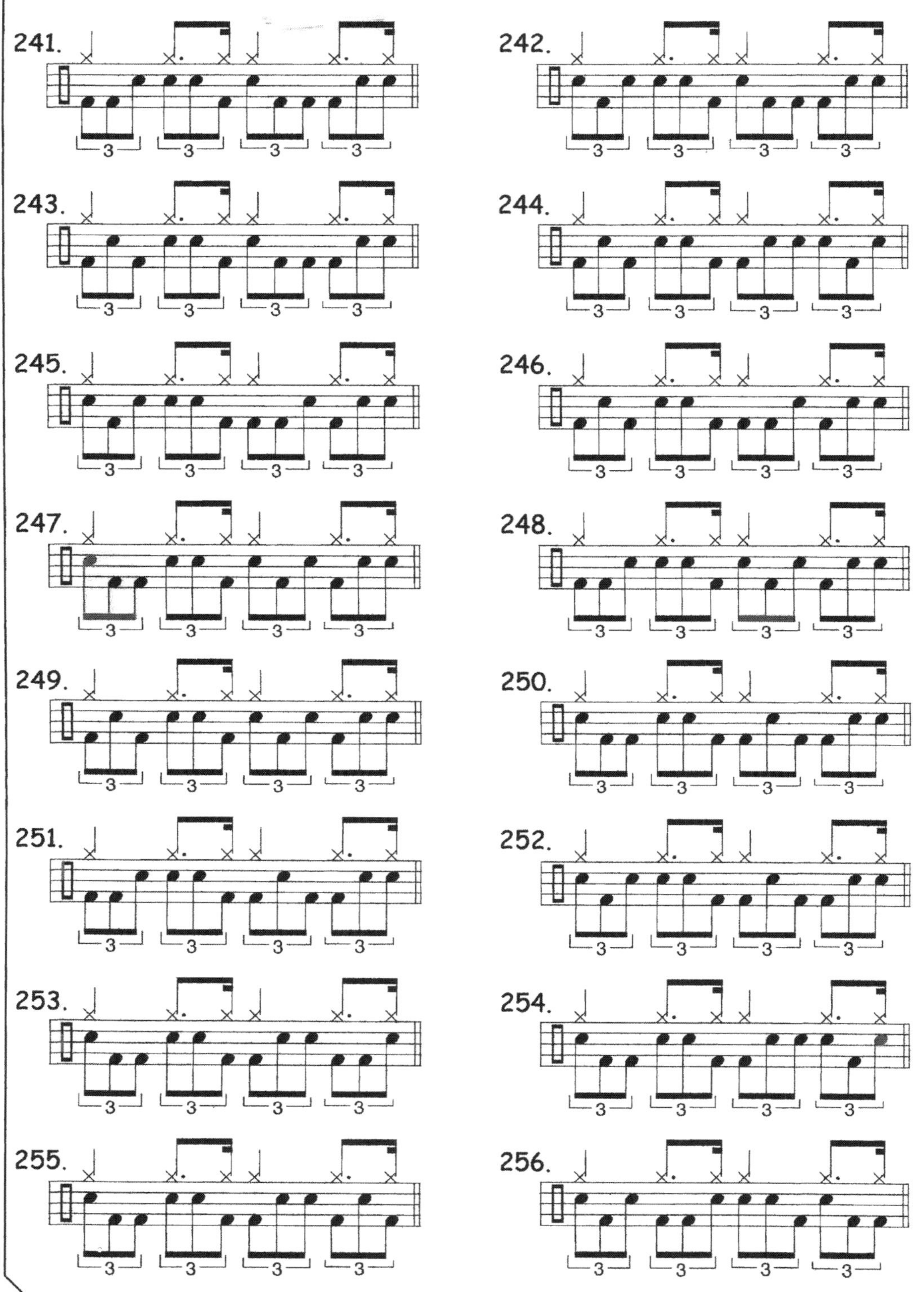

STEP C 8: TRIPLET INDEPENDENCE: SNARE & BASS DRUM

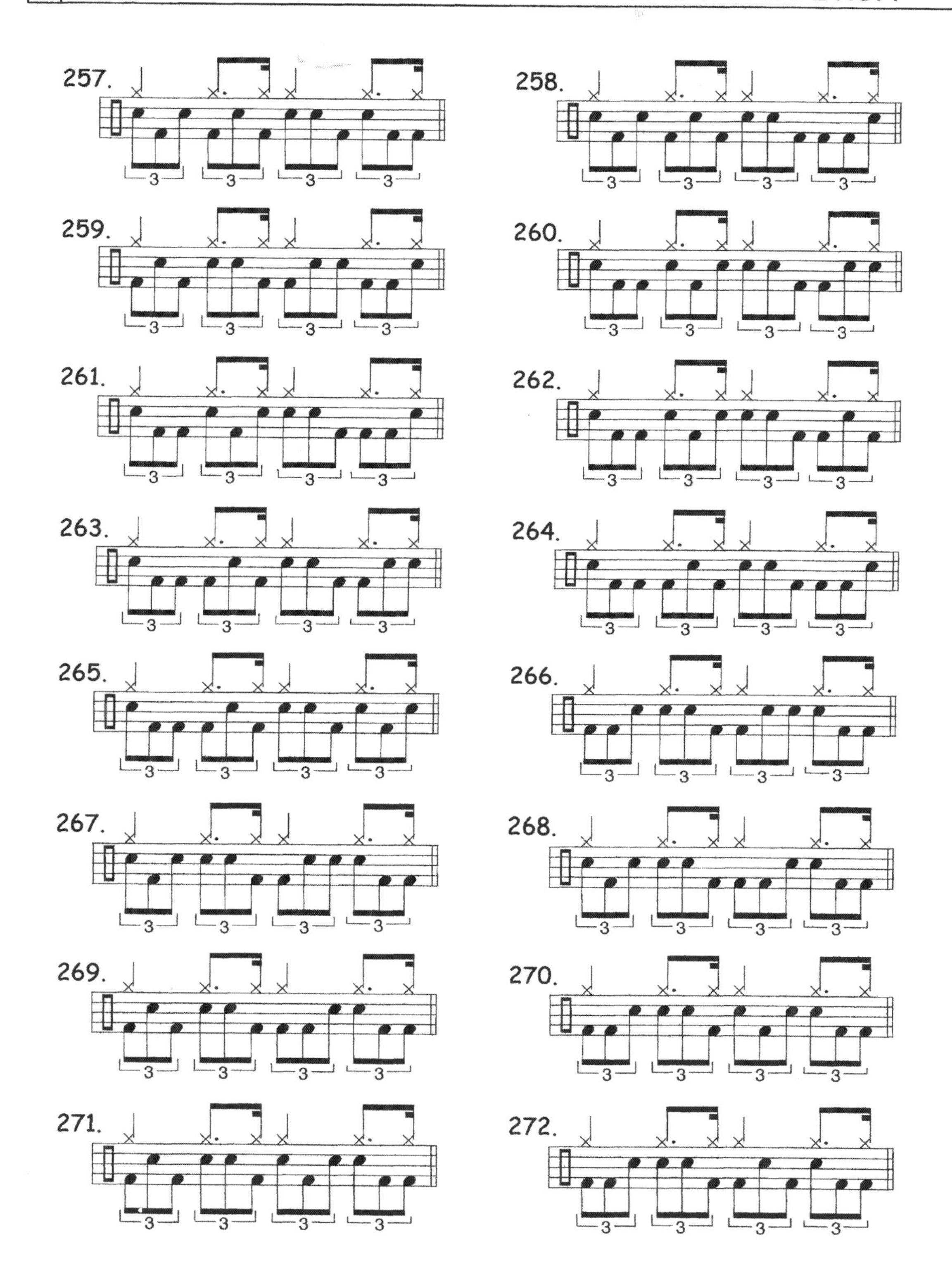

Step C 8: Triplet Independence: Snare & Bass Drum

STEP C 9: BROKEN TRIPLETS: SNARE & BASS DRUM

Follow these directions for pages 148 - 153.

- The exercises on the following four pages are to be played on the BD/RF and the SN/LH, against the jazz ride rhythm (RH/CYM) and hi-hat on 2 & 4 (LF).
- As you play the two exercises, sing the SN notes, using "tah," "dah," or "bop. Sing the BD part, using "boom" or "bom." Play each exercise with a **measure of "time"** in between. Repeat this sequence for each exercise. For example, exercise 1 looks like this:

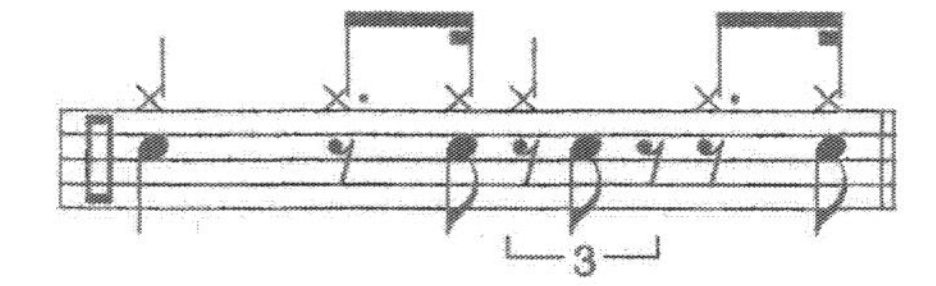

Here's how you will play it on the drumset:

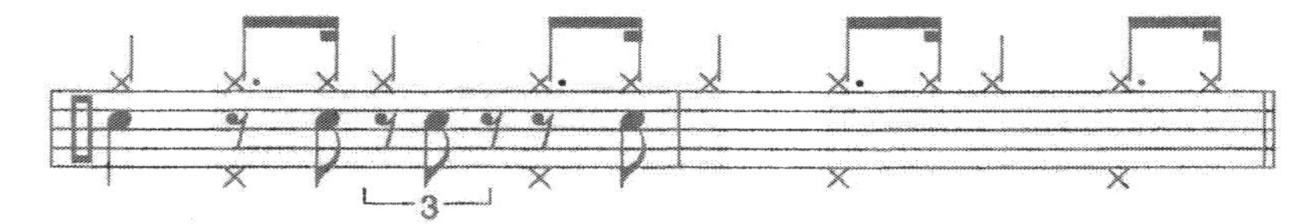

- Play these exercises against tracks 1 through 6 of the CD.

Drummer Counting Test

Q. How many drummer do you see here?

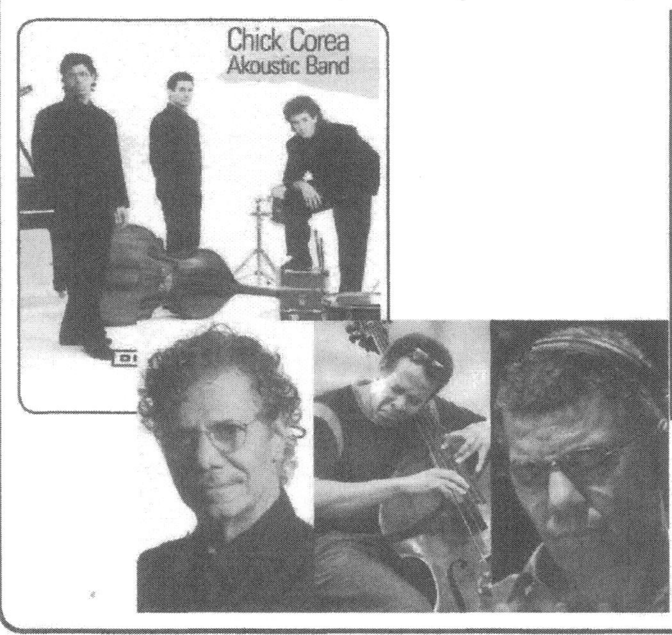

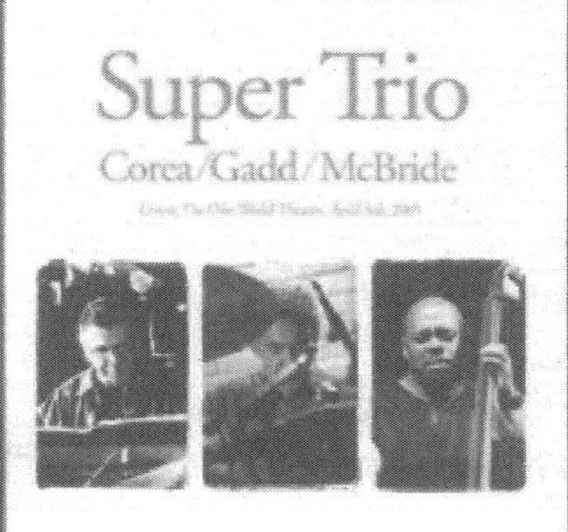

A. Four. Dave Weckl, Steve Gadd, Jack Dejonnette, and Chick Corea, who also plays drums

STEP C 9: BROKEN TRIPLETS: SNARE & BASS DRUM

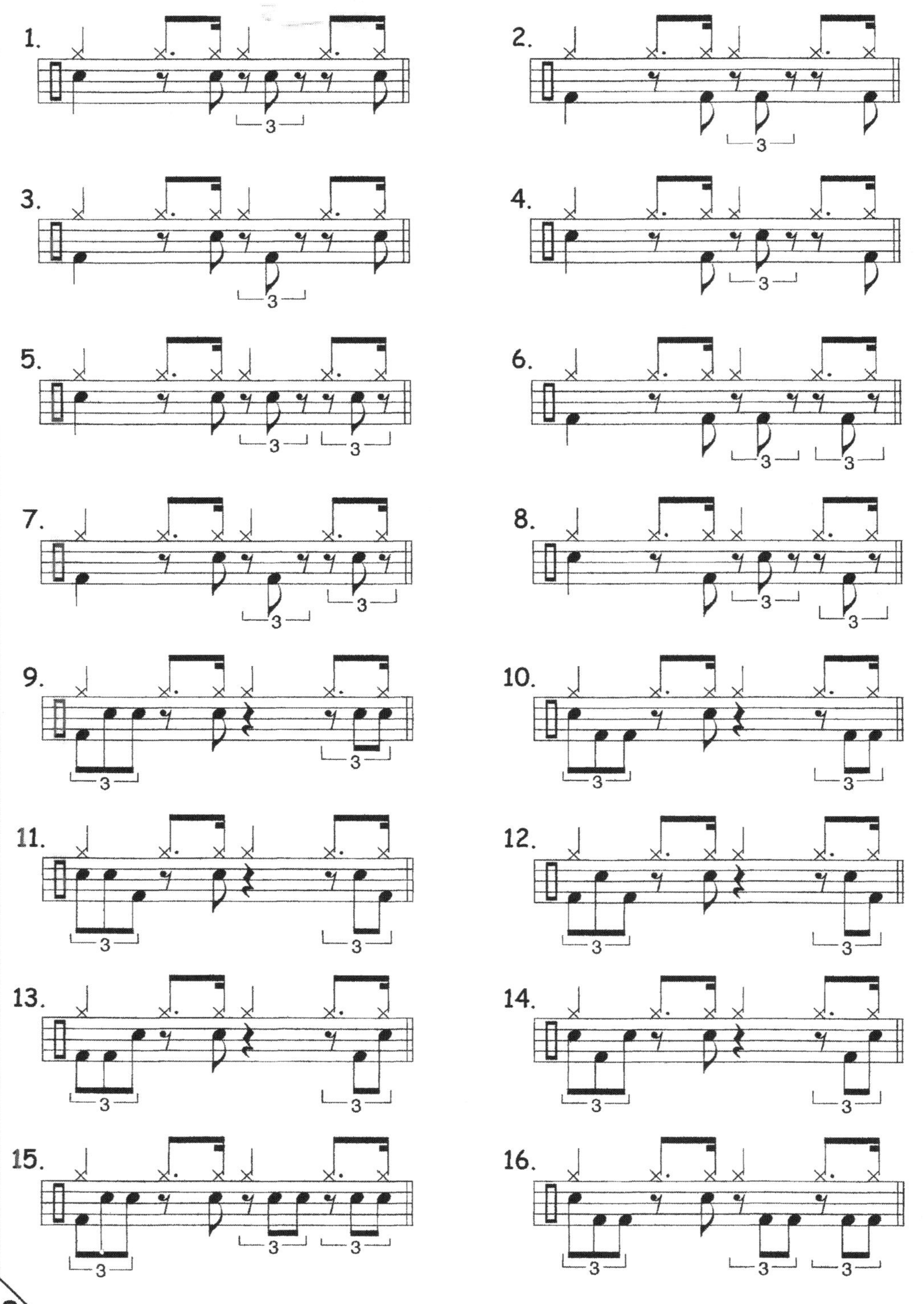

✓

STEP C 9: BROKEN TRIPLETS: SNARE & BASS DRUM

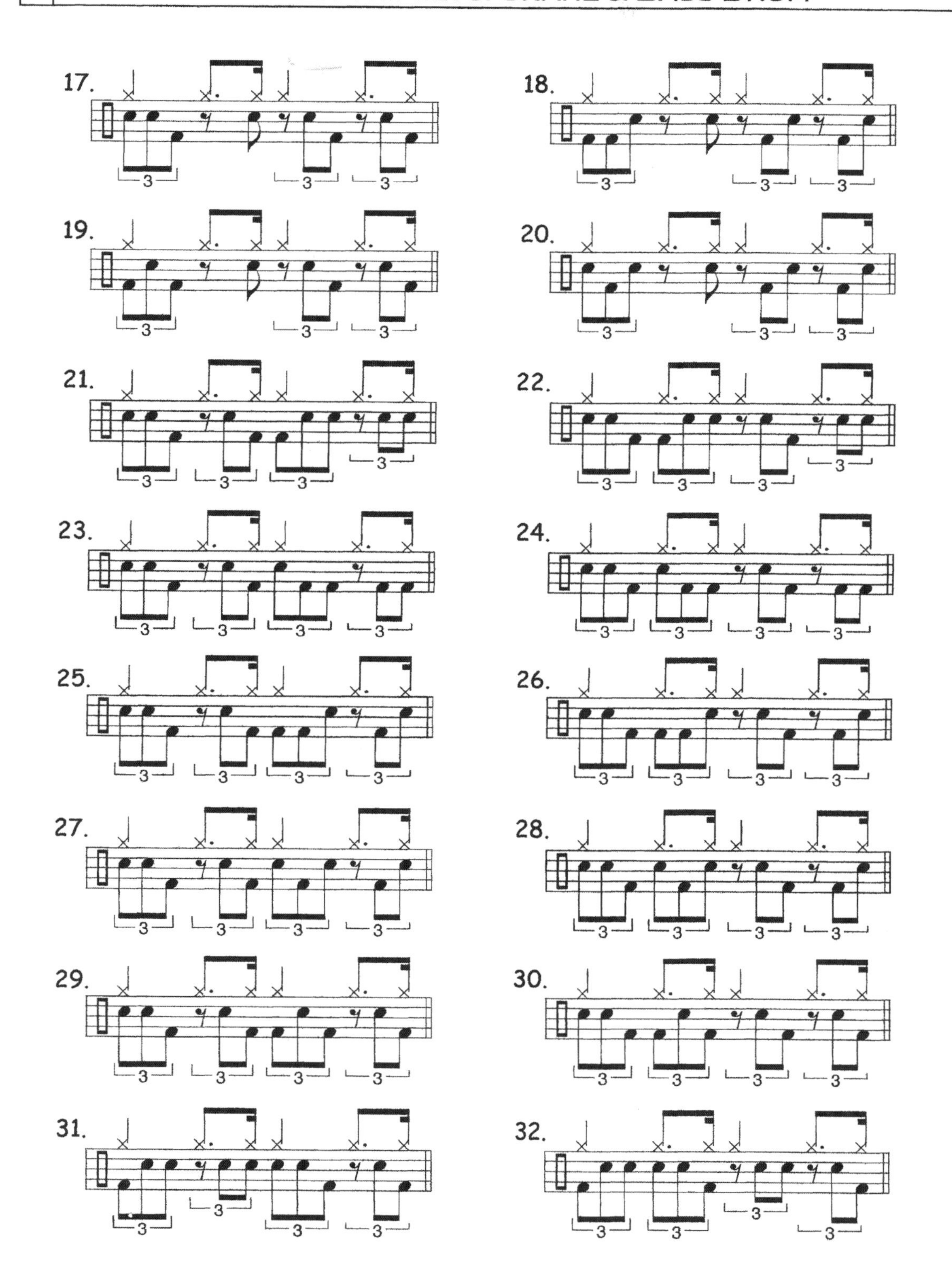

Step C 9: Broken Triplets: Snare & Bass Drum

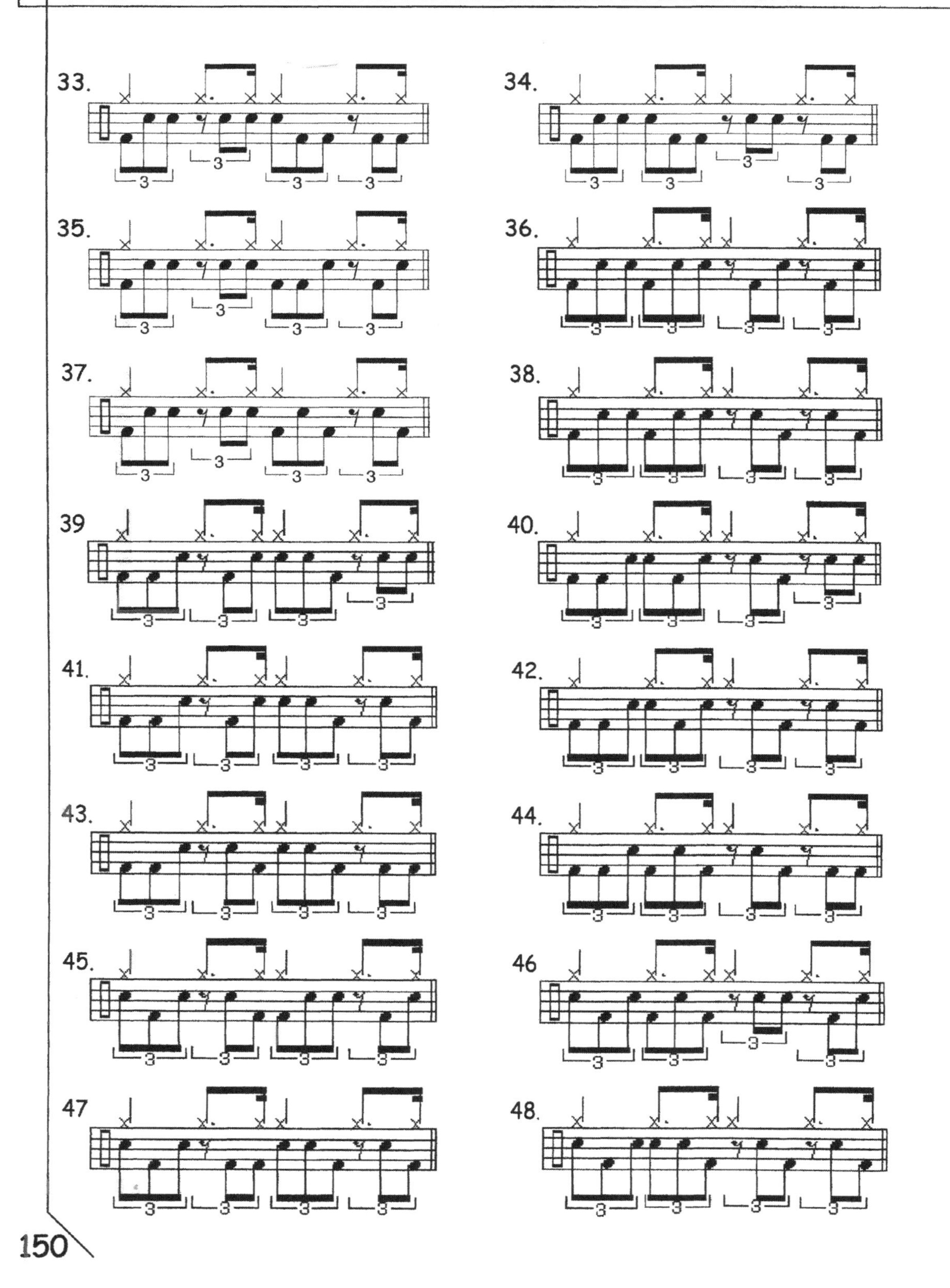

✓

Step C 9: Broken Triplets: Snare & Bass Drum

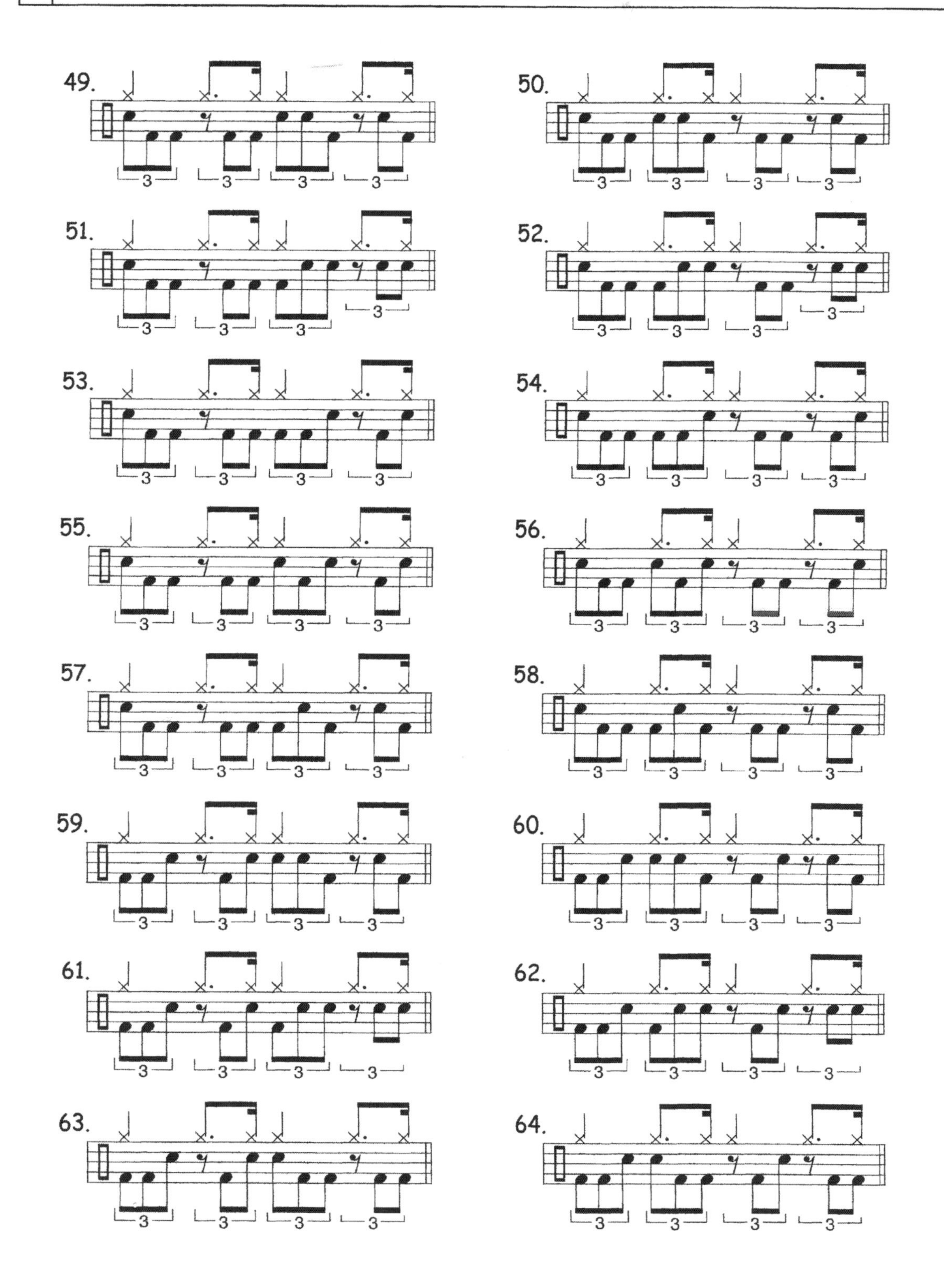

STEP C 9: BROKEN TRIPLETS: SNARE & BASS DRUM

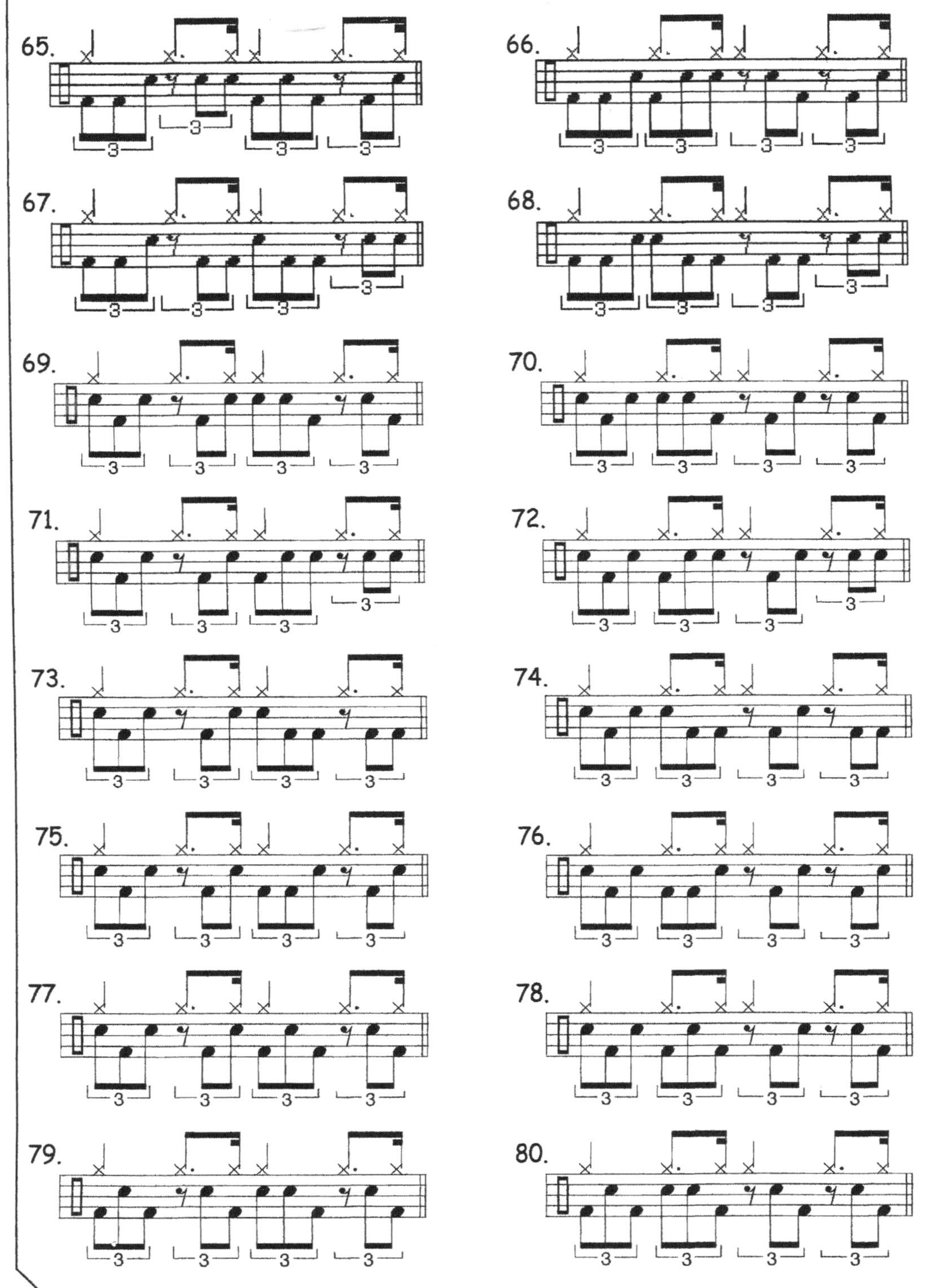

STEP C 9: BROKEN TRIPLETS: SNARE & BASS DRUM

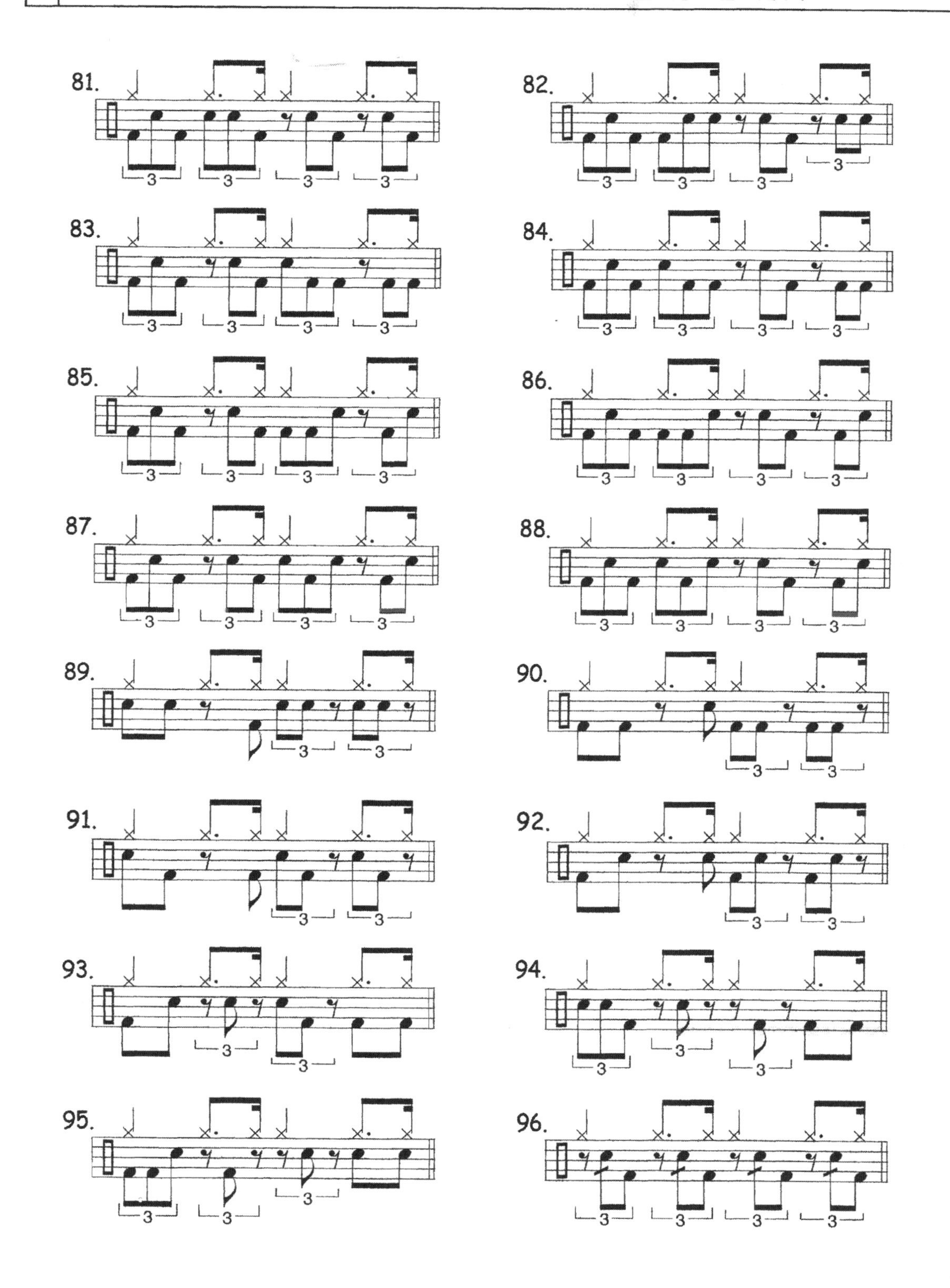

STEP C 10: TWO MEASURE COMP PATTERNS: SNARE AND BD

- Follow these directions for pages 155 - 156.

- The exercises on the following pages are to be played on the SN/LH and BD/RF, against the jazz ride rhythm (RH/CYM) and HH on 2 & 4 (LF).

- As you play each exercise, sing the SN and BD part, using "bop," "tah," or "dah" for the SN, "boom" or "bom" for the BD. Follow each two measure exercise with two measures of time" (ride cymbal and hi-hat).

  For example, exercise 1 looks like this:

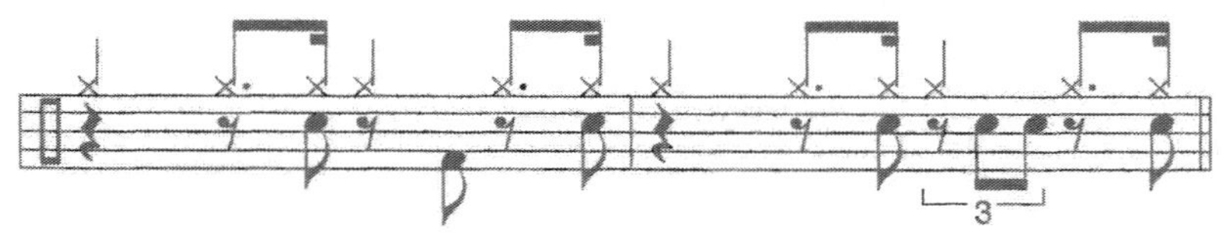

  Here's how you will play it on the drumset:

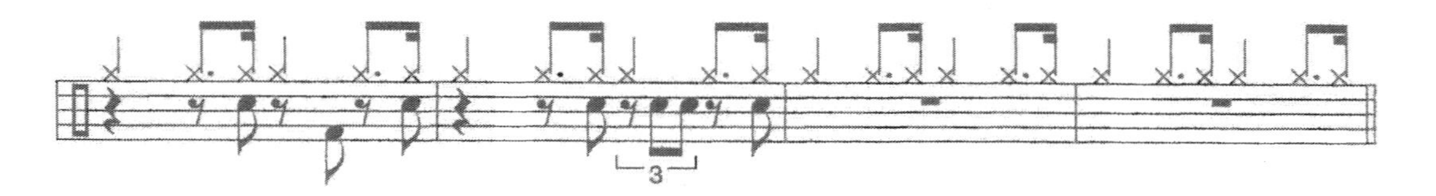

- Play these exercises against tracks 1 through 6 of the CD.

Dig Deeper

Originally in two volumes on VHS, this documentary is now available one one DVD. Hosted by Louis Bellson, "Legends Of Jazz Drumming" starts at the the beginning with Baby Dodds, and moves on from there. This is a treasure of jazz drumming history, and is highly recommended. The historical clips alone make this a worthy purchase.

Effortless Mastery: Liberating the Master Musician Within is a book for any musician who finds themselves having reached a plateau in their development. Werner, a masterful jazz pianist in his own right, uses his own life story and experiences to explore the barriers to creativity and mastery of music, and in the process reveals that "Mastery is available to everyone," providing practical, detailed ways to move towards greater confidence and proficiency in any endeavor.

STEP C 10: TWO MEASURE COMP PATTERNS: SNARE AND BD

9.
3
3
3
10.
3
3
3
11.
3
3
3
3
3
12.
3
3
3
13.
3
3
3
3
14.
3
3
3
15.
3
3
3
3
16.
3
3
3
3

Triplet Sticking Patterns
Cool Jazz
Rim Click
Bossa Nova
Samba
Afro-Cuban 6/8
Hard Bop
Ride Cymbal Variations
Interactive Phrasing: 8th Notes
Fusion
Mainstream
LF/HH Independence
Jazz Waltz
Interactive Phrasing: Triplets

STICKING FLUENCY - PART 2: TRIPLETS

On pages 94 - 97 you went through a series of swinging eighth note sticking exercises. Here comes another lengthy voyage for you: this time a series of 399 triplet patterns. Every accomplished drummer has gone through exercises such as these, and now its your turn.

Like the previous set of sticking patterns, it is recommended that you go through a certain amount every day (maybe a page) while you move on to other things. You can keep tabs on your progress with the checklists below. Later in the book we will return to this section for another application.

STEP D 1: STICK CONTROL/COORDINATION

- Play RF/BD quarter notes, LF/HH on "2" & "4" throughout.
- Play each exercise on pages 160 through 178 on the snare, playing eighth note triplets. Stay with each exercise until it feels smooth, relaxed, and flowing. Repeat each exercise on the snare until that pattern is reflexive and "locked in."
- Now play the pattern around the drumset, exploring the different sounds and combinations you can make.

Mark your progress

Page 160

1	2	3	4	5	6	7
8	9	10	11	12	13	14
15	16	17	18	19	20	21

Page 161

22	23	24	25	26	27	28
29	30	31	32	33	34	35
36	37	38	39	40	41	42

Page 162

43	44	45	46	47	48	49
50	51	52	53	54	55	56
57	58	59	60	61	62	63

Page 163

64	65	66	67	68	69	70
71	72	73	74	75	76	77
78	79	80	81	82	83	84

Page 164

85	86	87	88	89	90	91
92	93	94	95	96	97	98
99	100	101	102	103	104	105

Page 165

106	107	108	109	110	111	112
113	114	115	116	117	118	119
120	121	122	123	124	125	126

Page 166

127	128	129	130	131	132	133
134	135	136	137	138	139	140
141	142	143	144	145	146	147

Page 167

148	149	150	151	152	153	154
155	156	157	158	159	160	161
162	163	164	165	166	167	168

Page 168

169	170	171	172	173	174	175
176	177	178	179	180	181	182
183	184	185	186	187	188	189

Page 169

190	191	192	193	194	195	196
197	198	199	200	201	202	203
204	205	206	207	208	209	210

Page 170

211	212	213	214	215	216	217
218	219	220	221	222	223	224
225	226	227	228	229	230	231

Page 171

232	233	234	235	236	237	238
239	240	241	242	243	244	245
246	247	248	249	250	251	252

Page 172

253	254	255	256	257	258	259
260	261	262	263	264	265	266
267	268	269	270	271	272	273

Page 173

274	275	276	277	278	279	280
281	282	283	284	285	286	287
288	289	290	291	292	293	294

Page 174

295	296	297	298	299	300	301
302	303	304	305	306	307	308
309	310	311	312	313	314	315

Page 175

316	317	318	319	320	321	322
323	324	325	326	327	328	329
330	331	332	333	334	335	336

Page 176

337	338	339	340	341	342	343
344	345	346	347	348	349	350
351	352	353	354	355	356	357

Page 177

358	359	360	361	362	363	364
365	366	367	368	369	370	371
372	373	374	375	376	377	378

Page 178

379	380	381	382	383	384	385
396	387	388	389	390	391	392
393	394	395	396	397	398	399

STEP D 1: STICK CONTROL/COORDINATION: TRIPLETS

1.
R L R L R L R L R L R L

2.
L R L R L R L R L R L R

3.
R L L R L L R L L R L L

4.
L R R L R R L R R L R R

5.
R R L R R L R R L R R L

6.
L L R L L R L L R L L R

7.
R L R R L R R L R R L R

8.
L R L L R L L R L L R L

9.
R R R L L L R R R L L L

10.
L L L R R R L L L R R R

11.
R L R R L L R L R R L L

12.
L R L L R R L R L L R R

13.
R L R L R R R L R L R R

14.
L R L R L L L R L R L L

15.
R L R R R L R L R R R L

16.
L R L L L R L R L L L R

17.
R L R L L R R L R L L R

18.
L R L R R L L R L R R L

19.
R L R L L L R L R L L L

20.
L R L R R R L R L R R R

21.
R L L R L R R L L R L R

STEP D 1: STICK CONTROL/COORDINATION: TRIPLETS

22.
LRR LRL LRR LRL

23.
RLL LRL RLL LRL

24.
LRR RLR LRR RLR

25.
RLL LRR RLL LRR

26.
LRR RLL LRR RLL

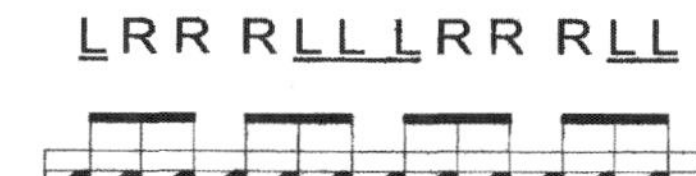

27.
RLL RRL RLL RRL

28.
LRR LLR LRR LLR

29.
RRL RLR RRL RLR

30.
LLR LRL LLR LRL

31.
RRL LRL RRL LRL

32.
LLR RLR LLR RLR

33.
RRL RLL RRL RLL

34.
RLR LRR RLR LRR

35.
RRL LLR RRL LLR

36.
LLR RRL LLR RRL

37.
RRR LRL RRR LRL

38.
LLL RLR LLL RLR

39.
RLR LRR LRL RLL

40.
LRL RLL RLR LRR

41.
RRL LRR LLR RLL

42.
LLR RLL RRL LRR

STEP D 1: STICK CONTROL/COORDINATION: TRIPLETS

43. RLR LRR LRL RLR

44. LRL RLL RLR LRL

45. RLR LRL RLL LRR

46. RLR LRL RLL RRL

47. RLR LRL RLL LLR

48. RLR LRL LRR RLL

49. RLR LRL LRR RRL

50. RLR LRL LRR LLR

51. RLR LRL RRL RLL

52. RLR LRL RRL LRR

53. RLR LRL RRL LLR

54. RLR LRL LLR RLL

55. RLR LRL LLR LRR

56. RLR LRL LLR RRL

57. RLR RLL LRL LRR

58. RLR RLL LRL RRL

59. RLR RLL LRL LLR

60. RLR RLL LRR LRL

61. RLR RLL LRR RRL

62. RLR RLL LRR LLR

63. RLR RLL RRL LRL

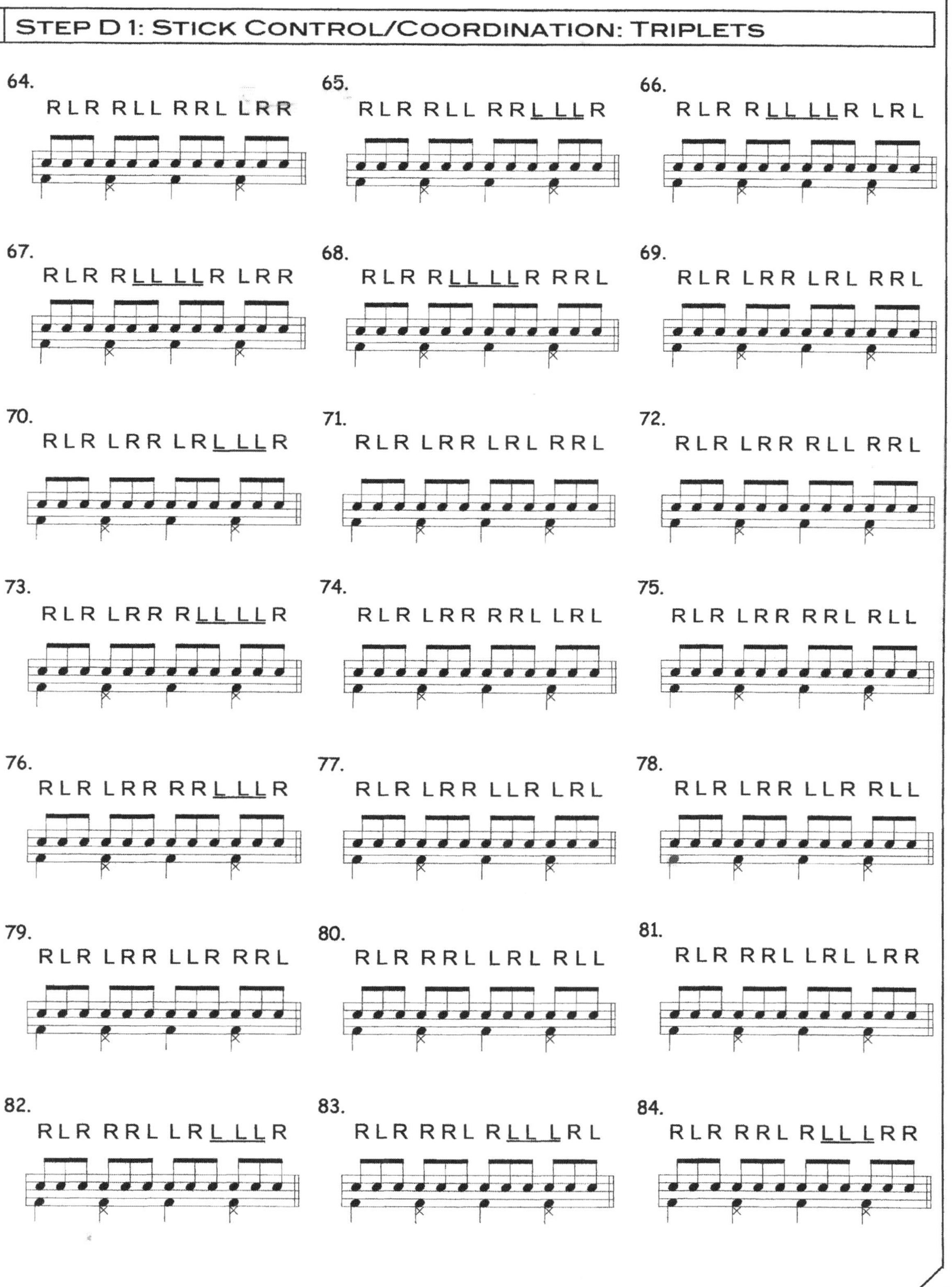
STEP D 1: STICK CONTROL/COORDINATION: TRIPLETS
64. RLR RLL RRL LRR
65. RLR RLL RRL LLR
66. RLR RLL LLR LRL
67. RLR RLL LLR LRR
68. RLR RLL LLR RRL
69. RLR LRR LRL RRL
70. RLR LRR LRL LLR
71. RLR LRR LRL RRL
72. RLR LRR RLL RRL
73. RLR LRR RLL LLR
74. RLR LRR RRL LRL
75. RLR LRR RRL RLL
76. RLR LRR RRL LLR
77. RLR LRR LLR LRL
78. RLR LRR LLR RLL
79. RLR LRR LLR RRL
80. RLR RRL LRL RLL
81. RLR RRL LRL LRR
82. RLR RRL LRL LLR
83. RLR RRL RLL LRL
84. RLR RRL RLL LRR

STEP D 1: STICK CONTROL/COORDINATION: TRIPLETS

85.

R L R R R L R L L L L R

86.

R L R R R L L R R L R L

87.

R L R R R L L R R R L L

88.

R L R R R L L R R L L R

89.

R L R R R L L L R L R L

90.

R L R R R L L L R R L L

91.

R L R R R L L L R L R R

92.

R L R L L R L R L R L L

93.

R L R L L R L R L L R R

94.

R L R L L R L R L R R L

95.

R L R L L R R L L L R L

96.

R L R L L R R L L L R R

97.

R L R L L R R L L R R L

98.

R L R L L R L R R L R L

99.

R L R L L R L R R R L L

100.

R L R L L R L R R R R L

101.

R L R L L R R R L L R L

102.

R L R L L R R R L R L L

103.

R L R L L R R R L L R R

104.

L R L R L R R L L L R R

105.

L R L R L R R L L R R L

✓

STEP D 1: STICK CONTROL/COORDINATION: TRIPLETS

106.
L R L R L R R L L L L R

107.
L R L R L R L R R R L L

108.
L R L R L R L R R R R L

109.
L R L R L R L R R L L R

110.
L R L R L R R R L R L L

111.
L R L R L R R R L L R R

112.
L R L R L R R R L L L R

113.
L R L R L R L L R R L L

114.
L R L R L R L L R L R R

115.
L R L R L R L L R R R L

116.
L R L R L L R L R R R L

117.
L R L R L L R L R L L R

118.
L R L R L L L R R R L R

119.
L R L R L L L R R R R L

120.
L R L R L L L R R L L R

121.
L R L R L L R R L R L R

122.
L R L R L L R R L L R R

123.
L R L R L L R R L L L R

124.
L R L R L L L L R R L R

125.
L R L R L L L L R L R R

126.
L R L R L L L L R R R L

Step D 1: Stick Control/Coordination: Triplets

127.
L R L L R R R L R R L L

128.
L R L L R R R L R R R L

129.
L R L L R R R L R L L R

130.
L R L L R R R L L R L R

131.
L R L L R R R L L R R L

132.
L R L L R R R L L L L R

133.
L R L L R R R R L R L R

134.
L R L L R R R R L R L L

135.
L R L L R R R R L L L R

136.
L R L L R R L L R R L R

137.
L R L L R R L L R R L L

138.
L R L L R R L L R R R L

139.
L R L R R L R L R R L L

140.
L R L R R L R L R L R R

141.
L R L R R L R L R L L R

142.
L R L R R L R L L R L R

143.
L R L R R L R L L L R R

144.
L R L R R L R L L L L R

145.
L R L R R L L R R R L R

146.
L R L R R L L R R R L L

147.
L R L R R L L R R L L R

STEP D 1: STICK CONTROL/COORDINATION: TRIPLETS

148.
LRL RRL LLR RLR

149.
LRL RRL LLR RLL

150.
LRL RRL LLR LRR

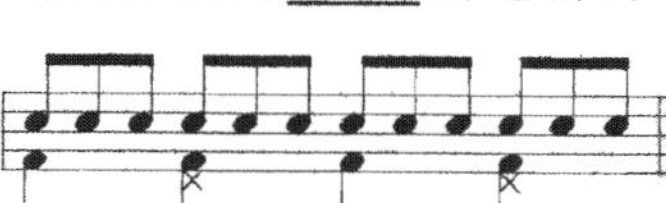

151.
LRL LLR RLR RLL

152.
LRL LLR RLR LRR

153.
LRL LLR RLR RRL

154.
LRL LLR RLL RLR

155.
LRL LLR RLL LRR

156.
LRL LLR RLL RRL

157.
LRL LLR LRR RLR

158.
LRL LLR LRR RLL

159.
LRL LLR LRR RRL

160.
LRL LLR RRL RLR

161.
LRL LLR RRL RLL

162.
LRL LLR RRL LRR

163.
RLL RLR LRL LRR

164.
RLL RLR LRL RRL

165.
RLL RLR LRL LLR

166.
RLL RLR LRR LRL

167.
RLL RLR LRR RRL

168.
RLL RLR LRR LLR

Step D 1: Stick Control/Coordination: Triplets

169.
R L L R L R R R L L R L

170.
R L L R L R R R L L R R

171.
R L L R L R R R L L L R

172.
R L L R L R L L R L R L

173.
R L L R L R L L R L R R

174.
R L L R L R L L R R R L

175.
R L L L R L R L R L R R

176.
R L L L R L R L R R R L

177.
R L L L R L R L R L L R

178.
R L L L R L L R R R L R

179.
R L L L R L L R R R R L

180.
R L L L R L L R R L L R

181.
R L L L R L R R L R L R

182.
R L L L R L R R L L R R

183.
R L L L R L R R L R R L

184.
R L L L R L L L R R L R

185.
R L L L R L L L R L R R

186.
R L L L R L L L R R R L

187.
R L L L R R R L R L R L

188.
R L L L R R R L R R R L

189.
R L L L R R R L R L L R

STEP D 1: STICK CONTROL/COORDINATION: TRIPLETS

190.
RLL LRR LRL RLR

191.
RLL LRR LRL RRL

192.
RLL LRR LRL LLR

193.
RLL LRR RRL RLR

194.
RLL LRR RRL LRL

195.
RLL LRR RRL LLR

196.
RLL LRR LLR RLR

197.
RLL LRR LLR LRL

198.
RLL LRR LLR RRL

199.
RLL RRL RLR LRL

200.
RLL RRL RLR LRR

201.
RLL RRL RLR LLR

202.
RLL RRL LRL RLR

203.
RLL RRL LRL LRR

204.
RLL RRL LRL LLR

205.
RLL RRL LRR RLR

206.
RLL RRL LRR LRL

207.
RLL RRL LRR LLR

208.
RLL RRL LLR RLR

209.
RLL RRL LLR LRL

210.
RLL RRL LLR RRL

STEP D 1: STICK CONTROL/COORDINATION: TRIPLETS

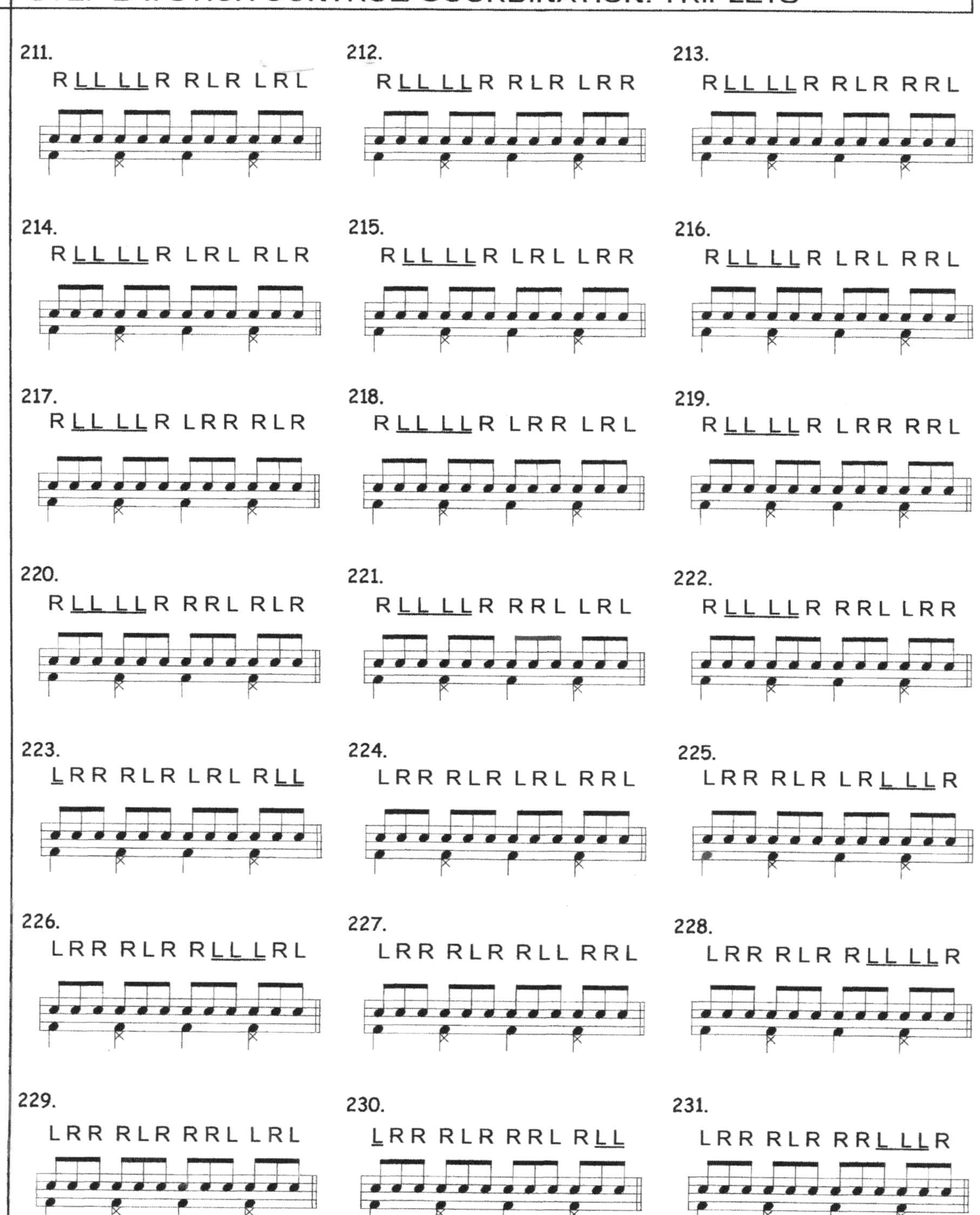

STEP D 1: STICK CONTROL/COORDINATION: TRIPLETS

232. LRR RLR LLR LRL

233. LRR RLR LLR RRL

234. LRR RLR LLR LLR

235. LRR LRL RLR RLL

236. LRR LRL RLR RRL

237. LRR LRL RLR LLR

238. LRR LRL RLL RLR

239. LRR LRL RLL RRL

240. LRR LRL RLL LLR

241. LRR LRL RRL RLR

242. LRR LRL RRL RLL

243. LRR LRL RRL LLR

244. LRR LRL LLR RLR

245. LRR LRL LLR RLL

246. LRR LRL LLR RRL

247. LRR RLL RLR LRL

248. LRR RLL RLR RRL

249. LRR RLL RLR LLR

250. LRR RLL LRL RLR

251. LRR RLL LRL RRL

252. LRR RLL LRL LLR

STEP D1: STICK CONTROL/COORDINATION: TRIPLETS

STEP D 1: STICK CONTROL/COORDINATION: TRIPLETS

274.
LRR LLR LRL RLR

275.
LRR LLR LRL RLL

276.
LRR LLR LRL RRL

277.
LRR LLR RLL RLR

278.
LRR LLR RLL LRL

279.
LRR LLR RLL RRL

280.
LRR LLR RRL RLR

281.
LRR LLR RRL LRL

282.
LRR LLR RRL RLL

283.
RRL RLR LRL RLL

284.
RRL RLR LRL LRR

285.
RRL RLR LRL LLR

286.
RRL RLR RLL LRL

287.
RRL RLR RLL LRR

288.
RRL RLR RLL LLR

289.
RRL RLR LRR LRL

290.
RRL RLR LRR RLL

291.
RRL RLR LRR LLR

292.
RRL RLR LLR LRL

293.
RRL RLR LLR RLL

294.
RRL RLR LLR RRL

STEP D 1: STICK CONTROL/COORDINATION: TRIPLETS

295.

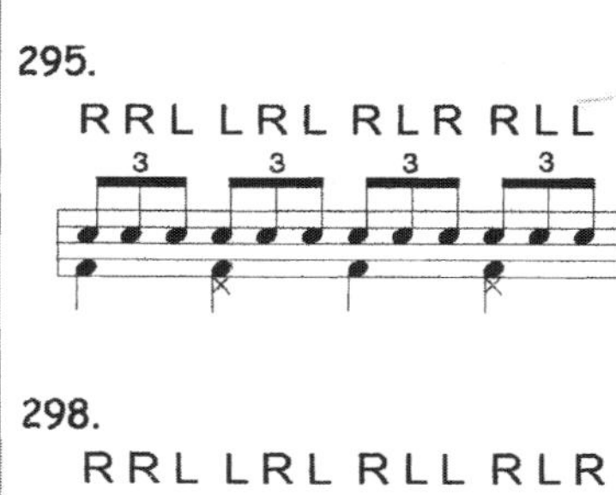

296.

297.

298.

299.

300.

301.

302.

303.

304.

305.

306.

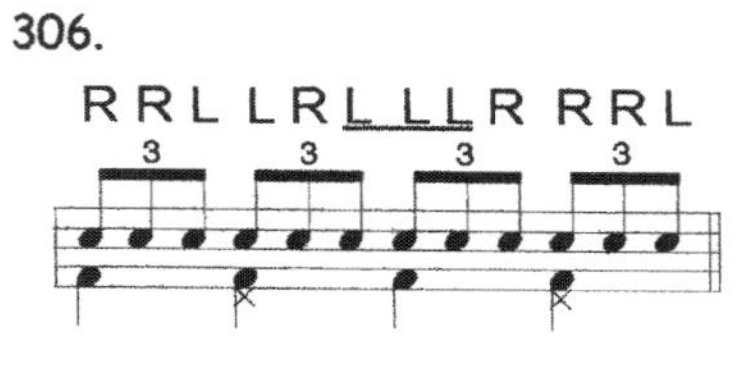

307.

308.

309.

310.

311.

312.

313.

314.

315.

STEP D 1: STICK CONTROL/COORDINATION: TRIPLETS

316.
RRL RLL LLR RLR

317.
RRL RLL LLR LRL

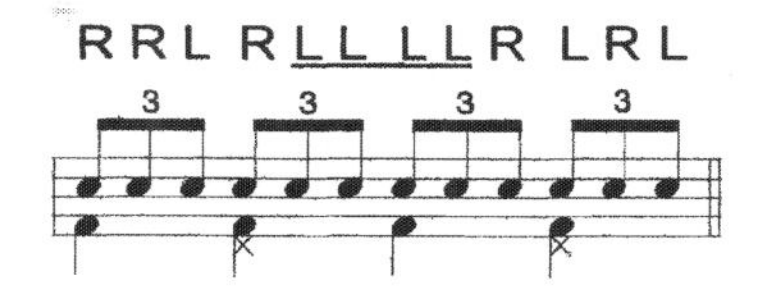

318.
RRL RLL LLR LLR

319.
RRL LRR RLR LRL

320.
RRL LRR RLR RLL

321.
RRL LRR RLR LLR

322.
RRL LRR LRL RLR

323.
RRL LRR LRL RLL

324.
RRL LRR LRL LLR

325.
RRL LRR RLL RLR

326.
RRL LRR RLL LRL

327.
RRL LRR RLL LLR

328.
RRL LRR LLR RLR

329.
RRL LRR LLR LRL

330.
RRL LLR RLR LRL

331.
RRL LLR RLR RLL

332.
RRL LLR RLR LRR

333.
RRL LLR LRL RLR

334.
RRL LLR LRL RLL

335.
RRL LLR LRL LRR

336.
RRL LLR RLL RLR

STEP D 1: STICK CONTROL/COORDINATION: TRIPLETS

337.
RRL LLR RLL LRL

338.
RRL LLR RLL LRR

339.
RRL LLR LRR RLR

340.
RRL LLR LRR LRL

341.
RRL LLR LRR RLL

342.
LLR RLR LRL RLL

343.
LLR RLR LRL LRR
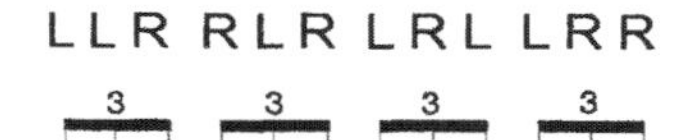

344.
LLR RLR LRL RRL

345.
LLR RLR RLL LRL

346.
LLR RLR RLL LRR

347.
LLR RLR RLL RRL

348.
LLR RLR LRR LRL

349.
LLR RLR LRR RLL

350.
LLR RLR LRR RRL

351.
LLR RLR RRL LRL

352.
LLR RLR RRL RLL

353.
LLR RLR LLR LRR

354.
LLR LRL RLR RLL

355.
LLR LRL RLR LRR

356.
LLR LRL RLR RRL

357.
LLR LRL RLL LRL

STEP D 1: STICK CONTROL/COORDINATION: TRIPLETS

358.
LLR LRL RLL LRR

359.
LLR LRL RLL RRL

360.
LLR LRL LRR RLR

361.
LLR LRL LRR RLL

362.
LLR LRL LRR RRL

363.
LLR LRL RRL RLR

364.
LLR LRL RRL RLL

365.
LLR LRL RRL LRR

366.
LLR RLL RLR LRL

367.
LLR RLL RLR LRR

368.
LLR RLL RLR RRL

369.
LLR RLL LRL RLR

370.
LLR RLL LRL LRR

371.
LLR RLL LRL RRL

372.
LLR RLL LRR RLR

373.
LLR RLL LRR LRL

374.
LLR RLL LRR RRL
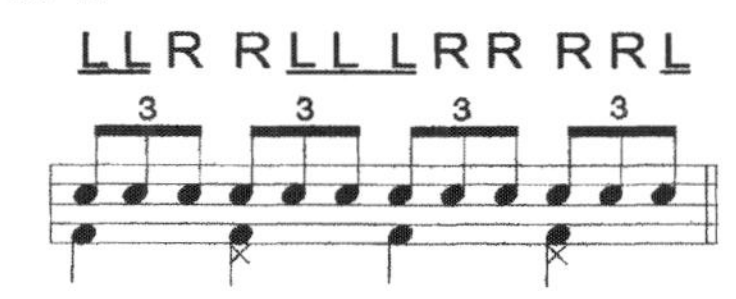

375.
LLR RLL RRL RLR

376.
LLR RLL RRL LRL

377.
LLR LRR RLR LRL

378.
LLR LRR RLR RLL

STEP D 1: STICK CONTROL/COORDINATION: TRIPLETS

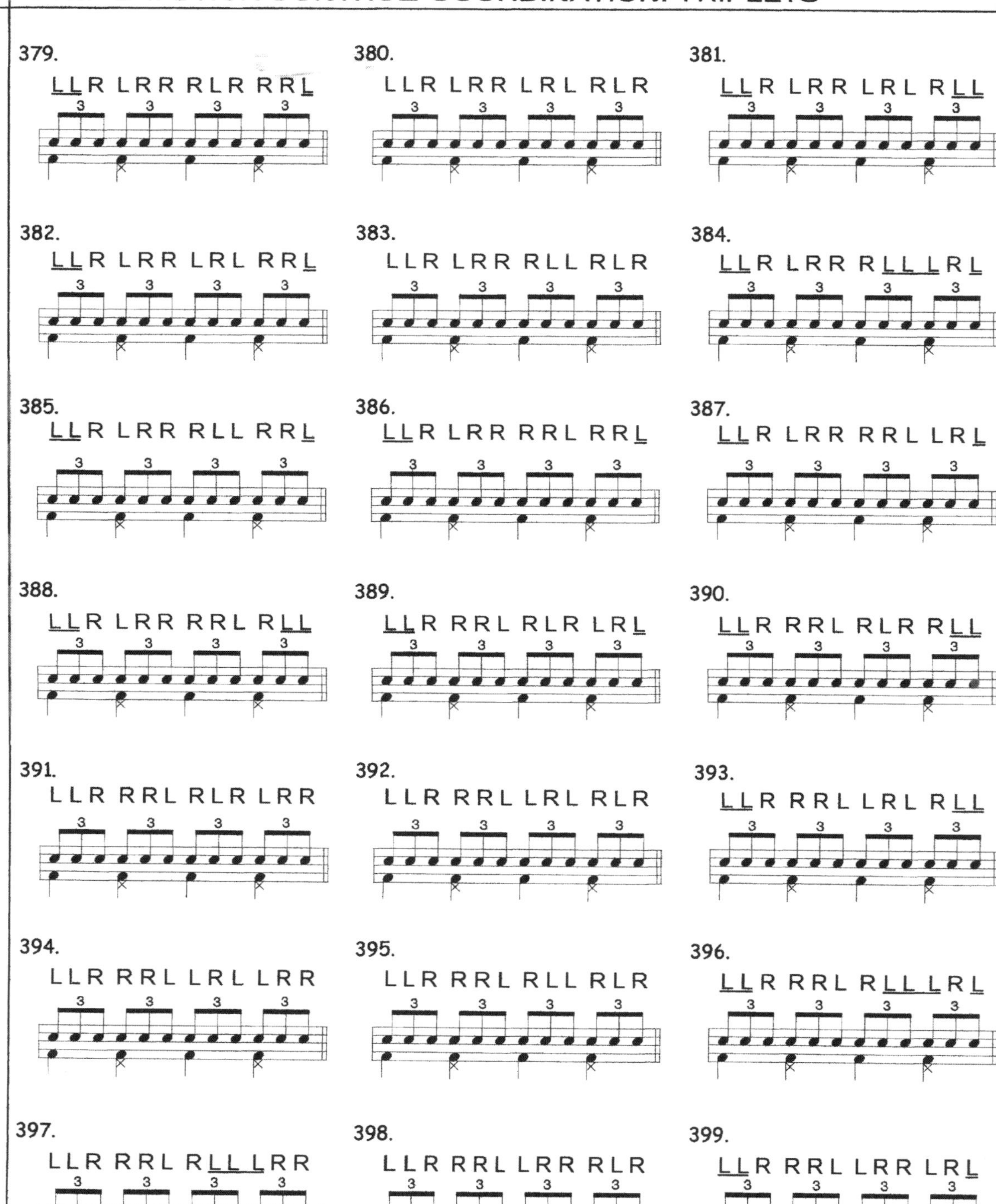

Soloing

Louie Bellson, Buddy Rich, Max Roach, and many other jazz drummers put soloing near the bottom of a list of priorities a jazz drummer must attend to. It was Louie Bellson who said that if you couldn't swing a band, you could do the solo at the end of the night, while another drummer would have to be hired to back the band the other three and a half hours. Yet these and other drummers were terrific soloists also. I believe that it was their very sense of priorities that made them wonderful soloists, for their attention to form, feel, tempo, and the other musicians informed their own solos. Several years ago I attended a workshop given by Alan Dawson (see page 192), where he soloed while singing the melody to "Satin Doll," thereby tying his solo to the song form for all to hear. Being young at the time, I was properly impressed, but found out later that all competent jazz drummers incorporate the same mental trick when they solo. It is important that jazz drummers learn to solo against the form of a song. Here are some practice ideas that will help you reach that goal.

- Apply the ear training exercises on pages 102 - 105 to the drumset. Instead of answering the notes on the piano, play jazz time for the first two measures, as you listen for the phrase, then play that phrase on any part of the set during the next two measure, while keeping time with the hi-hat on '2' & '4'. Do this against tracks 7 - 10 of the CD. Relax, and allow for the space between notes. If the phrase consists of just one note, play just that one note.

- Now repeat the above set of exercises, playing jazz time for the first two measures as you listen for the phrase. For the next two measures repeat the phrase on the drumset, playing the notes with the right hand on any part of the set, while keeping time with the hi-hat on '2' & '4'. Fill in the rests with swinging eighth notes with any combination of left and right hands as well as bass drum. Go back to keeping time and continue with the next phrase.

- To begin to get a feel for playing against a song's form, start by soloing against simple nursery or children's songs (seriously - the concept is the same as against jazz standards). Try to sing aloud while you are soloing. This may prove to be a bigger challenge than it seems. Sample songs: "Mary Had A Little Lamb," "Farmer In The Dell," "Row, Row, Row Your Boat," "If You're Happy And You Know It," etc. When this level is mastered, try combining any two songs to create a longer song form.

- Become familiar with jazz standards by listening to recordings, and singing the melody afterwards. You could also have a musician friend play the melody for you, and even play the melody over your soloing.

- Vocalist Bobby McFerrin recommends this idea, as so do I: Set a timer for ten minutes, and play any idea that comes to you. Go exploring, this time without regard to form. See what a blank slate brings forth. You will surprise yourself with the ideas you come up with, and those ideas will add to your musical vocabulary, and you will become more adept at spontaneous creativity.

STEP D 2: READ "COOL JAZZ"

COOL JAZZ

The Pendulum Swings. In our society, things tend to shift back and forth. When one trend has been embraced and then explored to the point of saturation, a trend in the other direction can be expected. During the late '40s and early '50s, several jazz musicians started playing music that was more subdued and subtle, with melodic lines that were more flowing than the angular lines of bop. Many musicians, like Miles Davis and Stan Getz, who had played bop, moved to the new trend with a good deal of commercial success. Because some of these musicians were based in California at the time, this style of music was also known as "West Coast Jazz." Pianist Lennie Tristano, alto saxophonist Lee Konitz, and baritone saxophonist Gerry Mulligan were early and influential practitioners of cool jazz.

Miles Davis. Miles Davis was born in 1926 in Alton, Illinois, and began playing the trumpet at age 13. While attending Julliard School of Music in New York, Davis heard Charlie Parker and was mesmerized by both Parker and bebop music. Soon Parker and Davis were roommates as well as bandmates. The mid '40s in New York was the time and place of bop's incubation, and Davis was there among the originators. When Dizzy Gillespie ended his partnership with Charlie Parker, Parker put together a quintet in 1947 that featured Davis on trumpet and Max Roach on drums.

Two years later Davis put a nonet (a nine piece group) to record an album which became known as *The Birth of the Cool*. The music, which was smoother, lighter, and more arranged than the bop of the time, set the tone for the cool jazz movement to come. After a terrible bout with heroin addiction, Miles retreated to his father's farm and cleaned himself up cold turkey. He was now ready to change the jazz world.

1955 was a turning point in Davis' life. His mentor, Charlie Parker died that year. As if guided by some unseen hand, Davis then heard alto saxophonist Julian "Cannonball" Adderly, and was struck by his soulful sound. At the Newport Jazz Festival, Davis wowed the crowd with his muted rendition of Monk's "After Midnight." He is signed with Columbia Records, and forms an historic combo, the Miles Davis Quintet. The lineup includes the legendary John Coltrane on saxophone and "Philly" Joe Jones (not the Basie drummer) on drums. Davis would later recall, "the music that we were playing... was so bad that it used to send chills through me at night."

Davis' aptitude at bringing together just the right combination of musicians proved timely in 1958. Coltrane had gone through his own personal rehab, and was back with Miles, now joined by Cannonball Adderly on alto, Red Garland on piano, Paul Chambers on bass, and Philly Joe Jones on drums. The results: a breakthrough album, *Milestones*, in which the title cut introduced the listeners to something new: modal jazz.

The group's next recording, *Kind of Blue* (1959), brought modal jazz to its highest expression, and became one of the most critically acclaimed *and* commercially successful albums in jazz history. The album was a logical step in a series of stylistic changes that Davis

Modal jazz: Music in which the frequent chord changes which characterize most of jazz are replaced by modes, or scales. This approach to improvisation gave the soloist a freer, and yet still demanding, platform to create.

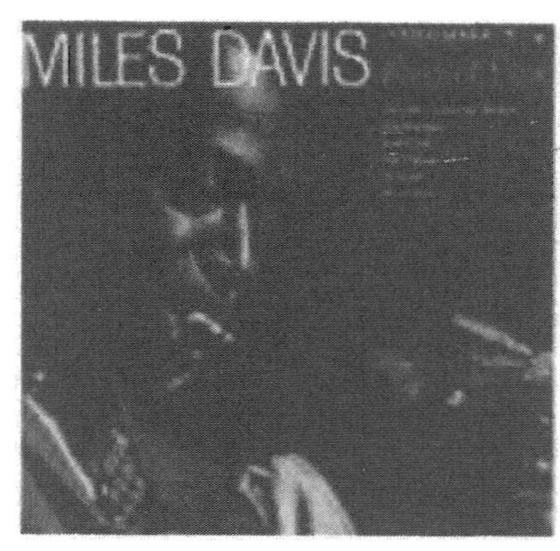

would make throughout his career. The personnel on *Kind of Blue* was now different: Two pianists were used on different cuts, Wynton Kelly and Bill Evans. Bluesy alto saxophonist Julian "Cannonball" Adderley and energetic tenor saxopahonist John Coltrane were a perfect balance for Miles' subdued and delicate tone. Paul Chambers was the bassist, and Jimmy Cobb was now in the drummer's seat. Much of the album's critical and commercial success stems from the spontanaity and atmosphere exhibited in the recording. The songs were sketched out literally hours before, and there were no rehearsals. The freshness of the group's sound is still evident on hearing it nearly half a century later. Two of the album's five cuts have long become standards: "So What" and "All Blues."

Miles, Philly Joe & the Philly Joe Lick

Joseph Rudolph (Philly Joe) Jones was Miles Davis' favorite drummmer, and one the most historically significant bop and post-bop drummers in jazz. Because he was from Philadelphia (born there in 1923), and to distinguish himself from Count Basie's well known drummer Jo Jones, he became known as "Philly Joe." Philly Joe was Miles Davis' drummer from 1952-1958. That band, known as "The Quintet," was regarded by many as the greatest group in jazz history. Always intuitively musical, Jones raised the level of playing of whomever he was playing with. During his career, Jones performed and recorded with Tadd Dameron, John Coltrane, Sonny Rollins, Hank Mobley, Dexter Gordon, Cannonball Adderly, Wynton Kelly, Bill Evans, Wes Montgomery, Freddie Hubbard, and of course, Miles Davis. From 1958 on he led his own band. In 1968 he moved to England and established himself as a teacher. Returning to the states, Jones was involved in several performing and recording projects. He passed away in 1985 of a heart attack in his hometown of Philadelphia.

One playing technique that Jones used frequently was simply to keep time on the ride cymbal and place a crosstick on the fourth beat of each measure. This had a relaxing effect on the music being played. Miles was so taken with this pattern that he dubbed it the "Philly lick."

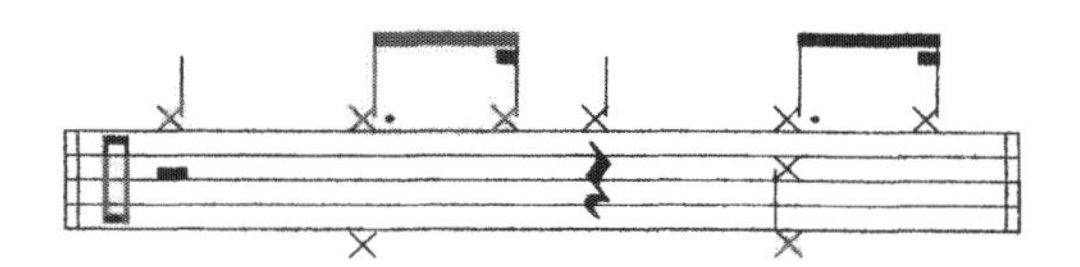

Above: The "Philly Lick." Left: Philly Joe Jones, getting that "great Gretsch sound." Many jazz drummers in the '50s and '60s played and endorsed Gretsch.

See page 186 for more info on the crosstick or rim-click.

To be Continued. . . Miles Davis spearheaded significant stylistic changes in jazz history, and his story continues later in this book.

Dave Brubeck. Dave Brubeck was born on December 6, 1920 in Concord, California, and grew up on his parents' cattle ranch. Though his mother pressed him with classical training, it was skill at improvising, a strong interest in rhythms, and an inability to learn to read music that moved him toward jazz. Indeed, it was the sound of the various ranch machines on the ranch that created an interest in odd meters and polyrhythms. After studying music at two colleges with a stint in the army in between, Brubeck made his first recordings, with an avant-garde octet (they didn't gig much, as might be expected), and a much more popular trio, which did work a lot in the Bay Area. It was alto saxophonist Paul Desmond who persuaded Brubeck to expand the group into a quartet. Joe Morello became the drummer in 1956, and Eugene Wright became the bassist two years later. Soon the Brubeck quartet was the most popular jazz band in the country, with them now recording for Columbia (Miles Davis' label), touring heavily (many college campus concerts), and Brubeck appearing on the cover of Time Magazine. This trajectory of success culminated in the 1959, with the album *Time Out*, a collection of songs, none of them in 4/4. Brubeck had asked Paul Desmond to write a song that would feature their drummer, Joe Morello, and Desmond came up with "Take Five," a song in 5/4 that featured a dynamic solo by Morello, played over a piano and bass ostinato. The album was a surprise smash (Columbia was reluctant to release it), and "Take Five," released as a single, became a Top Forty hit, a very rare feat for a jazz recording. Follow-up albums stayed in keeping with the "odd time" theme: *Time Further Out, Time In Outer Space,* and *Time Changes*. Other thematic recordings: *Jazz Impressions of Japan, Jazz Impressions of Spain*, etc., as well as various live recordings (*At Carnegie Hall*, 1963, being one of their best), kept Columbia Records happy and the group in the public eye.

The always exhuberant
Dave Brubeck

Polyrhythms: Two or more rhythms played at the same time. Drummers, by virtue of their instrument, play polyrhythms all the time. The study of polyrhythms, however is open-ended and can become extremely complex.

Avant-Garde (AH-vahnt GARD): An example of art that steps outside of conventional boundaries and parameters. Also refers to the group of people who are involved in breaking those boudaries. All art forms (music, painting, film, etc.) have their boundary breakers, and nowadays what they do is described as "pushing the envelope." But being unconventional and interesting at the same time without appearing gratuitous is a tricky business, and a challenge for those who venture there. From the French, meaning literally, "before the guard."

Voted Most Unlikely To Succeed

History is full of ironic examples of people being misjudged before they became successful. It is well known that Albert Einstein was viewed by his teachers as slow and dimwitted. He basically was a high school dropout. The Beatles were rejected by every major label before their manager finally landed them a recording contract. The founder of the publishing company that published this book, Mel Bay, was a working guitarist with a trunk full of guitar instruction books. When all the major publishing companies refused to publish his book, he simply started his own company. When Dave Brubeck attended the University of the Pacific, he was nearly expelled when it was discovered that he could not read music. Other professors came forward on his behalf. Still, he was given a diploma with the stipulation that he would never teach piano!

One of the best selling jazz albums of all time, this was also the golden age of album cover art, was it not?

Joe Morello. Joe Morello was born in Springfield, Massachusetts on July 17, 1929. His early experiences certainly set the stage for later success. From birth on he had very poor eyesight. He started a prodigious study of the violin at the age of six, and performed with the Boston Symphony Orchestra just three years later. After meeting and hearing the great violinist Jascha Heifetz, and realizing he could never reach that level of musical mastery, Joe turned to the drums. He studied the drums with the same discipline he had for the violin, and could not have had better teachers. First, Joe Sefcik, a local pit drummer, who modeled for Joe the idea of the working professional, playing any situation. Then he studied in Boston with the great George Lawrence Stone, the author of the classic book "Stick Control." Stone was so taken with his young student that he dedicated his second book, "Accents And Rebounds," to him. It was from Stone that Joe learned technique and reading, and he came to realize his future was in jazz, not classical or show percussion. Joe's reputation grew, and he spent some time on the road with several groups.

Joe decided to move New York, and was soon creating a buzz among other musicians. Gigs with such reputable musicians as Johnny Smith, Stan Kenton, and Marian McPartland followed. He then turned down offers to join the big bands of Benny Goodman and Tommy Dorsey, and went with the chance to tour with the Dave Brubeck Quartet for two months. The two month gig turned into a twelve and one-half stay. It is revealing that during this time of success, Joe continued his studies, this time with Billy Gladstone.

Possessing flawless technique with a blend of keen musical insight and melodic phrasing, Joe was a model for many drummers of what a musician/drummer does. He appeared on over 120 albums, half of which were with Dave Brubeck. In later years Joe continued the tradition his teachers had set for him earlier, and also became a teacher of reknown, doing clinics, writing books, and recording instructional videos as well as giving private lessons.

Joe Speaks His Mind

"When your hand is relaxed, your thumb isn't squeezing against your first finger and your wrist isn't at some funny angle. The stick just rests in the hand in a very natural position. When you strike a practice pad, you should be able to hear the ring of the wood stick. The average person chokes the stick, and that comes through on the drum. The whole thing is relaxation and letting the sticks do most of the work."

Quoted by Rick Mattingly

Jascha Changes Joe's Mind

The legendary Jascha Heifetz, the second violinist to enter this drum book. This book almost received a PG-13 rating, but was deemed by the book review board to have too much sax and violins. We are appealing that judgement.

Joe, More Joe, And Even Mojo

Left: it's always a good idea to play close to the bass player. Check out Joe's cool canister throne. Center: Joe's form was perfect. Right: Joe playing his wide-open tuned, silver sparkle Ludwigs. Bottom: A sample four measures of Joe's comping during "Take Five."

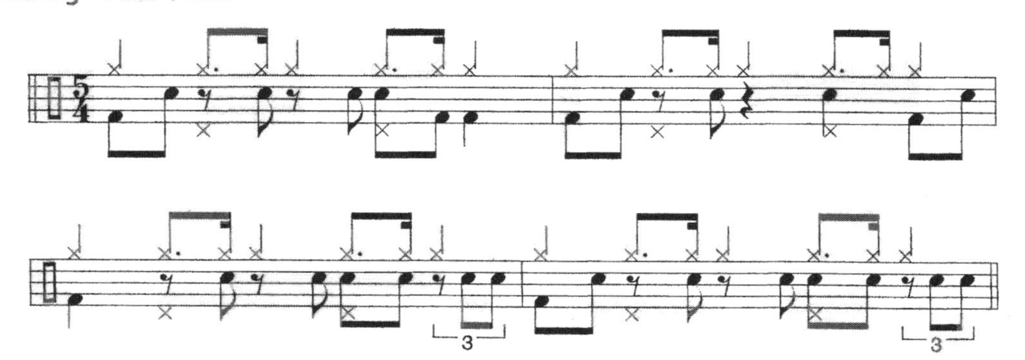

We bring you this commercial message

Both Miles Davis and Dave Brubeck broke a lingering stereotype about the music business and jazz that persists today: the idea that "good" jazz should not be a commercial success, and that if an artist is successful, then the music must not be as valid or as "good" as music that is not as popular. Louis Armstrong was particularly dismissed by some critics and a younger generation of jazz musicians who might have forgotten his singular contributions to the development of jazz. The fact that he was an immensely popular entertainer clouded their judgement. Some of the same critics who lauded Dave Brubeck's music before his success later found fault with it, even though he had not changed his style at all.

The bottom line is this: If someone's brand of jazz finds favor with the public and is commercially successful, we should not begrudge that person's success, but be happy that someone in music is getting a check cut. Maybe someday you will be getting such a check cut. But whether you do or not shouldn't affect your efforts, your musical vision, or the integrity of the results.

The Cool School Alumni

Claude Thornhill
Modern Jazz Quartet
Miles Davis with Bill Evens
Chico Hamilton
Shelly Manne
Dave Brubeck Quartet
Gerry Mulligan
Lee Konitz
George Shearing
Lennie Tristano

THE BOYS FROM BRAZIL

Brazilian music has had a long and intricate heritage unique to itself. From the late '50s to the early '60s, Brazilians took a break from the samba to make a new music called bossa nova. Through a series of circumstances, the trend caught on in the United States, and this subtle music dovetailed perfectly with the cool jazz at the time.

João Gilberto,a popular singer in Rio, had developed an understated style of singing and guitar playing, after years of singing lively and loud. At the same time, a pianist/composer/arranger named Antonio Carlos Jobim was hacking out a respectable living by arranging music for a record company. In 1958, Jobim acheived acclaim with his contributions to a movie called *Black Orpheus*, which won an Oscar that year. Soon thereafter, Jobim wrote a song with a tricky melody called "Desafinado" (meaning: slightly off-key). When Gilberto recorded the song, a musical partnership was born. The dominant writer of bossa novas and the primary singers of these songs helped spark a bossa nova boom in Brazil.

When guitarist Charlie Byrd and tenor saxophonist Stan Getz recorded Brazilian music both jointly and separately, their recordings helped create a major interest in bossa nova in the United States. Indeed, it was Stan Getz' recording session in 1964 with Jobim and Gilberto (along with Gilberto's wife, Astrud, bassist Tommy Williams, and drummer Milton Banana) that put bossa nova on the pop charts with the all time bossa nova hit, "The Girl From Ipanema," and one of the most successful jazz albums of all time, *Getz/Gilberto*. Pretty soon everyone was on the bossa nova train, with even Frank Sinatra recording an album with Jobim, and other Jobim compositions became standards in the jazz repertoire.

Stan Getz

Bossa Nova Standards:

"The Girl From Ipanema
"Desafinado"
"Corcavado"
"Wave"
"Day In The Life Of A Fool"
"Meditation"
"Watch What Happens"

Playing the Rim Click

One of the several extra sounds a drummer gets from his set is called a "rim click" or "cross-stick." To get this sound, turn the stick in your left hand around so the butt end of the stick is facing toward the snare. The tip end of the stick stays on the drum as the butt end of the stick is struck against the rim. The result is a hollow, wooden sound, unique to itself, but somewhere between the sound of claves and a low pitched wood block.

The trick to a click. The stick is held "upside down" with the butt end facing away from you. The left hand lightly pinches the stick between the thumb and forefinger with all four fingers splayed outward (see right).

The entire left hand rests on the drum while holding the stick down. Position the stick so that the tip sits on the drumhead approximately one inch from the rim (below, left). Placing the tip too far either way degrades the sound you want. The wrist and tip of the stick both act as a hinge, lifting the butt end of the stick up and down to produce the click (below, right).

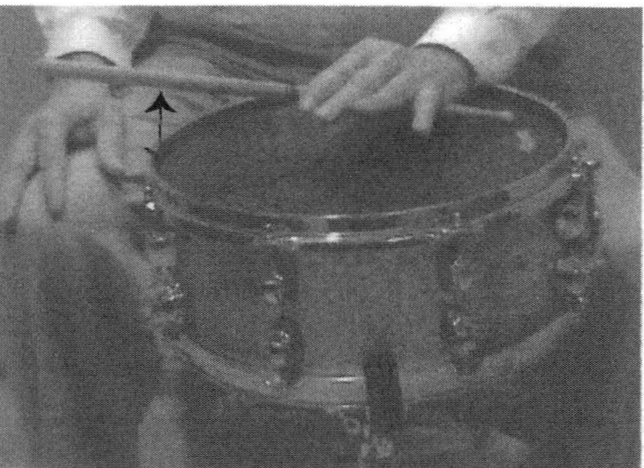

PLAYING THE BOSSA NOVA

Imitation is the sincerest form of flattery. The drumset, like jazz, baseball, fast food, and rock music, is a good old American invention. Just as other countries adopted all of the above items through their own cultural filters, *we* do the same when we adopt things from other countries. Just compare a Taco Bell restaurant with an authentic Mexican restaurant, and you'll see what I mean (actually I like both restaurants, depending on the mood)

Traditional latin music employs several percussion instruments instead of a drumset. The drumset player uses different parts of the set to simulate the different latin sounds. The steady pulsation of the maracas can be matched by playing eighth notes on the snare with the brush. The sound of the claves can be mimicked by playing a rim click on the snare. This Brazilian rhythm is based on a variant of the clave pattern:

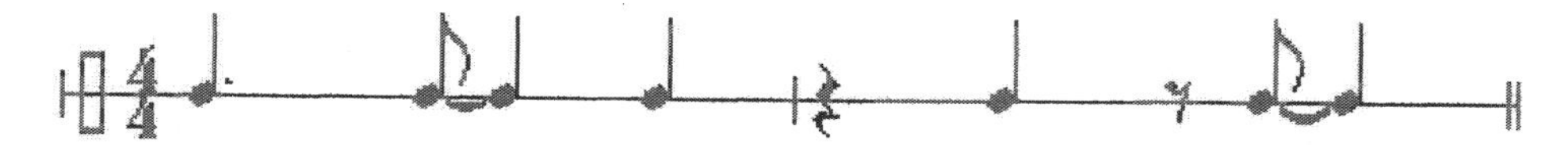

In a standard drumset application, the right hand usually plays straight eighth notes on the snare with a brush, or on the hi-hat or cymbal with a stick or brush, while the left hand plays the above pattern with snare drum rim clicks:

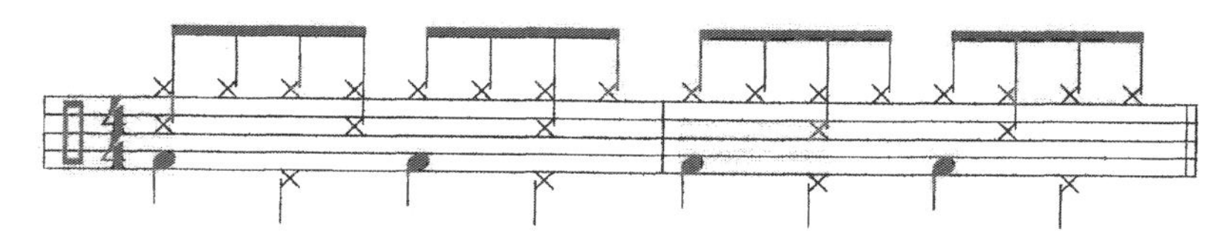

The two measure pattern can be reversed, and, if desired, the bossa nova and be livened up by augmenting the bass drum pattern:

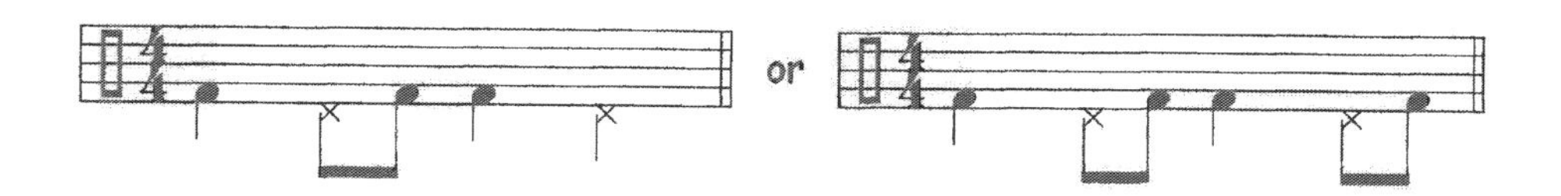

Great Insight From Peter Erskine:

"We spend thousands of hours learning to play our instrument and trying to get some level of mastery. Then after a while, you realize it's not quite the physical sporting event it was when you first started out, and you learn to stop wrestling and fighting your instrument. I tell my students that the whole thing is a lot simpler than you may be prepared to believe. Just play what you would like to hear next. I think when you put it in that context, it demystifies the whole thing."

International Musician, January, 2011

BOSSA NOVA - NOVA = BOSSA

Sometimes a chart or composition suggests playing in the bossa nova style rather than a strict bossa nova. This is referred to as a "bossa," and is usually acheived by playing eighth notes with the right hand on the hi-hat or cymbal, and improvised rim click patterns on the snare.

The following 16 measure exercise is an example of drumming in a bossa style.

PLAYING THE SAMBA

The samba is another import from Brazil, by way of Africa. Like many styles of music, it originated as a dance, and its beginnings can be traced to the early 20th century. It has a lively feel to it, and is felt "in two," with a slight emphasis on the second beat. This articulation is a little subtle, and can be realized by vocalizing the dotted-eighth/16th note bass drum line, emphasizing the "2" of the count:"one - - a **TWO** - - a one - - a **TWO** - - a (etc.)"

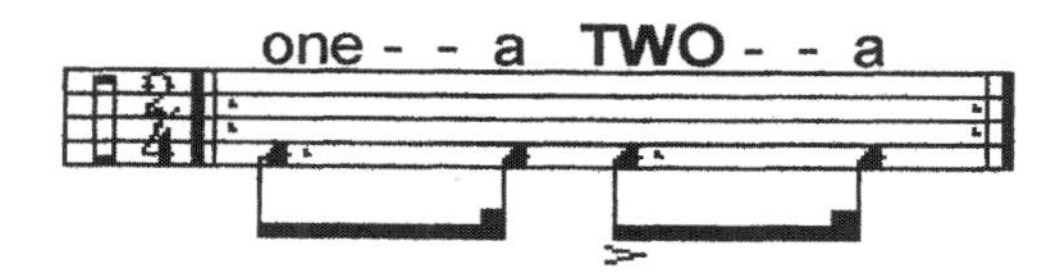

Now place the LF/HH on all the upbeats ("ands"):

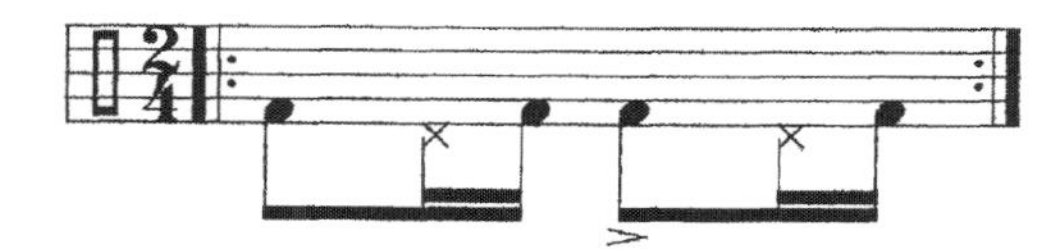

Practice the bass drum/hi-hat ostinato as you count, and this will color your articulation as you apply other accent patterns.

Now let's transpose to **4/4** time, and add one more ostinato on the ride cymbal:

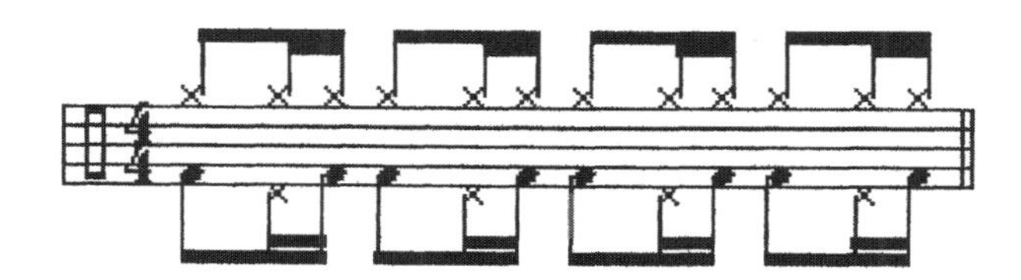

When you have these three limbs "locked in." you are ready for the first three examples:

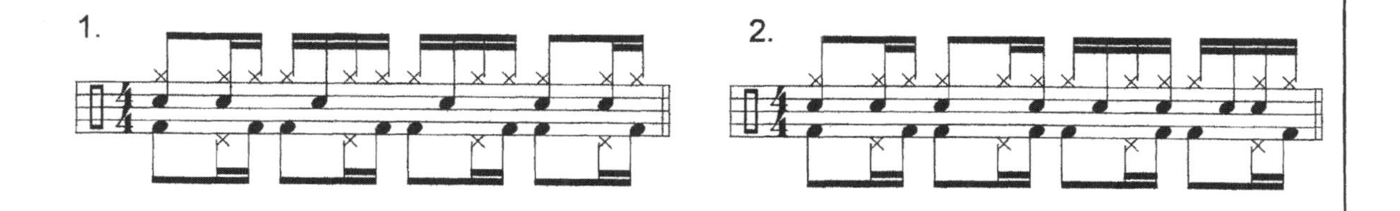

STEP D 6: PLAYING THE SAMBA

Samba #3 features some syncopated accents at the end of the measure:

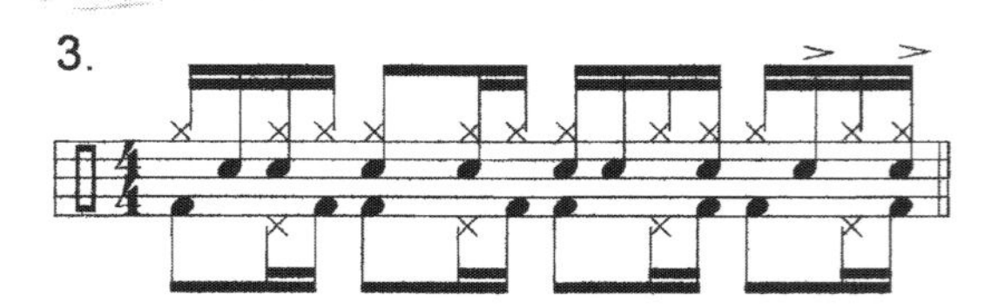

For sambas 4 & 5, play hand-to-hand 16ths (RLRL, etc.), using sticks or brushes.

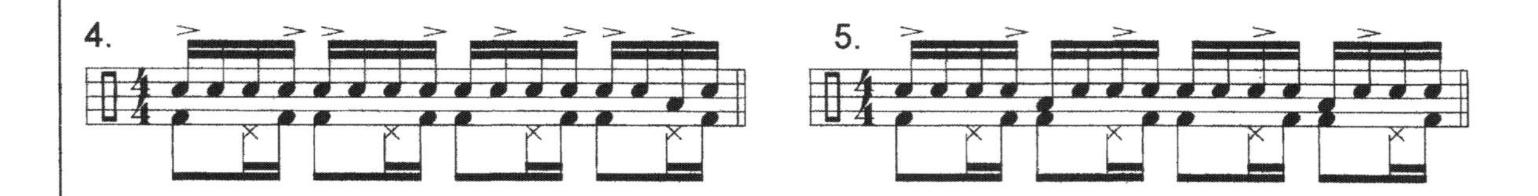

For samba 6, the RH moves around the drums while the LH plays snare clicks. Watch the sticking.

Sometimes both hands play a unison pattern:

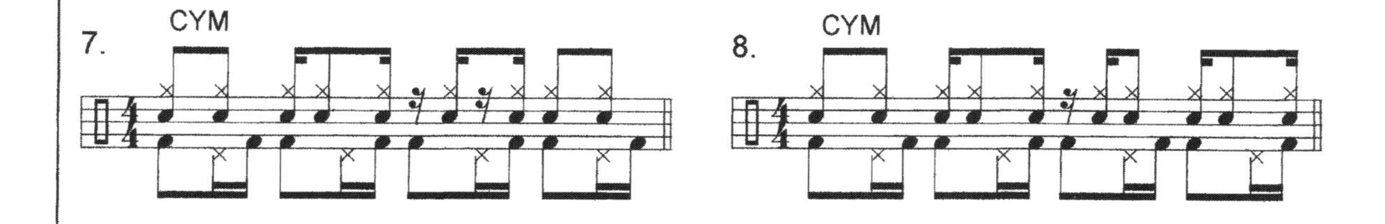

AFRO-CUBAN 6/8

Many years ago I attended a workshop given by the great drummer-educator Alan Dawson (see next page). The first thing he did was demonstrate the following afro-cuban groove:

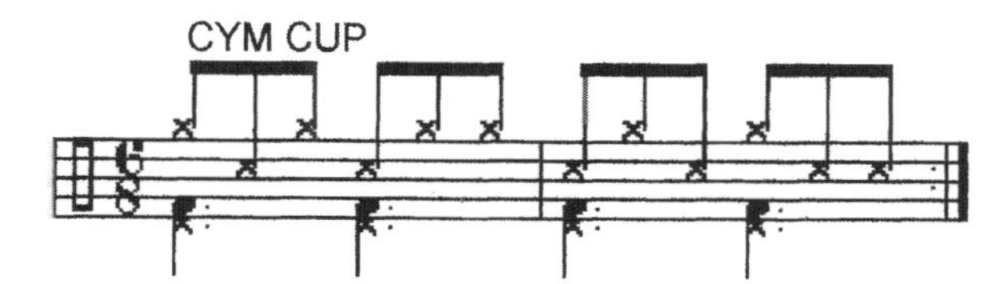

He then asked us to describe what he was doing. We were too intimidated to respond, so he informed us that all he was doing was the double paradiddle. It was like the light was turned on, seeing that it was just a basic rudiment applied on two surfaces. That experience reinforced in me the idea that the mastery of patterns is vital to good drumming.

Like the samba, the afro-cuban 6/8 can be mastered in a deeper way if preparatory steps are taken. First, master the cymbal cup part, with the bass drum on the downbeat to anchor the feel:

Now add a snare click on the second measure to balance it further:

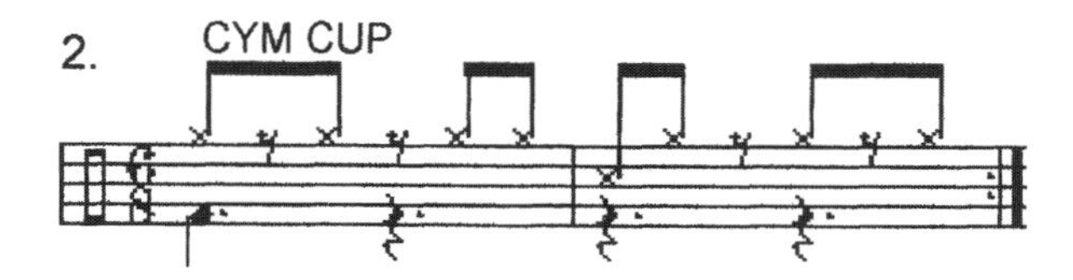

Add LF/HH on the beat, fill in the remaining rests with snare clicks, with an optional BD on the last eighth note:

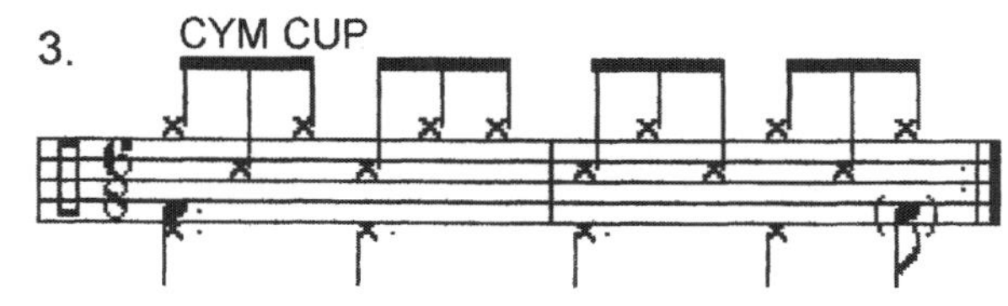

Now feel free to experiment, placing the LH notes on different parts of the set.

STEP D 7: PLAYING AFRO-CUBAN 6/8

This pattern was used in recordings by Santana:

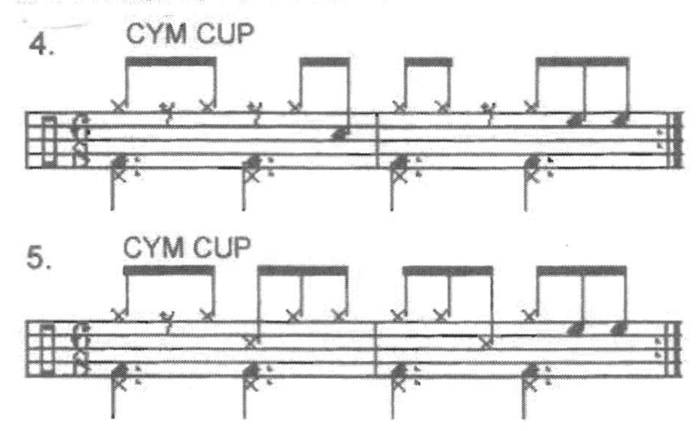

Art Blakey (see page193) used this pattern. Notice the LF/HH playing the upbeats:

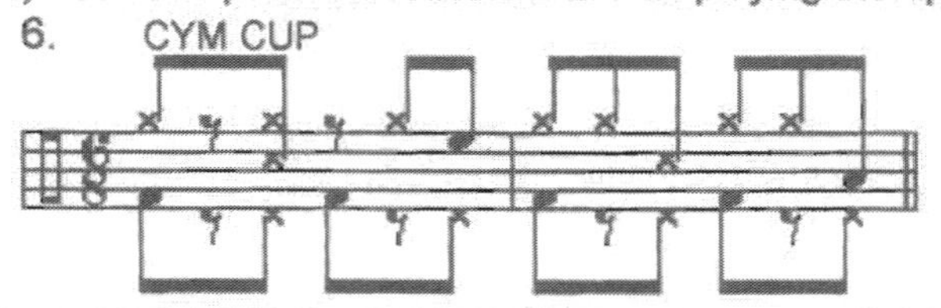

Some Notable Latin Percussionist/Drummers

Airto
Alex Acuña
Don Alias
Robby Ameen
Julio Barreto
Ray Barretto
Ignacio Berroa
Jimmy Branly
Luis Conte
Paulinho Da Costa
Sammy Figueroa Richie

Horacio Hernandez
Giovanni Hidalgo
Tito Puente
Marc Quiñones
Walfredo Reyes
Walfredo Reyes, Jr.
Bobby Sanabria
Poncho Sanchez
Efrain Toro
Nana Vasconcelos
Glen Velez

More on Alan Dawson

When Joe Morello left the Dave Brubeck Quarter in 1968, he was replaced by Alan Dawson. Dawson made his own mark in the group, but was already well known as a Boston-based master drum instructor with an impressive list of students who would later make their own history: Tony Williams, Terri Lyne Carrington, Vinnie Colaiuta, Steve Smith, and Kenwood Dennard. Dawson felt that practicing the brushes enhanced one's stick technique and had a routine called his "Rudimental Ritual." He also advocated a melodic/structural approach to both comping and soloing by singing the melody while drumming. Alan Dawson died in 1996.

STEP D 8: READ "HARD BOP" & "HARD BOPPERS OF NOTE"

HARD BOP

The bop scene of the late '40s subdivided into two styles in the '50s: cool jazz (discussed on page 180), and hard bop. These two styles were quite distinct from each other: whereas cool jazz went toward a more arranged, classically influenced as subtle approach, hard bop went in the other direction, with a raw, hard driving, sometimes funky feeling. Major exponents of hard bop included **Cifford Brown**, tenor saxophonist **Sonny Rollins**, pianist **Horace Silver**, alto saxophonist **Cannonball Adderly**, and his brother, cornetist **Nat Adderly**. Drummer **Art Blakey** (10/11/1919 - 10/16/1990) also belongs on the list, as he was a primary innovator in both his roles as drummer and bandleader. Blakey interacted with his soloists in an intense and driving fashion. One interesting trademark was his hi-hat independence: Blakey would occasionally break out of the standard backbeat pattern, and actually incorporate the hi-hat as an independent voice against the ride cymbal. Many of Blakey's sidemen went on to make names for themselves: Clifford Brown, Freddie Hubbard, Wayne Shorter, Chuck Mangione, Horace Silver, Keith Jarrett, and Wynton Marsalis. Other drummers who were known for hard bop drumming included **Philly Joe Jones** (who distinguished himself as a member of Miles Davis' group from 1952 to 1958), **Louis Hayes**, **Roy Haynes**, **Mikey Roker**, **Jimmy Cobb**, and **Frankie Dunlop**.

Art Blakey's pattern to "A Night In Tunisia," a standard he became strongly associated with:

Art Blakey, Philly Joe Jones (see next page), and many other jazz drummers of the time favored Gretsch Drums. The company's slogan then was "That Great Gretsch Sound!"

Hard Boppers of Note

Drummer **MaxRoach** and trumpeter **Clifford Brown** partnered together to form a burning quinted that lasted barely two years because of a tragic accident: Brown was killed in an automobile adcident in 1956.

After his cool phase and another bout with drugs, **Miles Davis** returned with perhaps the most definitive jazz band of the time: Red Garland on piano, Paul Chambers on bass, **Philly Joe Jones** on drums, and tenor saxophonist **John Coltrane**. Coltrane's strenuous solos contrasted with Davis' more restrained appraoch, sometimes with conflict. There is a well known story of an occasion when Coltrane's solo was too much for Miles. Coltrane said to Miles, "I can't stop playing." "Try taking the horn out of your mouth," was Miles' reply.

Sonny Rollins was always an adventurous tenor saxophonist, willing to explore to the fullest of his abilities, and sometimes when not satisfied with the results, willing to withdraw from the public for extended periods of time. Prior to recording classic albums under his own name, Rollins paid his dues playing with the likes of Thelonious Monk, Charlie Parker, Bud Powell, Art Blakey, the Modern Jazz Quartet, and Miles Davis. In 1956, Rollins released *Saxophone Colossus* (which featured Max Roach on drums), one of jazz' most acclaimed albums. One of the cuts, "St. Thomas," became a jazz standard.

Horace Silver, a pianist who was an early alumnus of Art Blakey's Jazz Messengers, became known for his percussive rhythmic style of playing. His well known compositions included "The Preacher," "Doodlin'," "Opus de Funk," "Senor Blues," "Nica's Dream," "Sister Sadie" and "Song for my Father."

Other hard bop musicians: Cannonball Adderley, Donald Byrd, Sonny Clark, Lou Donaldson, Kenny Drew, Benny Golson, Dexter Gordon, Johnny Griffin, Joe Henderson, Andrew Hill, Freddie Hubbard, Jackie McLean, Charles Mingus, Blue Mitchell, Hank Mobley, Lee Morgan, and Sonny Stitt.

Notable recordings:

Walkin', Miles Davis
Blue Train, John Coltrane
Moanin', Art Blakey
Finger Poppin', Horace Silver
Work Song, Nat Adderley
Soul Station, Hank Mobley
Ready for Freddie, Freddie Hubbard
Page One, Joe Henderson
Soul Station, Hank Mobley
Go,Dexter Gordon
Ready for Freddie, Freddie Hubbard
The real McCoy, McCoy Tyner

RIDE CYMBAL VARIATIONS

In any art form, nothing is static, and it wasn't long before early jazz drummers began playing permutations and variations of the ride cymbal pattern. This, along with phrasing, accents, and BD/SN interactions, led to a freer, spontaneous flow of the time. Joe Morello called it "skating."

Follow these directions for pages 195 - 196.

- Each exercise consists of 2 measures of the standard ride cymbal pattern, followed by 2 measures of a ride cymbal variation.
- Play each exercise against the CD tracks 1 - 6. Repeat each exercise several times. Maintain LF/HH on "2" and "4" throughout.
- As each exercise is mastered, feel free to "pepper" your playing with accents and BD and SN notes.

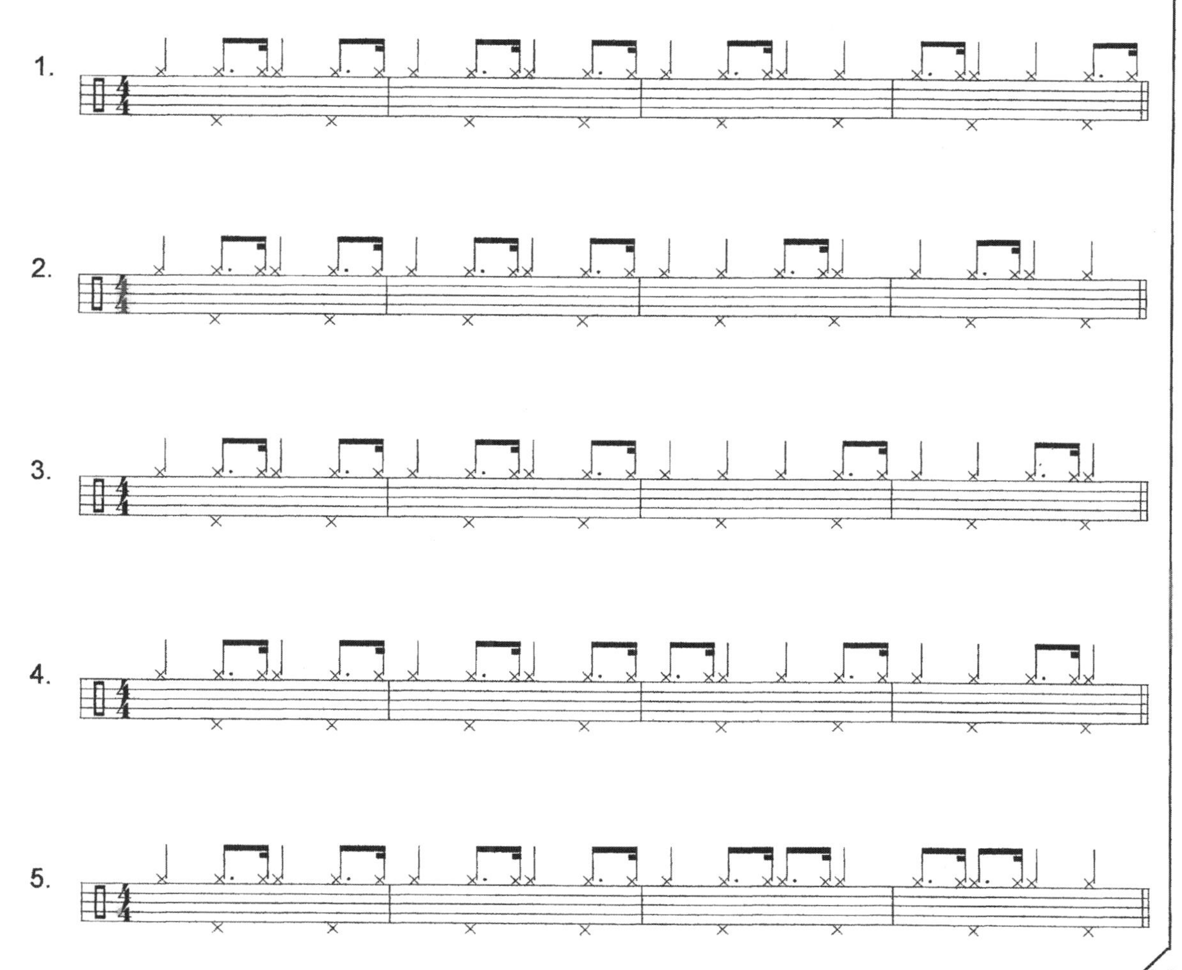

Step D 9: Ride Cymbal Variations

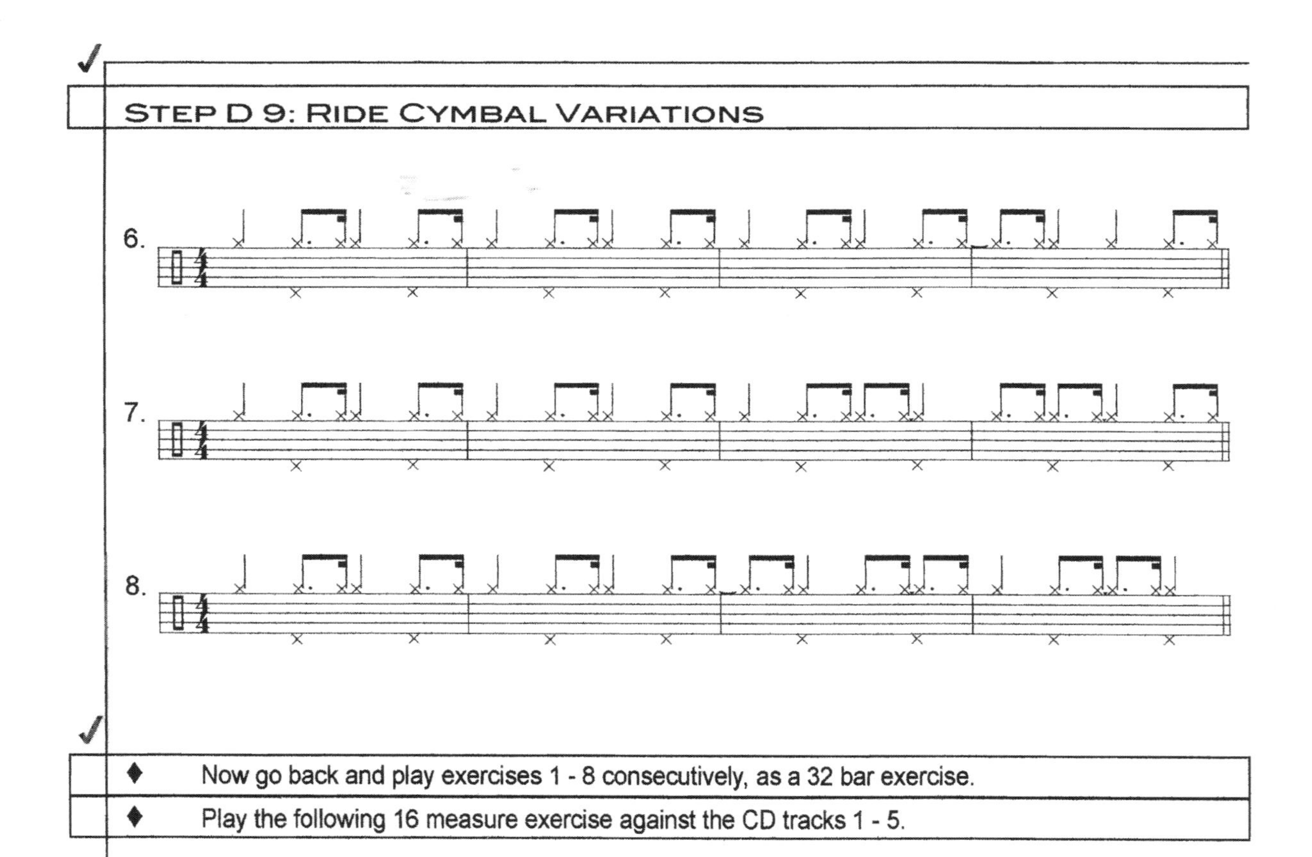

- Now go back and play exercises 1 - 8 consecutively, as a 32 bar exercise.
- Play the following 16 measure exercise against the CD tracks 1 - 5.

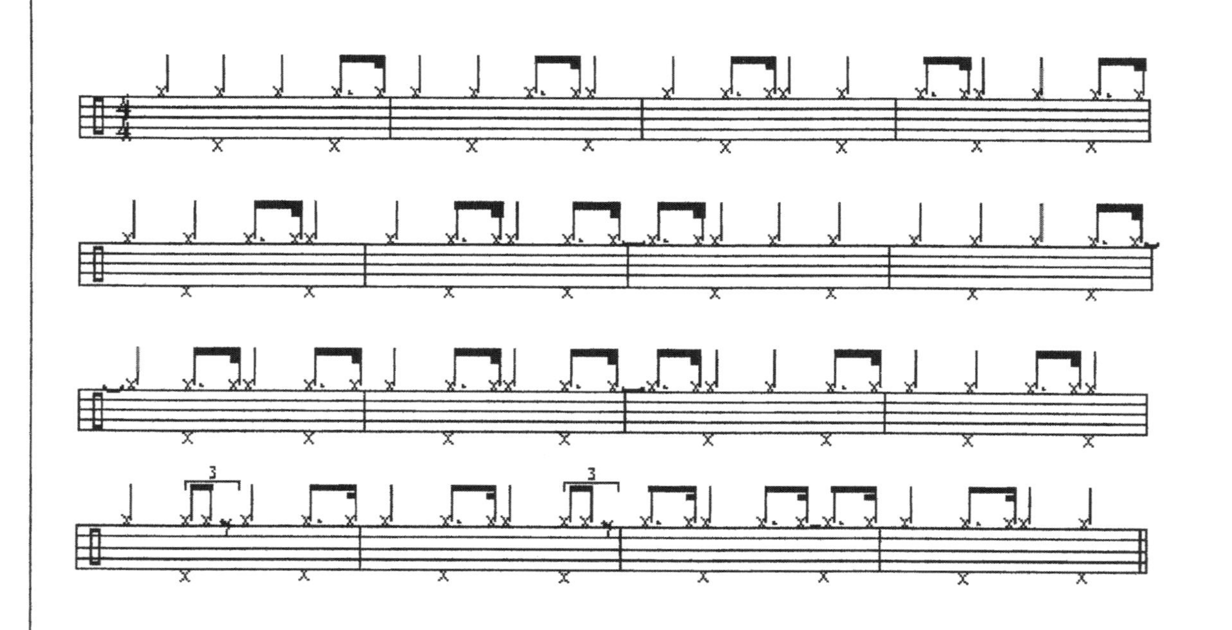

MAINSTREAM

Jazz hits the pop charts.

At this point, jazz made great inroads into public acceptance. In the mid '60s, bop guitarist Wes Montgomery's covers of popular tunes sold very well. Cannonball Adderly's quintet had a major Top 40 hit with Josef Zawinul's "Mercy, Mercy, Mercy." As noted earlier, Brazilian music, particularly the bossa nova, was introduced to the United States by tenor saxophonist Stan Getz in 1963, with his recording of "The Girl From Ipanema," a collaboration between Getz and writer/pianist Antonio Carlos Jobim and guitarist Joao Gilberto. Gilberto's wife Astrus sang the English lyrics, and this recording also made the Top 40 charts. "Ipanema" and other bossa novas of the time, with their subtle melodies and clever chord progressions, were a welcome change of pace for many jazz fans. The bossa nova was a natural extension of the cool period, and opened the door for jazz mergings with other latin rhythms, especially the samba. Flutist Herbie Mann was also influenced by latin rhythms, and sold many albums with his renditions of popular songs.

Bill Evans, a talented pianist who contributed to Miles Davis' *Kind of Blue* album, formed his own trio, whose musicians interacted with each other with a depth rarely seen. Evans had a fondness for pretty waltzes, and his tender rendition of two Disney Studio tunes, "Someday My Prince Will Come" and "Alice In Wonderland,"influenced many pianists soon to make their own mark, among them Herbie Hancock, Chick Corea, and Keith Jarrett. Drummer Paul Motian contributed to the Evans Trio with great taste and subtlety. His brushwork was crisp, and he brought out different sounds with his hi-hat, including the "splash" effect, in which the cymbals were released immediately upon light contact, allowing them to ring freely.

You really had to listen.

It's Never Too Late To Start

Wes Montgomery (1923-1968) began playing the guitar at the late age of 19, after he heard Charlie Christian play. He had a unique style of playing octave solos with his thumb. Joe Pass said, "To me, there have been only three real innovators on the guitar - Wes Montgomery, Charlie Christian, and Django Reinhardt."

MILES AND COLTRANE

It is impossible to exclude Miles Davis in discussing different styles of jazz that developed, as in many cases it was his recording of many landmark albums that pioneered various styles. It was as if, in choosing certain musicians to play with, and certain pieces to record, Davis anticipated where jazz was going. In 1955, Davis formed a quintet that included saxophonist John Coltrane, whose improvisational genius took bop to the edge of atonality, with every melodic idea of ther remotest relationship explored at a furious pace. In 1959, Coltrane appeared the landmark Miles album *Kind of Blue* (see pages 178-179), in which a single chord or mode would be employed for eight or sixteen measures at a time, giving the soloist great freedom to improvise. "So What," a cut from the album that became a jazz standard, is an example of modal jazz. The album featured pianist Bill Evans and drummer Jimmy Cobb, who stayed with Davis until 1963.

After his stint with Miles Davis from 1955-1957, John Coltrane spent a year with Thelonious Monk, then returned to Davis from 1958-1960, during the recording of *Kind of Blue*. Although he had recorded many albums under his own name, by 1960 he was ready to lead his own group. Coltrane released several albums - among them: the landmark *Giant Steps* (1959) which took bop to the extreme, *A Love Supreme* (1964), and *Ascension* (1965), the culmination of his search for total freedom in jazz.

The nature of jazz often requires a musician to be an itinerant wanderer - playing with various combinations of other musicians as he develops and finds his own voice. However, sometimes a musician is so strongly associated with another, that the partnership is viewed as historic. So it was with Elvin Jones and his drumming with John Coltrane.

Camco Drum Ad

THE ELVIN ERA

Elvin Jones was born in Pontiac, Michigan, in 1927, and his fascination with drums began early in life when he would watch circus marching bands go by his house. He played drums in the high school band, then served in the army. Upon his return, be bought a drumset with $35.00 dollars that he borrowed, and began his career. His discography includes over 500 albums with many artists, but, as mentioned in the above paragraph, it was with his association with John Coltrane that make him a significant figure in jazz history.

Jones matched Cotrane's freedom and intensity with his own, and changed drumming history with his own sense of time, fusing looseness of swing with the evenness of latin, sometimes referred to as "Elvin Latin." He incorporated what some have called a "circular" style of drumming, using rolling triplets, continuous polyrhythms, and a never-ending stream of ideas. In later years Jones led his own groups with great success. He died in 2004.

What Others Said About Elvin:

"He was a supreme drummer who was doing things that were totally different than anyone else. When I hear Elvin's music, I hear the pyramids, I hear African and pre-Columbian music, and I hear the future. Elvin is the beat of life itself, and his music transcends 'clever' or 'cute' or any superlatives."

Carlos Santana

"He is mother earth, coming alive with syncopation."

Louie Bellson

The Tony Era

For many musicians, and not just drummers, Tony Williams represented a bridge between jazz and the ever expanding rock scene, as well as being a consummate musician whose influence remains today. Born in Chicago, but raised in Boston, Williams' first mentor was his father, a gigging saxophonist who often took the young boy to the clubs he was performing in. After sitting in some sessions and showing real potential, he began drum lessons with Allan Dawson (see page 190) at age eleven. By age sixteen, he was already a professional musician, working with saxophonist Jackie McLean. Word of Williams' talent was spreading, and he was invited to join Miles Davis' new group. It was with Davis' group that the jazz world on a much larger scale took notice. Like the other members of the group, Williams was a groundbreaking musician, not content with the drummer's traditional role of time-keeper, but as an interactive participant, interjecting polyrhythmic phrases and metric modulations that kept the music ever fresh and exciting.

Williams left the Davis group and started the Tony Williams Lifetime, which featured guitarist John McLaughlin, organist Larry Young, and later bassist Jack Bruce. Because Williams was a fan of rock music as much as jazz, that group was not constrained by stylistic boundaries, and fused jazz, rock, and R&B, becoming a model for future fusion groups. Their first album, *Emergency*, was received with mixed reviews at first, but today is regarded as the emergence of a new style of music. The band's lineup went through various changes through the years (Allan Holdsworth was a later guitarist). After the group's run, Williams studied composition and played with Herbie Hancock's V.S.O.P. band. In the '80s, Williams took to heading his own band, with his own compositions featured. The music world was shocked when Williams died in 1997, from a heart attack following gall bladder surgery. To this day, Williams remains one of the most influential drummers in the history of jazz.

Tony Starts A Trend. As early as 1966 (while still with Miles Davis), on "Freedom Jazz Dance," from the Miles Smiles album, Williams pioneered a timekeeping trend by playing straight quarter notes on the hi-hat with his left foot (as opposed to the standard "two" and "four" hi-hat pattern). Overall, Williams played assertively, with great diversity and sensivity, influencing hundreds of jazz and rock drummers.

FUSION

During the mid '60s, rock music underwent a phase of unprecedented mergings. With rock music being taken seriously more than it had before, several jazz artists began attempts at fusing jazz with the syncopated funk elements of rock (especially as played by James Brown with his band, and Sly Stone). Two popular bands with horn sections emerged by the end of the decade: Chicago and Blood, Sweat, & Tears. The terms "fusion" or "jazz-rock" began to be used to describe such music. Once again, Miles Davis, along with his musicians, were at the forefront of a new jazz style.

In 1963, Miles Davis revamped his group with a new rhythm section: pianist Herbie Hancock, bassist Ron Carter, and drummer Tony Williams, who was only seventeen at the time. Besides comprising one of the most cohesive rhythm sections in the history of jazz. Each musician would be significant in the sylistic advances of his respective instrument. Hancock and Carter were both in demand as session musicians, appearing on literally hundreds of albums. Hancock went on to front several groups to play his own compositions, which included "Maiden Voyage," "Watermelon Man," and "Chameleon."

When Worlds Collide. During this period of experimentation, some hallmark albums were released, among them *Bitches Brew*, by Miles Davis (which featured drummer Lenny White) in 1969, a highly accaimed album which combined electronic instruments and funk rhythms with high energy improvisation. Band leader Don Ellis brought a unique big band approach to jazz-rock with his emphasis on odd-time signatures, exotic influences, and use of quarter-tones. Two rock groups who made a tremendous impact by utilizing horn sections with a jazz flavor were Chicago and Blood, Sweat, & Tears (featuring drummers Danny Seraphine and Bobby Colomby, respectively). Blood, Sweat, & Tears had a number one hit, "Spinning Wheel," from their second album, in 1969. Chick Corea, one of the most gifted pianists in the fusion genre, formed a group called Return to Forever. Corea, a drummer also, played piano percussively, and his songs had their own rhythmical trademarks that made them popular among musicians. "Spain" was perhaps Corea's most poplular composition.

John McLaughlin, mentioned earlier as guitarist for Tony Williams' Lifetime, went off on his own to form the Mahavishnu Orchestra, which featured the dynamic and powerful Billy Cobham as drummer. It was primarily through his association with the Mahavishnu Orchestra that Cobham gained the status he now enjoys, although prior to this he also worked with Billy Taylor and Miles Davis. Cobham's dynamic, two-fisted powerhouse style was enhanced by his rudimental background and his ambidexitry, enabling him to lead off with either hand.

Another model group for jazz-rock musicians was the Weather Report, a group of virtuosos which included pianist Joe Zawinul, saxophonist Wayne Shorter, and Miroslav Vitous on bass. Alphonse Mouzon played drums and percussionist Airto Moriera added exotic effects, contributing to the Weather Report sound, which featured highly interactive roles between soloist and accompanist, so much so that sometimes the distinction was difficult to perceive. Zawinul once stated, "We always solo and we never solo." Successive musicians who made their mark with the Weather Report were bassist Jaco Pastorious and drummers Alex Acuña and Peter Erskine.

What They Said About Jazz

"Jazz is not the kind of music you are going to learn to play in three or four years or that you can just get because you have some talent for music."
Wynton Marsalis

"Imitate,
assimilate,
and innovate."
Clark Terry

"There was a period which I refer to as the 'Golden Age of Jazz,' which sort of encompasses the middle Thirties through the Sixties, we had a lot of great innovators, all creating things which will last the world for a long, long time."
Sonny Rollins

"Risk is at the heart of jazz. Every note we play is a risk."
Steve Lacy

"One thing I like about jazz, kid, is that I don't know what's going to happen next. Do you?"
Bix Beiderbecke

"The pulse will come alive if you attach it in relation to the melody."
Ed Thigpen

"The most attractive thing a musician can be is to be comfortable to play with."
Peter Erskine

"Jazz consumes you to learn to play it, and I'm still trying to learn. It's an ongoing process, with different levels of learning through-out your life"
Bob Magnusson

"The stories from 1975 on are not finished and there is no resolve. I could spend 50 hours on the last 25 years of jazz and still not do it justice."
Ken Burns

✓

STEP D 12: LEFT FOOT HI-HAT INDEPENDENCE

Up to this point, all the exercises concerning SN or BD independence kept the LF/HH on 2 & 4 of the measure. Indeed, the playing of the hi-hat on the backbeat is an historical and stylistic part of jazz drumming, and is a crucial component of the swing feel. Ever since bebop, however, drummers have felt free to occasionally deviate from that standard and use the hi-hat as a temporary comping statement, just as the snare and bass drum have been doing.

- ♦ Follow these directions for pages 203 - 205.
- ♦ Play these exercises as written, against CD tracks 1 - 6.
- ♦ Play each exercise 4 times, before moving to the next one.
- ♦ The exercises are in two measure phrases, to demonstrate that in most cases, the LF/HH reverts back to "2" and "4" after the comp statement:

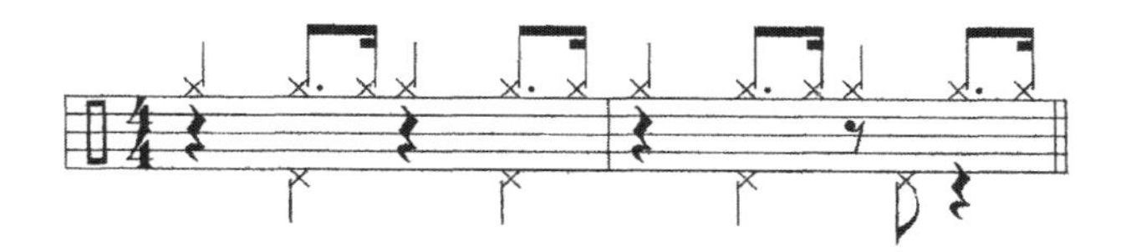

- ♦ When this symbol
  O
  is written below the note, the hi-hat is to be played as a "splash." This is acheived by bringing up the left foot immediately when the cymbals come into contact, creating a "splash" effect. The hi-hat cymbals remain open until the next comp note, or until they resume playing on 2 & 4:

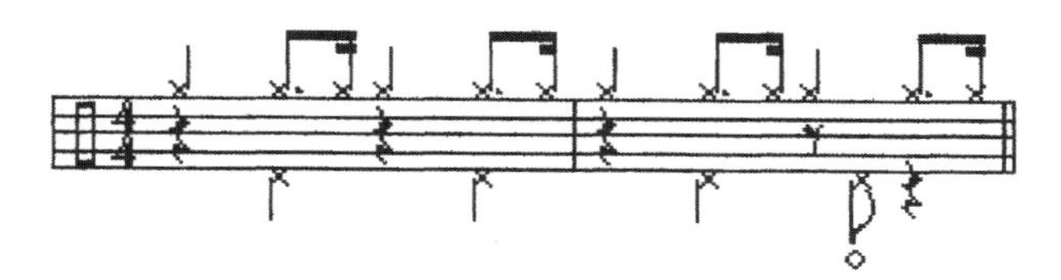

Something To Think About

No Drummer Is An Island - Elvin Jones with John Coltrane. Tony Williams with Miles Davis. Most historically significant drummers are considered so because of how they:
1. collaborated with
2. supported
3. responded to
4. interacted with
5. played with . . . other musicians.

Step D 12: Left Foot Hi-Hat independence

1.

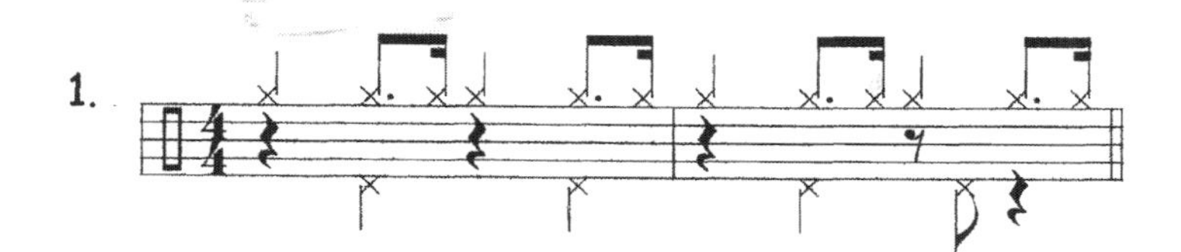

2.

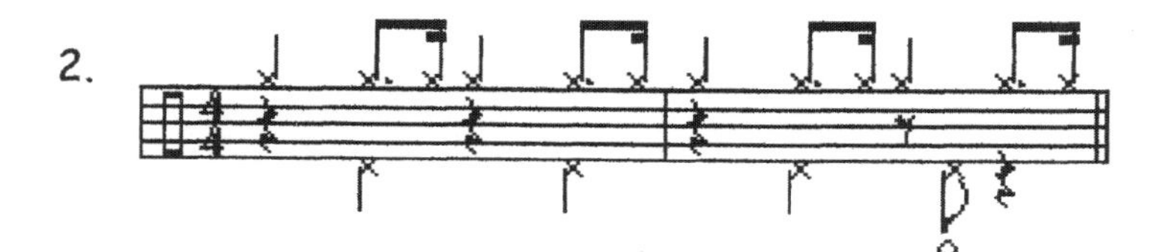

3.

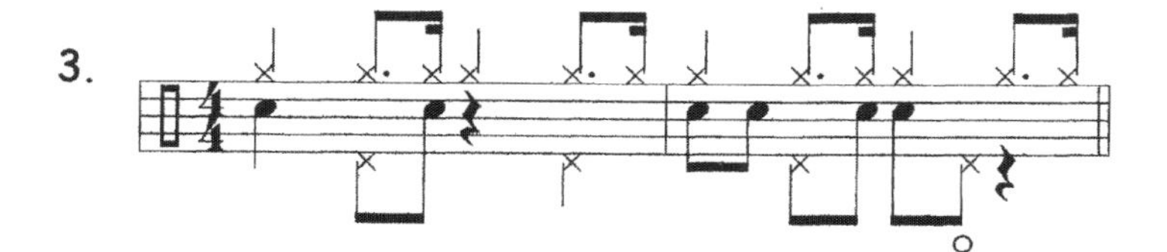

4.

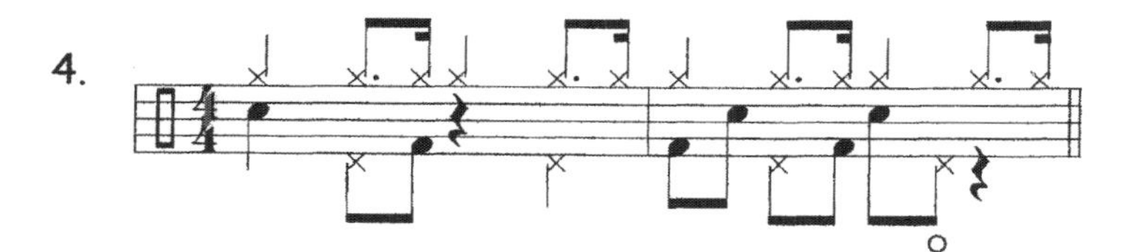

5.

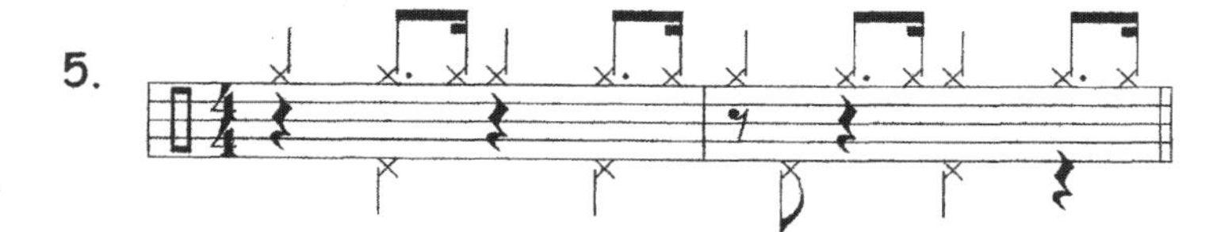

6.

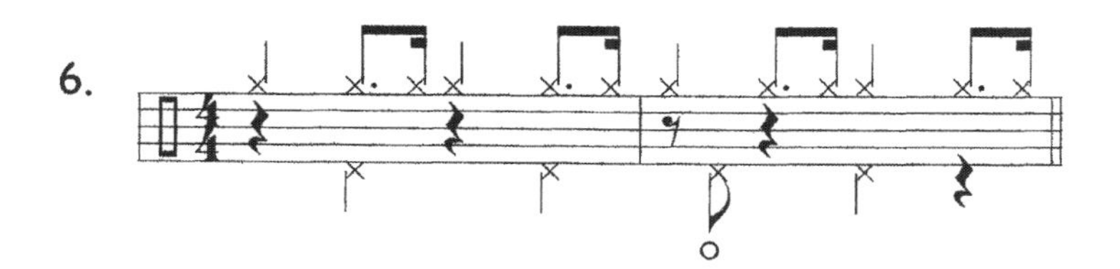

7.

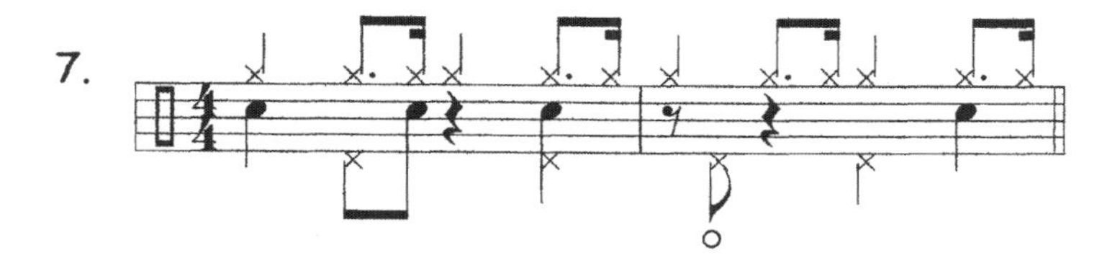

Step D 12: Left Foot Hi-Hat independence

8.

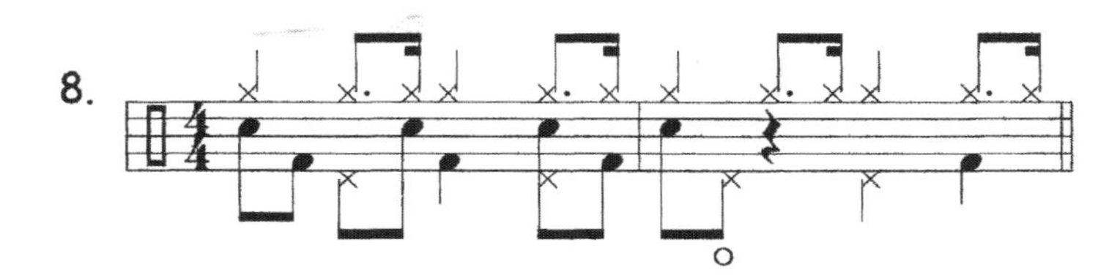

9.

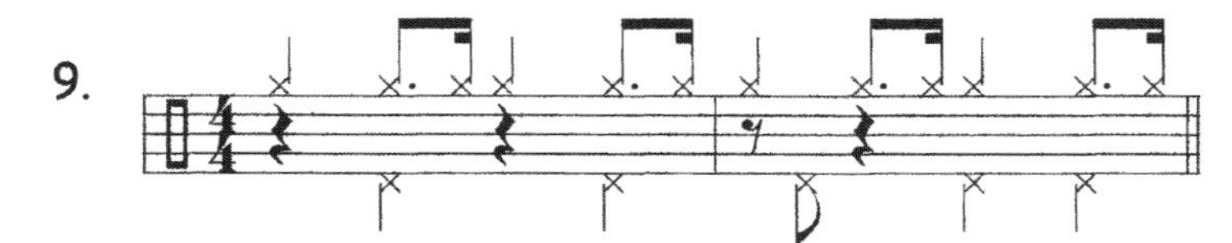

10.

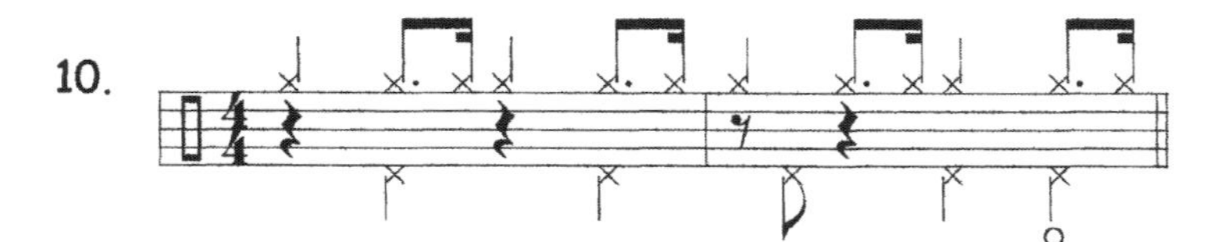

11.

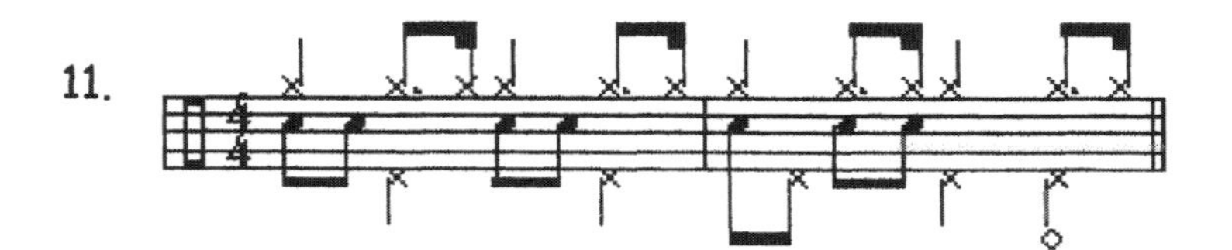

12.

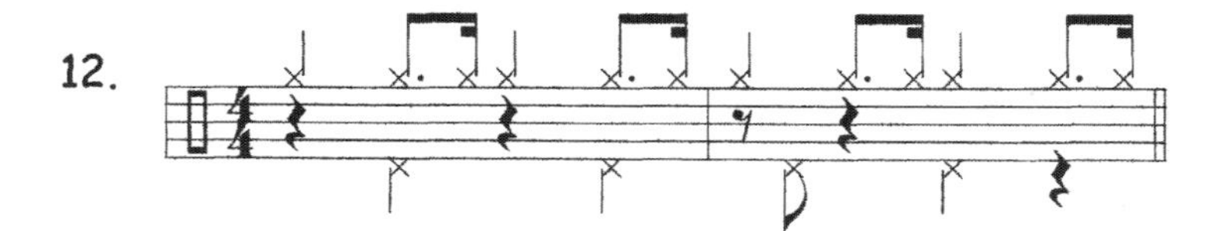

13.

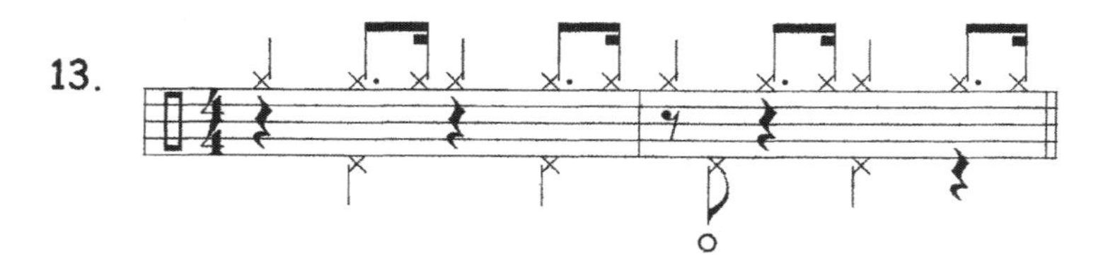

14.

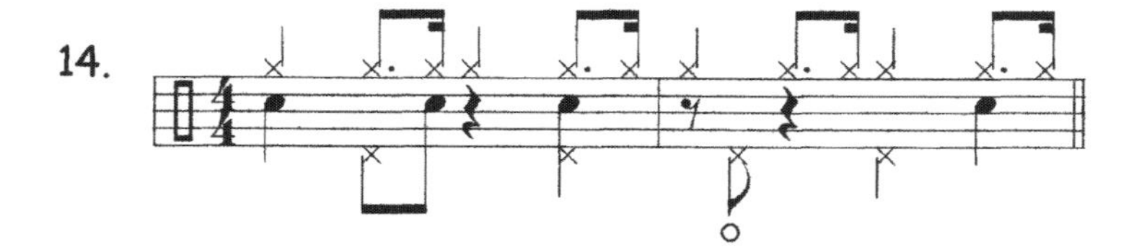

✓

Step D 12: Left Foot Hi-Hat Independence

15.

16.

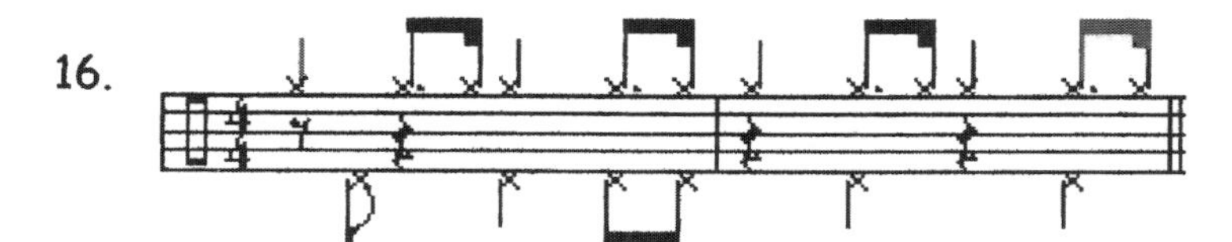

17.

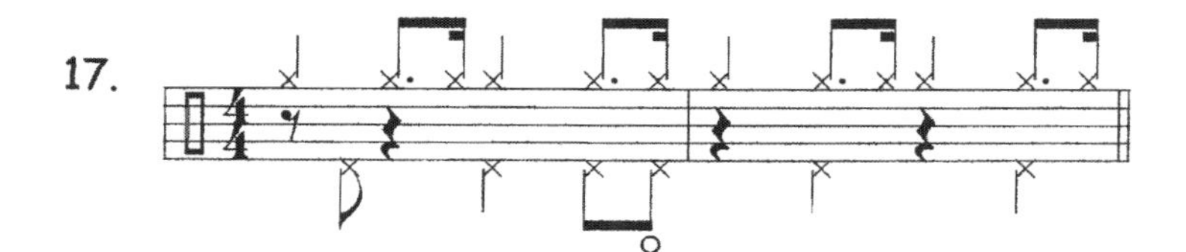

18.

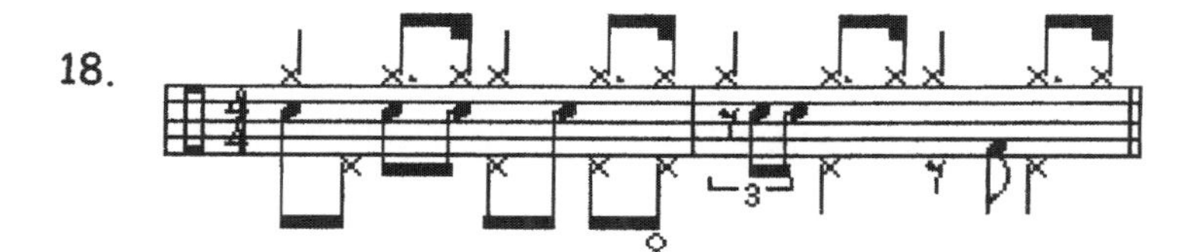

19.

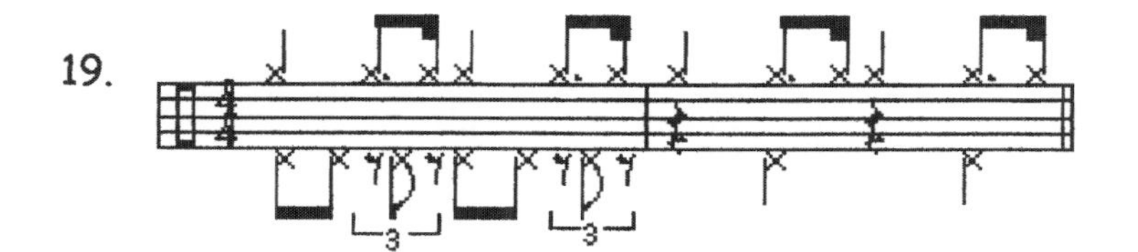

20.

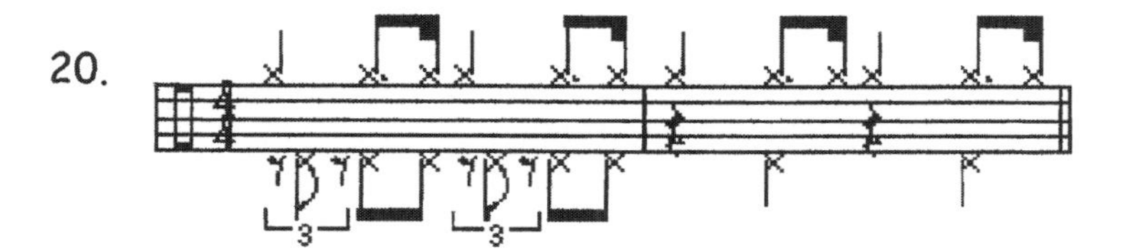

21.

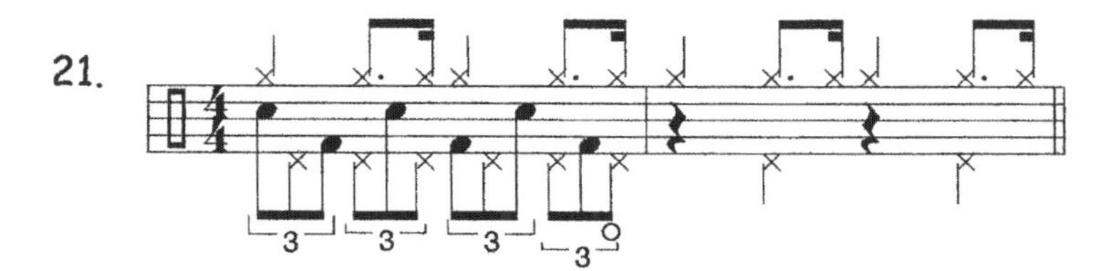

"The Drum Also Waltzes" is a well known solo by Max Roach, as well as a reminder that jazz music is often performed in 3/4 time. In fact, many standards are jazz waltzes (see bottom of the next page).

- Follow these directions for the following page.
- Play these exercises against CD track 11
- LF/HH plays on beat 2 of each measure.*
- Play each exercise twice in succession, follwed by two measures of "time."

For example, exersise 1 looks like this:

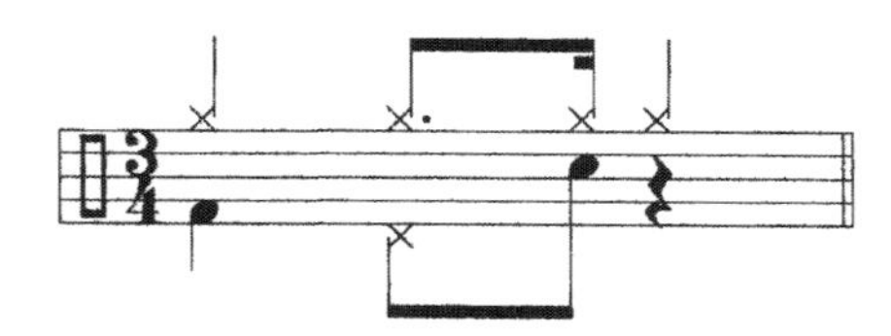

and would be played like this:

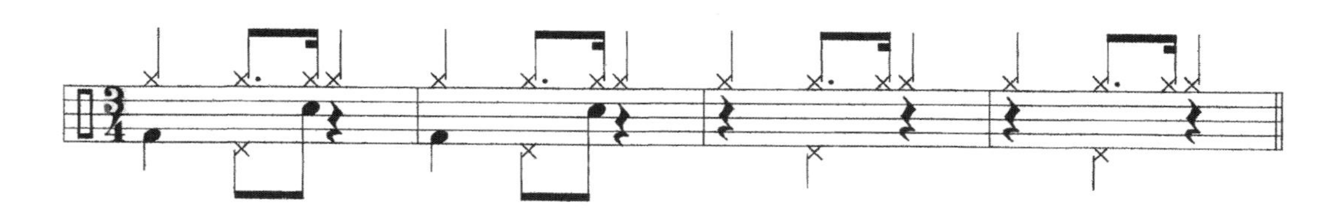

---

* Just as a drummer is free on occasion to break from the traditional standard of playing LF/HH on "2" & "4" to other patterns, so can a drummer playing a jazz waltz can also deviate from the standard "2" with the LF. Other patterns that have been used:

1. Playing on "3":

2. Playing on "2" & "3":

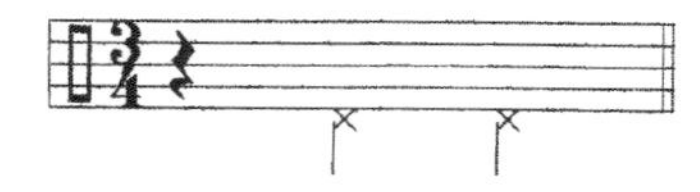

3. Occasionally, drummers have superimposed a duple (every other beat) pattern against the jazz waltz:

STEP D 13: JAZZ WALTZ PATTERNS

1. 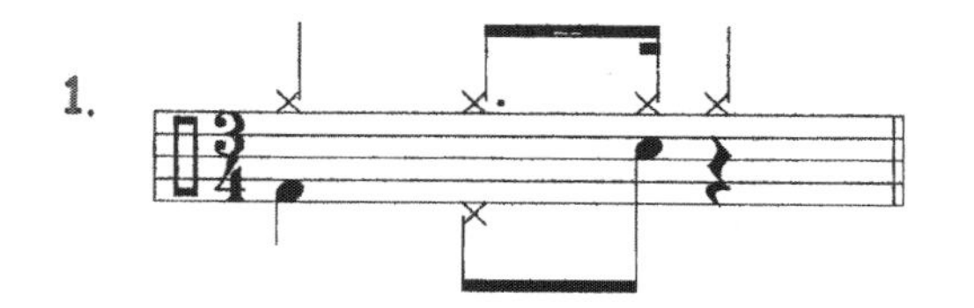

2. 

3. 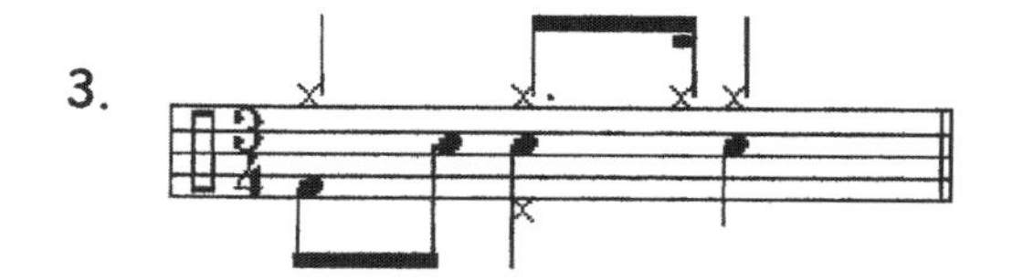

4. 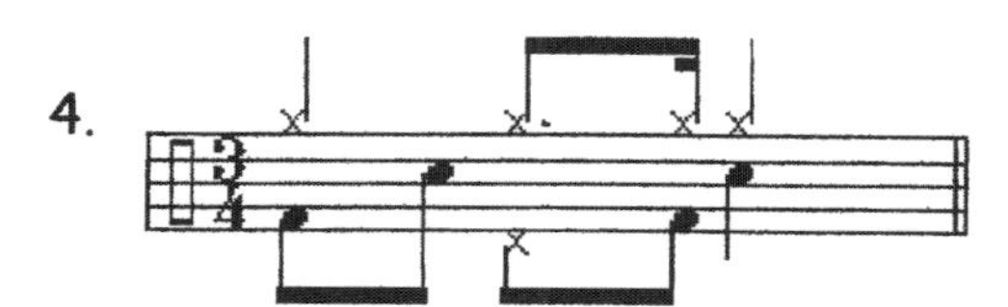

5. 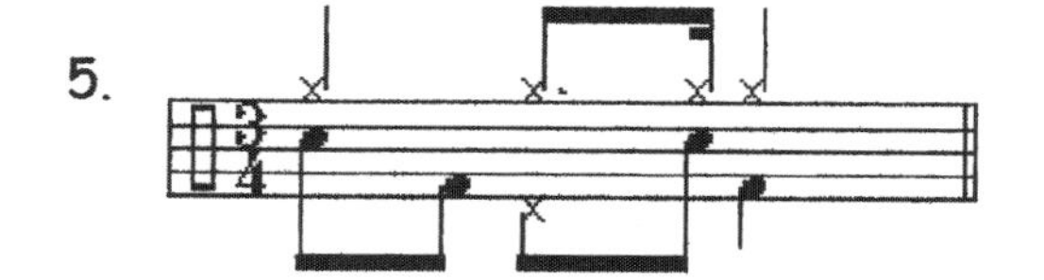

6. 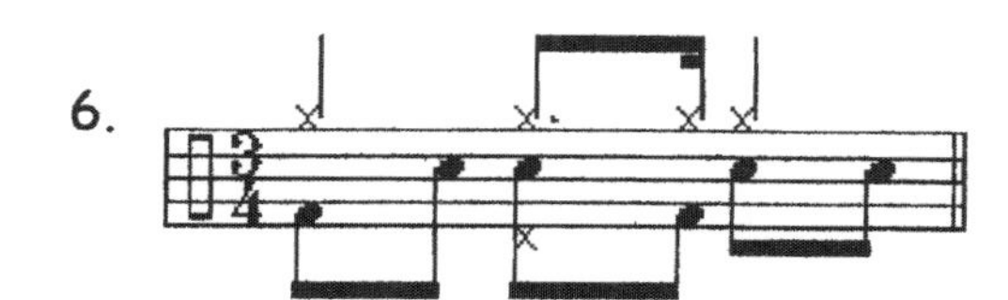

7. 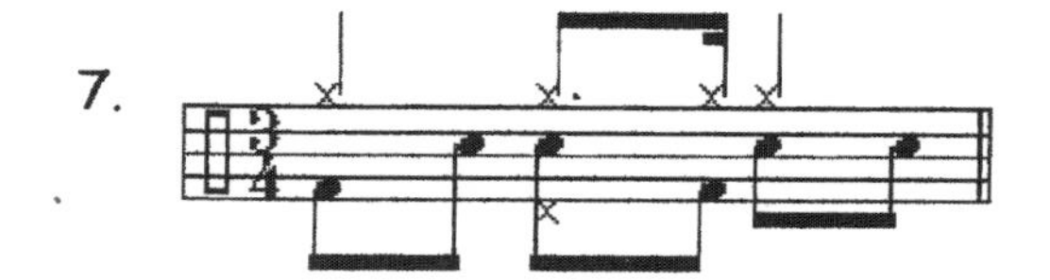

8. 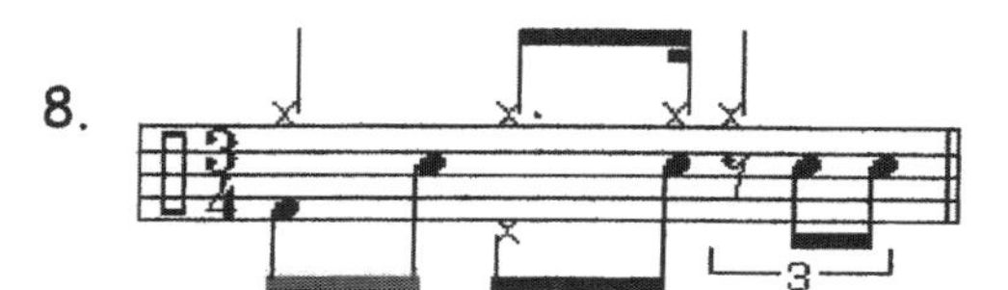

9. 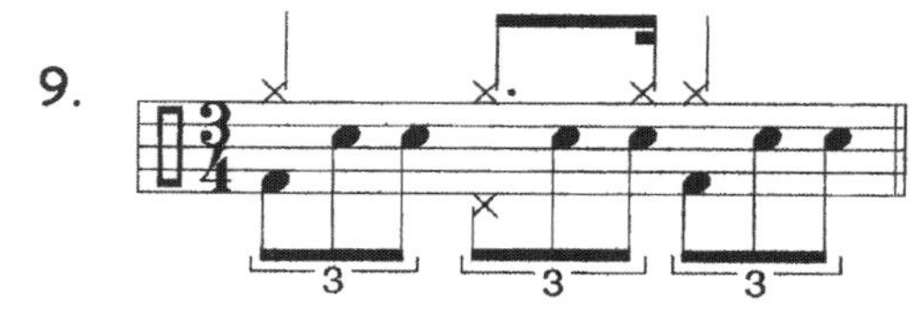

10. 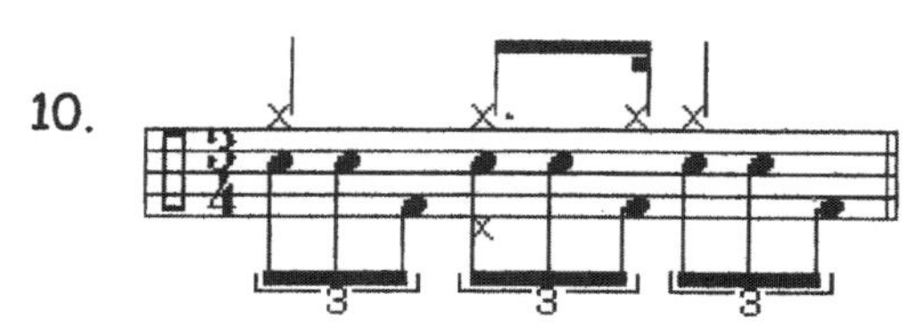

11. 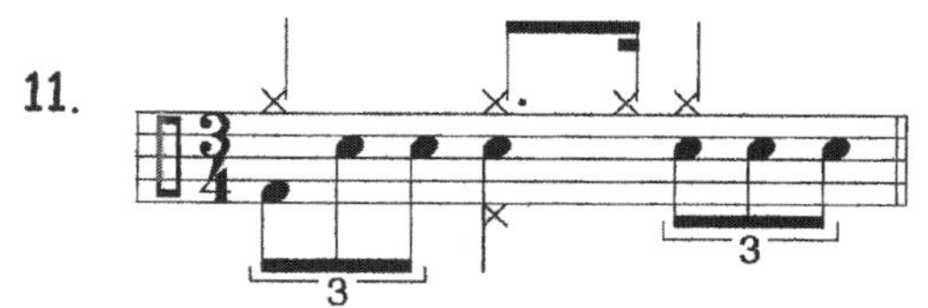

12. 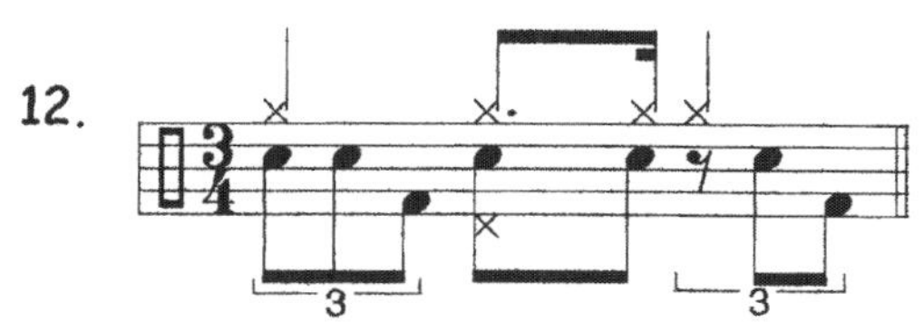

Jazz Waltz Standards:

"Alice in Wonderland"
"All Blues" (Miles Davis)
"Bluesette" (Toots Thielemans)
"Emily" (Bill Evans)
"Greensleeves"
"Maxine"
"My Favorite Things" (recorded by John Coltrane)
"Someday My Prince Will Come" (recorded by Miles Davis)
"A Taste Of Honey"
"Tenderly"
"Valse Hot"
"Waltz For Debby" (Bill Evans)
"Window" (Chick Corea)

STEP D 14: INTERACTIVE PHRASING: EIGHTH NOTE TRIPLETS

The exercises in this step relate to the eighth note triplet sticking patterns on pages 158 through 176. Each pattern will be expressed as a rhythmic phrase on ther drumset, as follows.

- Play two measures of jazz time.

- Play each sticking exercise for two measures on the set, with each "R" on RH/CYM and RF/BD simultaneously, and each "L" on the LH/SN. LF/HH plays on "2" and "4."

  Exercise one on page 158 looks like this:

and should be played like this:

- For those patterns that feature **three** successive underlined L's, substitute "L R L" on the snare in its place. For example, exercise 9 looks like this:

and should be played like this:

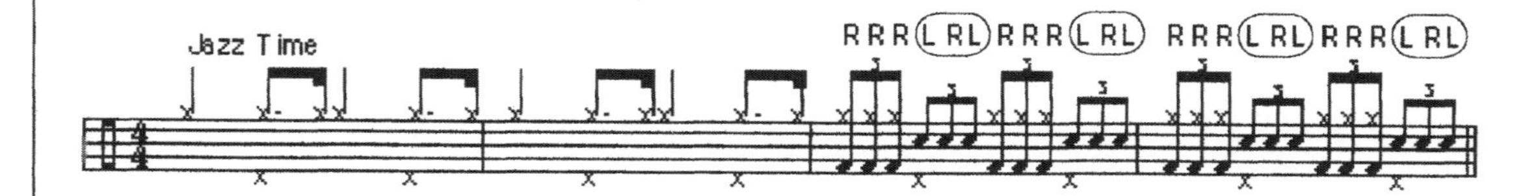

♦ For those patterns that feature **four** successive underlined L's, substitute "L R L L" on the snare in its place. For example, exercise 67 looks like this:

and should be played like this:

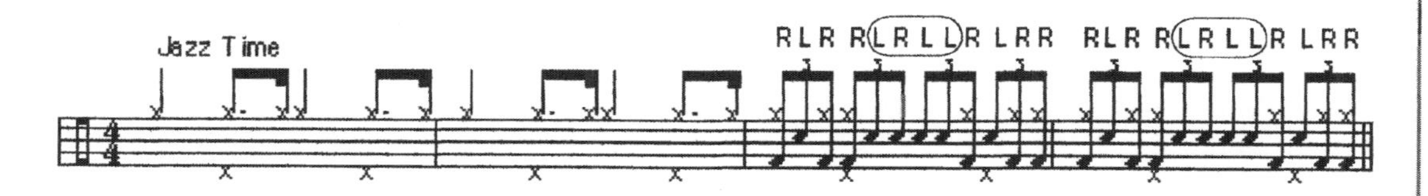

♦ The stickings for all the triplet patterns are listed below for your convenience. You can check them off as you go.

Page 158

1. RLR-LRL-RLR-LRL
2. LRL-RLR-LRL-RLR
3. RLL-RLL-RLL-RLL
4. LRR-LRR-LRR-LRR
5. RRL-RRL-RRL-RRL
6. LLR-LLR-LLR-LLR
7. RLR-RLR-RLR-RLR
8. LRL-LRL-LRL-LRL
9. RRR-LLL-RRR-LLL
10. LLL-RRR-LLL-RRR
11. RLR-RLL-RLR-RLL
12. LRL-LRR-LRL-LRR
13. RLR-LRR-RLR-LRR
14. LRL-RLL-LRL-RLL
15. RLR-RRL-RLR-RRL
16. LRL-LLR-LRL-LLR
17. RLR-LLR-RLR-LLR
18. LRL-RRL-LRL-RRL
19. RLR-LLL-RLR-LLL
20. LRL-RRR-LRL-RRR
21. RLL-RLR-RLL-RLR

Page 159

22. LRR-LRL-LRR-LRL
23. RLL-LRL-RLL-LRL
24. LRR-RLR-LRR-RLR
25. RLL-LRR-RLL-LRR
26. LRR-RLL-LRR-RLL
27. RLL-RRL-RLL-RRL
28. LRR-LLR-LRR-LLR
29. RRL-RLR-RRL-RLR
30. LLR-LRL-LLR-LRL
31. RRL-LRL-RRL-LRL
32. LLR-RLR-LLR-RLR
33. RRL-RLL-RRL-RLL
34. RLR-LRR-RLR-LRR
35. RRL-LLR-RRL-LLR
36. LLR-RRL-LLR-RRL
37. RRR-LRL-RRR-LRL
38. LLL-RLR-LLL-RLR
39. RLR-LRR-LRL-RLL
40. LRL-RLL-RLR-LRR
41. RRL-LRR-LLR-RLL
42. LLR-RLL-RRL-LRR

Page 160

43. RLR-LRR-LRL-RLR
44. LRL-RLL-RLR-LRL
45. RLR-LRL-RLL-LRR
46. RLR-LRL-RLL-RRL
47. RLR-LRL-RLL-LLR
48. RLR-LRL-LRR-RLL
49. RLR-LRL-LRR-RRL
50. RLR-LRL-LRR-LLR
51. RLR-LRL-RRL-RLL
52. RLR-LRL-RRL-LRR
53. RLR-LRL-RRL-LLR
54. RLR-LRL-LLR-RLL
55. RLR-LRL-LLR-LRR
56. RLR-LRL-LLR-RRL
57. RLR-RLL-LRL-LRR
58. RLR-RLL-LRL-RRL
59. RLR-RLL-LRL-LLR
60. RLR-RLL-LRR-LRL
61. RLR-RLL-LRR-RRL
62. RLR-RLL-LRR-LLR
63. RLR-RLL-RRL-LRL

Page 161

64. RLR-RLL-RRL-LRR
65. RLR-RLL-RRL-LLR
66. RLR-RLL-LLR-LRL
67. RLR-RLL-LLR-LRR
68. RLR-RLL-LLR-RRL
69. RLR-LRR-LRL-RRL
70. RLR-LRR-LRL-LLR
71. RLR-LRR-LRL-RRL
72. RLR-LRR-RLL-RRL
73. RLR-LRR-RLL-LLR
74. RLR-LRR-RRL-LRL
75. RLR-LRR-RRL-RLL
76. RLR-LRR-RRL-LLR
77. RLR-LRR-LLR-LRL
78. RLR-LRR-LLR-RLL
79. RLR-LRR-LLR-RRL
80. RLR-RRL-LRL-RLL
81. RLR-RRL-LRL-LRR
82. RLR-RRL-LRL-LLR
83. RLR-RRL-RLL-LRL
84. RLR-RRL-RLL-LRR

Page 162

85. RLR-RRL-RLL-LLR
86. RLR-RRL-LRR-LRL
87. RLR-RRL-LRR-RLL
88. RLR-RRL-LRR-LLR
89. RLR-RRL-LLR-LRL
90. RLR-RRL-LLR-RLL
91. RLR-RRL-LLR-LRR
92. RLR-LLR-LRL-RLL
93. RLR-LLR-LRL-LRR
94. RLR-LLR-LRL-RRL
95. RLR-LLR-RLL-LRL
96. RLR-LLR-RLL-LRR
97. RLR-LLR-RLL-RRL
98. RLR-LLR-LRR-LRL
99. RLR-LLR-LRR-RLL
100. RLR-LLR-LRR-RRL
101. RLR-LLR-RRL-LRL
102. RLR-LLR-RRL-RLL
103. RLR-LLR-RRL-LRR
104. LRL-RLR-RLL-LRR
105. LRL-RLR-RLL-RRL

Page 163

106. LRL-RLR-RLL-LLR
107. LRL-RLR-LRR-RLL
108. LRL-RLR-LRR-RRL
109. LRL-RLR-LRR-LLR
110. LRL-RLR-RRL-RLL
111. LRL-RLR-RRL-LRR
112. LRL-RLR-RRL-LLR
113. LRL-RLR-LLR-RLL
114. LRL-RLR-LLR-LRR
115. LRL-RLR-LLR-RRL
116. LRL-RLL-RLR-RRL
117. LRL-RLL-RLR-LLR
118. LRL-RLL-LRR-RLR
119. LRL-RLL-LRR-RRL
120. LRL-RLL-LRR-LLR
121. LRL-RLL-RRL-RLR
122. LRL-RLL-RRL-LRR
123. LRL-RLL-RRL-LLR
124. LRL-RLL-LLR-RLR
125. LRL-RLL-LLR-LRR
126. LRL-RLL-LLR-RRL

Page 164

127. LRL-LRR-RLR-RLL
128. LRL-LRR-RLR-RRL
129. LRL-LRR-RLR-LLR
130. LRL-LRR-RLL-RLR
131. LRL-LRR-RLL-RRL
132. LRL-LRR-RLL-RRL
133. LRL-LRR-RRL-RLR
134. LRL-LRR-RRL-RLL
135. LRL-LRR-RRL-LLR
136. LRL-LRR-LLR-RLR
137. LRL-LRR-LLR-RLL
138. LRL-LRR-LLR-RRL
139. LRL-RRL-RLR-RLL
140. LRL-RRL-RLR-LRR
141. LRL-RRL-RLR-LLR
142. LRL-RRL-RLL-RLR
143. LRL-RRL-RLL-LRR
144. LRL-RRL-RLL-LLR
145. LRL-RRL-LRR-RLR
146. LRL-RRL-LRR-RLL
147. LRL-RRL-LRR-LLR

Page 165

148. LRL-RRL-LLR-RLR
149. LRL-RRL-LLR-RLL
150. LRL-RRL-LLR-LRR
151. LRL-LLR-RLR-RLL
152. LRL-LLR-RLR-LRR
153. LRL-LLR-RLR-RRL
154. LRL-LLR-RLL-RLR
155. LRL-LLR-RLL-LRR
156. LRL-LLR-RLL-RRL
157. LRL-LLR-LRR-RLR
158. LRL-LLR-LRR-RLL
159. LRL-LLR-LRR-RRL
160. LRL-LLR-RRL-RLR
161. LRL-LLR-RRL-RLL
162. LRL-LLR-RRL-LRR
163. RLL-RLR-LRL-LRR
164. RLL-RLR-LRL-RRL
165. RLL-RLR-LRL-LLR
166. RLL-RLR-LRR-LRL
167. RLL-RLR-LRR-RRL
168. RLL-RLR-LRR-LLR

Page 166

169. RLL-RLR-RRL-LRL
170. RLL-RLR-RRL-LRR
171. RLL-RLR-RRL-LLR
172. RLL-RLR-LLR-LRL
173. RLL-RLR-LLR-LRR
174. RLL-RLR-LLR-RRL
175. RLL-LRL-RLR-LRR
176. RLL-LRL-RLR-RRL
177. RLL-LRL-RLR-LLR
178. RLL-LRL-LRR-RLR
179. RLL-LRL-LRR-RRL
180. RLL-LRL-LRR-RRL
181. RLL-LRL-RRL-RLR
182. RLL-LRL-RRL-LRR
183. RLL-LRL-RRL-RRL
184. RLL-LRL-LLR-RLR
185. RLL-LRL-LLR-LRR
186. RLL-LRL-LLR-RRL
187. RLL-LRR-RLR-LRL
188. RLL-LRR-RLR-RRL
189. RLL-LRR-RLR-LLR

Page 167

190. RLL-LRR-LRL-RLR
191. RLL-LRR-LRL-RRL
192. RLL-LRR-LRL-LLR
193. RLL-LRR-RRL-RLR
194. RLL-LRR-RRL-LRL
195. RLL-LRR-RRL-LLR
196. RLL-LRR-LLR-LRL
197. RLL-LRR-LLR-RLR
198. RLL-LRR-LLR-RRL
199. RLL-RRL-RLR-LRL
200. RLL-RRL-RLR-LRR
201. RLL-RRL-RLR-LLR
202. RLL-RRL-LRL-RLR
203. RLL-RRL-LRL-LRR
204. RLL-RRL-LRL-LLR
205. RLL-RRL-LRR-RLR
206. RLL-RRL-LRR-LRL
207. RLL-RRL-LRR-LLR
208. RLL-RRL-LLR-RLR
209. RLL-RRL-LLR-LRL
210. RLL-RRL-LLR-RRL

Page 168

211. RLL-LLR-RLR-LRL
212. RLL-LLR-RLR-LRR
213. RLL-LLR-RLR-RL
214. RLL-LLR-LRL-RLR
215. RLL-LLR-LRL-LRR
216. RLL-LLR-LRL-RRL
217. RLL-LLR-LRR-RLR
218. RLL-LLR-LRR-LRL
219. RLL-LLR-LRR-RRL
220. RLL-LLR-RRL-RLR
221. RLL-LLR-RRL-LRL
222. RLL-LLR-RRL-LRR
223. LRR-RLR-LRL-RLL
224. LRR-RLR-LRL-RRL
225. LRR-RLR-LRL-LLR
226. LRR-RLR-RLL-LRL
227. LRR-RLR-RLL-RRL
228. LRR-RLR-RLL-LLR
229. LRR-RLR-RRL-LRL
230. LRR-RLR-RRL-RLL
231. LRR-RLR-RRL-LLR

Page 169

232. LRR-RLR-LLR-LRL
233. LRR-RLR-LLR-RRL
234. LRR-RLR-LLR-LLR
235. LRR-LRL-RLR-RLL
236. LRR-LRL-RLR-RRL
237. LRR-LRL-RLR-LLR
238. LRR-LRL-RLL-RLR
239. LRR-LRL-RLL-RRL
240. LRR-LRL-RLL-LLR
241. LRR-LRL-RRL-RLR
242. LRR-LRL-RRL-RLL
243. LRR-LRL-RRL-LLR
244. LRR-LRL-LLR-RLR
245. LRR-LRL-LLR-RLL
246. LRR-LRL-LLR-RRL
247. LRR-RLL-RLR-LRL
248. LRR-RLL-RLR-RRL
249. LRR-RLL-RLR-LLR
250. LRR-RLL-LRL-RLR
251. LRR-RLL-LRL-RRL
252. LRR-RLL-LRL-LLR

Page 170

253. LRR-RLL-RRL-RLR
254. LRR-RLL-RRL-LRL
255. LRR-RLL-RRL-LLR
256. LRR-RLL-LLR-RLR
257. LRR-RLL-LLR-LRL
258. LRR-RLL-LLR-RRL
259. LRR-RRL-RLR-LRL
260. LRR-RRL-RLR-RLL
261. LRR-RRL-RLR-LLR
262. LRR-RRL-LRL-RLR
263. LRR-RRL-LRL-RLL
264. LRR-RRL-LRL-LLR
265. LRR-RRL-RLL-RLR
266. LRR-RRL-RLL-LRL
267. LRR-RRL-RLL-LLR
268. LRR-RRL-LLR-RLR
269. LRR-RRL-LLR-LRL
270. LRR-RRL-LLR-RLL
271. LRR-LLR-RLR-LRL
272. LRR-LLR-RLR-RLL
273. LRR-LLR-RLR-RRL

Page 171

274. LRR-LLR-LRL-RLR
275. LRR-LLR-LRL-RLL
276. LRR-LLR-LRL-RRL
277. LRR-LLR-RLL-RLR
278. LRR-LLR-RLL-LRL
279. LRR-LLR-RLL-RRL
280. LRR-LLR-RRL-RLR
281. LRR-LLR-RRL-LRL
282. LRR-LLR-RRL-RLL
283. RRL-RLR-LRL-RLL
284. RRL-RLR-LRL-LRR
285. RRL-RLR-LRL-LLR
286. RRL-RLR-RLL-LRL
287. RRL-RLR-RLL-LRR
288. RRL-RLR-RLL-LLR
289. RRL-RLR-LRR-LRL
290. RRL-RLR-LRR-RLL
291. RRL-RLR-LRR-LLR
292. RRL-RLR-LLR-LRL
293. RRL-RLR-LLR-RLL
294. RRL-RLR-LLR-RRL

Page 172

295. RRL-LRL-RLR-RLL
296. RRL-LRL-RLR-LRR
297. RRL-LRL-RLR-LLR
298. RRL-LRL-RLL-RLR
299. RRL-LRL-RLL-LRR
300. RRL-LRL-RLL-LLR
301. RRL-LRL-LRR-RLR
302. RRL-LRL-LRR-RLL
303. RRL-LRL-LRR-LLR
304. RRL-LRL-LLR-RLR
305. RRL-LRL-LLR-RLL
306. RRL-LRL-LLR-RRL
307. RRL-RLL-RLR-LRL
308. RRL-RLL-RLR-LRR
309. RRL-RLL-RLR-LLR
310. RRL-RLL-LRL-RLR
311. RRL-RLL-LRL-LRR
312. RRL-RLL-LRL-LLR
313. RRL-RLL-LRR-RLR
314. RRL-RLL-LRR-LRL
315. RRL-RLL-LRR-LLR

Page 173

316. RRL-RLL-LLR-RLR
316. RRL-RLL-LLR-LRL
318. RRL-RLL-LLR-LLR
319. RRL-LRR-RLR-LRL
320. RRL-LRR-RLR-RLL
321. RRL-LRR-RLR-LLR
322. RRL-LRR-LRL-RLR
323. RRL-LRR-LRL-RLL
324. RRL-LRR-LRL-LLR
325. RRL-LRR-RLL-RLR
326. RRL-LRR-RLL-LRL
327. RRL-LRR-RLL-LLR
328. RRL-LRR-LLR-RLR
329. RRL-LRR-LLR-LRL
330. RRL-LLR-RLR-LRL
331. RRL-LLR-RLR-RLL
332. RRL-LLR-RLR-LRR
333. RRL-LLR-LRL-RLR
334. RRL-LLR-LRL-RLL
335. RRL-LLR-LRL-LRR
336. RRL-LLR-RLL-RLR

Page 174

337. RRL-LLR-RLL-LRL
338. RRL-LLR-RLL-LRR
339. RRL-LLR-LRR-RLR
340. RRL-LLR-LRR-LRL
341. RRL-LLR-LRR-RLL
342. LLR-RLR-LRL-RLL
343. LLR-RLR-LRL-LRR
344. LLR-RLR-LRL-RRL
345. LLR-RLR-RLL-LRL
346. LLR-RLR-RLL-LRR
347. LLR-RLR-RLL-RRL
348. LLR-RLRLRR-LRL
349. LLR-RLR-LRR-RLL
350. LLR-RLR-LRR-RRL
351. LLR-RLR-RRL-LRL
352. LLR-RLR-RRL-RLL
353. LLR-RLR-LLR-LRR
354. LLR-LRL-RLR-RLL
355. LLR-LRL-RLR-LRR
356. LLR-LRL-RLR-RRL
357. LLR-LRL-RLL-LRL

Page 175

358. LLR-LRL-RLL-LRR
359. LLR-LRL-RLL-RRL
360. LLR-LRL-LRR-RLR
361. LLR-LRL-LRR-RLL
362. LLR-LRL-LRR-RRL
363. LLR-LRL-RRL-RLR
364. LLR-LRL-RRL-RLL
365. LLR-LRL-RRL-LRR
366. LLR-RLL-RLR-LRL
367. LLR-RLL-RLR-LRR
368. LLR-RLL-RLR-RRL
369. LLR-RLL-LRL-RLR
370. LLR-RLL-LRL-LRR
371. LLR-RLL-LRL-RRL
372. LLR-RLL-LRR-RLR
373. LLR-RLL-LRR-LRL
374. LLR-RLL-LRR-RRL
375. LLR-RLL-RRL-RLR
376. LLR-RLL-RRL-LRL
377. LLR-LRR-RLR-LRL
378. LLR-LRR-RLR-RLL

Page 176

379. LLR-LRR-RLR-RRL
380. LLR-LRR-LRL-RLR
381. LLR-LRR-LRL-RLL
382. LLR-LRR-LRL-RRL
383. LLR-LRR-RLL-RLR
384. LLR-LRR-RLL-LRL
385. LLR-LRR-RLL-RRL
386. LLR-LRR-RRL-RRL
387. LLR-LRR-RRL-LRL
388. LLR-LRR-RRL-RLL
389. LLR-RRL-RLR-LRL
390. LLR-RRL-RLR-RLL
391. LLR-RRL-RLR-LRR
392. LLR-RRL-LRR-RLR
393. LLR-RRL-LRL-RLL
394. LLR-RRL-LRL-LRR
395. LLR-RRL-RLL-RLR
396. LLR-RRL-RLL-LRL
397. LLR-RRL-RLL-LRR
398. LLR-RRL-LRR-RLR
399. LLR-RRL-LRR-LRL

A Final Word

Bassist Bob Magnusson once described the history of jazz and its performers as a stream, constantly changing as new performers bring their own creativity to their performances, informed by the giants of the past and the inspiration of their mentors and peers. I would like to invite you to join that stream now, by playing jazz where you can. There are plenty of other musicians just like you, anxious to sharpen their skills by experience. I do hope this book has been a great help to you, but one can only swim by jumping in the water. So come on in, the water's fine. And best wishes for your drumming future!

"You only get better by playing." Buddy Rich

Printed in Great Britain
by Amazon